Darshan with Swami Narayanananda

Darshan with Swami Narayanananda

Darshan with Swami Narayanananda Copyright © 2022 by Maribeth Gray

All rights reserved. No part of this book may be used or reproduced in any manner whatsoever without the written permission of the author except in the case of brief quotations embodied in critical articles and reviews.

    The information in this book is distributed on an "as is" basis, without warranty. Although every precaution has been taken in the preparation of this work, neither the author nor the publisher shall have any liability to any person or entity with respect to any loss or damage caused or alleged to be caused directly or indirectly by the information contained in this book.

First Edition

Paperback: 978-0-9963389-5-0
eBook: 978-0-9963389-6-7
Hardcover: 978-0-9963389-7-4

Swami Narayanananda, age 70

Table of Contents

Introduction	9
Darshans	11
Glossary	307
Brief Biography of Swami Narayanananda	317

Darshan with Swami Narayanananda

Introduction

The original book, "Darshan with Swami Narayanananda, 1973" was created by Sashi, a long-time disciple of Swami Narayanananda, affectionately identified in this book as Swamiji. The book of darshans was printed long ago with only a few copies given by Sashi to her closest disciple friends. It has been said that Swamiji expressed an interest in having this book of darshans published.

Swami Narayanananda first went to Denmark from India in the summer of 1971 after his many Danish disciples, who visited him in India, convinced him that he and his teachings were needed in the west. Swamiji's work began at his ashram in the small town of Gylling, Denmark where he established a Free Spiritual Training Camp that first summer. Swamiji welcomed all sincere Truth-Seekers to stay at the camp and participate in the four daily meditations, study groups, hatha yoga classes and daily private darshan. In the early years, there were talks every evening followed by meditation with Swamiji. He returned to Denmark every summer for 17 years but many consider the summer of 1973 to be the "Golden Summer" because of the focus on his main teachings as written in his book, "The Secrets of Mind-Control". This book contains only some of the darshans from that summer.

Swami Narayanananda teaches that brahmacharya and mind-control are necessary to attain the aim of life known as Freedom or Nirvikalpa Samadhi. Brahmacharya is only possible with mind-control and is necessary for the rising of the kundalini shakti to the sahasrara chakra where spiritual Enlightenment takes place. Swami Narayanananda teaches that whenever possible, brahmacharya should be practiced and encouraged those living a family or householder life to have a regulated sexual life. Mind-control makes the mind pure, subtle

and one-pointed so one can get a glimpse of the true Self. The three main practices to achieve mind-control are:
1. Living a pure, simple and holy (ethical) life,
2. Mantra-jap: repetition of the mantra,
3. Meditation: constantly taking the Divine name (mantra) and living in the Divine Form.

It is impossible to describe Swamiji – his presence, his compassion, his energy, his love. He offered his teachings freely and gave everyone the tools and the guidance needed to be totally Free in this very life. It was a rare and great opportunity to meet Swamiji and spend time with him. Subtle but profound transformations took place under his guidance that continue to this day – fifty years later.

The intention of this new edition is to make the darshans available to a greater number of Truth-Seekers. Every effort has been made to reflect the sacred atmosphere where the talks took place. Editing has only been done to increase clarity.

Darshan with Swami Narayanananda
(Reading from: "The Secrets of Mind-Control"
written by Swami Narayanananda,)

June 3, 1973
Camp rules. *The camp is arranged for the purpose of giving all sincere truth-seekers a practical training in mind-control as a means to attaining the highest Truth – Nirvikalpa Samadhi. Meditation is the central activity of the camp and ashram. One must be strict in keeping the daily meditation, etc.*
Swamiji: So, I am not forcing anyone. You must know that. All these things have come from you people. This is all your own choice. To come to this line nobody has compelled you. It is all your own selection. So, you must willingly take up the work, every one of you. It is your duty to follow it. It will help you or else it has no meaning to come to a camp in this cold weather, lying down on the ground. If you want to be easy-going, to live an easy life, it has no meaning. For an easy life, you could have stayed in Copenhagen or some other place and made yourself happy. Or, if your aim is to eat, drink and be happy, that also you could do more in the city, than in a town out in the country like this. Do your best and follow the rules. Don't waste your time.

We remember when we were young and doing sadhana. We had not even a single second to waste. If anybody was to come and speak to us, we will ask, "Have you got any important work or something?" If there was any gossip, we would turn them out from a distance. I had no time. I used to say — "Get away." Whoever it may be, it may be our best friend but we had no compromise with it. So, in that way, every one of you must be strong. Don't waste your time. Go on with your mantra-jap and meditation. Little by little, keep it up. In these three months, you can change completely, if you work hard. It is not mere exaggeration. You will understand it actually. Many of your weaknesses can be rooted out even in fifteen days if you live the pure life of brahmacharya. Actually, you can see it in their faces. There will be so much change. So, we are giving a push in that way. Make the best use of the time. You can't always get that kind of opportunity. Now, you have to make use of it but not by force. If you do a thing by force, you are a slave. If you do it willingly, you are a free man. Suppose nobody is asking you to do any work and you willingly go to the garden and work hard. Then you have the pleasure. If someone compels you to do the work, that means you are a slave there. Freedom means to do the thing willingly. So here, it is your own choice, your Freedom to do it willingly. It will help you.

Reading: *The Self (Jivatman) is the ruling monarch in the living body and It lives only as a witness. Imagine that you are standing still on the bank of a tank and your reflection is seen on the water surface. Though you are standing still, your reflection trembles with the ripples on the water surface. You do see and witness the movements of the reflection but are not, in the least, affected by them. Such is the relation between the Jivatman (Self) and the mind, the senses, the body and the sense-objects.*

Swamiji: The Self in the body remains as a witness only. How to prove it? Suppose you take some other examples also. In the waking–state this world of names and forms looks to you as real as anything. From the waking-state, you go to dream-state, then the dreaming world appears as real as anything else to you. From these two stages, you go to the third one. That is the deep-sleep-state where there are no dreams. You are having sound sleep. Then you totally forget the waking-state world and the dream-state-world. You are in the third state. During the deep-sleep-state, you are breathing, blood circulation is there, nerve currents are working, and still, you have no understanding about anything. There may be so much noise outside. There may be light inside. You have no idea of anything of the external world. What happens there? Life is there but you have no experience whatsoever. The mind is absent during the deep-sleep-state. It goes back to the Self and remains merged momentarily. Without the mind, you have no experience of this world at all. So, it proves that mind is everything. The universe is nothing but a projection of your own mind. Secondly, it proves that though the Self lives in the body, it remains as a witness only. It does not take part either in good or bad things.

Suppose that before going to sleep you have received some good or bad news. In deep-sleep you forget both. There is neither sorrow nor joy. But when you get up again, you make a bridge there. The sorrow or joy comes up. You begin to laugh or weep once again. What becomes of the sorrow or joy when you are sleeping? The news you forget totally. Though life was functioning, you had no idea about your sorrow or joy. This clearly indicates that though the Self remains in the body, it remains as a witness only. Then who is the cause of all this destruction for you? Your own mind is the cause. That is why we have to put so much stress on mind-control. With a purified mind, a well-controlled mind, a regulated mind, you are in heaven. You enjoy peace and bliss – actually it is heaven. With an impure mind you are in hell really. So, heaven and hell are within you. The Self does not take part in good or bad things. The merits and demerits are always the same. Then who is having this Freedom? Freedom is in the mind only. When you go to the state of Nirvikalpa Samadhi, there is not a thing called Freedom, because if you are bound, then only you can become free. You are not at all bound. Your True Nature is Freedom already. So, who is there to bind you but your dirty mind? By identifying yourself with the dirty mind and ego, you appear as a bound person. Now, get rid of this delusion. How? By controlling your mind. Mind-control is a necessity. Without controlling the mind, you cannot understand anything. You will be in hell always. You are suffering and suffering. There is no end to your misery. The mind is only an instrument of the Self. It gets its life and light from the Self.

The mind by itself cannot know the universe without the senses. You have five senses. It is just like electricity coming from a dynamo going to a powerhouse. From there, so many wires are coming. Then you have five switches here in the room with light burning in different colours. These are like your own five senses. The senses by themselves cannot work. If they can work, they must work in sleep also. It is a clear proof. When you are in deep-sleep, there is no sensation at all. It means there was no mind,; so, the mind must be connected to the senses. The mind cannot work by itself. It must have life and light from the Jiva – your Self.

In order to control the mind, you have to regulate your life, exercise control over all your five senses in whatever you do such as eating, drinking, speaking, running, etc. There are so many unnecessary things. You are wasting your time for nothing. The mind has become weak and stupid. How? It runs through the five senses constantly and becomes very weak. The powers have become scattered all over the five senses. You want to eat tasteful things. You want to see beautiful objects. You want to hear beautiful songs. So, it has become very weak.

Now, what is meant by mind-control? You are bringing the whole force to one point. Samadhi means taking the ray of light back to the sun, as it were. You go back to your Source. When you go back there, you understand there is really only One Thing in the universe – that is God or your own Self. Sadhana means you are struggling to gain mind-control to get it one-pointed. So, every one of you must put stress on that one thing, sadhana, and do all other works also. When you go on doing, even the other work also becomes part of your sadhana. That is not a separate thing in that way. Is it clear?

Disciple: Not fully. How can the mind become weak from looking at beautiful things?

Swamiji: Beauty takes away your energy. If you can enjoy beauty as a master, but not as a slave, then I have no objection for it. When you go deeply, there is no beauty also. Beauty is within you. You paint it yourself and make it beautiful – that is all. The same beauty becomes ugly when you are sick. The very idea of beauty is so terrible for you. You don't want to see it. You find some usefulness and make it very beautiful. Another man, he does not want it. He finds it so ugly.

Disciple: For example, you go to nature and see something very beautiful. You get some very strong emotions because it is very beautiful.

Swamiji: That is all right.

Disciple: Is it not as a master you see this beauty?

Swamiji: Because the beautiful thing attracts you, you are seeing that thing. Afterwards, some other things attract you. You go after that thing. You are a slave there actually.

Disciple: But isn't nature a manifestation of God? Is that wrong?

Swamiji: It is all right that it is manifested. If you can see God in everything, then you have solved the whole problem. There is no difficulty. Why do you see only beauty in nature, in some part, not beauty in other things? See beauty in ugly things also, then. That is also God. So, when you come to that state, you go above all those things. Nothing can attract you.

Disciple: So, one should avoid going to such beautiful places?

Swamiji: I don't say that thing. You can have it but have control over it, I mean. Our aim is just to have whatever is necessary. There are so many things. A man going to cinema who is habituated to that cinema, he is a slave of going to that thing. Even if you tell him a thousand times, he can't avoid it. He wants to go. Even if he has no money, he will steal money and go. There are so many people of that kind, because they become so helpless. He may also say in that way as you argue, "I want to enjoy the cinema. I had good concentration." That is also one way. There are a variety of concentrations. When a man is reading a novel, the mind also gets concentrated there. In doing all sorts of evils, when for example, a robber is going to rob, the mind is also concentrated there.

What is wanted is concentration of the mind at will. If you want to concentrate on any particular thing you do it as a master – that requires practice. Even the animals or the insects have higher concentration than human beings. Many during their mating season, watch them, they forget their life even. There is so much concentration in sense-pleasures; but they cannot do this concentration of mind at will. Many of the greatest men, so-called worldly great men, it may be scientists, they have concentration in different ways – not at will. They cannot do what you want. Here they lack. Many of them go mad when they lose their beloved pet objects. Even the greatest scientists, they are so helpless there. So, the aim of sadhana is concentration of mind at will on anything you want. If you don't want it, withdraw from it. And, if you want it, engage it to work there. In that way you are a master. In seeing beauty in nature, something else is dragging you. You have a sort of concentration on a set of objects. It is not at will. It is lacking there. You are not a master. You are a slave there. Even if you don't want it, the thing attracts you. You want to see it. That is the difference. Is it clear now?

Disciple: Yes.

Reading: *As ripples and waves are to a calm water surface of a lake, so are the desires and thoughts to a calm and serene mind.*
Swamiji: So, if you want to reflect your own True Nature, the mind must be calm and quiet. It is just like ripples making the water shaky. The reflection is already there but you can't catch your reflection. Likewise, the mind becomes unsteady, weak and stupid. You can't do any work with such a mind. Many people want to work but their mind is going here and there. It runs like a young, restless monkey.
Disciple: Swamiji, where in the mind do we experience the world?
Swamiji: You project the scene in the brain center. Mind and brain are two distinct things, you must know. All the senses have their common center there and it is projected there. The mind catches and projects the scene in a subtle way that is called chitta akasa – mental akasa. Suppose you close your eyes, the whole universe is there, You are seeing a photo. It is just like if you hold a mirror towards the forest, it projects the scene in a proportional way. Similarly, the mind projects the scene in the brain center. In the same way in the dream world, you project the scene in the lower brain. Is it clear?
Disciple: Yes.

June 4, 1973
Reading: *Likewise, until and unless one's mind is made pure, one-pointed and calm, one cannot get a glimpse of one's true Self.*
Swamiji: Do all of you catch this point? Yesterday we were explaining it. Suppose I am standing here and we have a big tub of water. If the water is steady, you can see the reflection. On the other hand, if you have put some colour in it and then again you stir it, you have made it shaky. So, though the reflection is still on the water surface, you don't see it. Here, the Self can be compared to the person standing here and the water in the tub can be compared to the mind and putting colour into it. That is, we have committed so many sins in the past and that

has made it so impure. It has given a colour to the whole mind. Now, besides that, you have made it shaky. It means you have so many unfulfilled desires. You want this thing, that thing, everything you want. It is running this side, that side. It is not steady, so you fail to catch your True Nature – your true reflection. That is what is meant by that parable. Is it clear?

Disciple: Yes. Once upon a time, the water surface must have been clear?

Swamiji: Once upon a time, if you can find it out, that is an end of everything. That is an end of your God also. If you can find out when this creation began, actually when you go to the last state, there is no creation. The whole thing comes with the mind and everything dies with the mind. As it is, you see so many things. When you go to mind-control, you go to the state of Samadhi. There is an end of everything. The question does not arise at all. When you go to that point, there is not a thing called Freedom because you are already free. Then, when there is no Freedom, there is no bondage also; but, as it is for ordinary people, bondage is there. He is suffering. He is so miserable. So, this is a dilemma. How, when and where has no meaning. You cannot give any satisfactory explanation. Nobody has given the answer yet and nobody will give it. Then you could say, "When God was created." That will bring confusion there. You understand it?

Disciple: Yes, but...

Swamiji: There is no but. Ignorance makes you put all those questions. When you go to the highest, there are no questions.

Disciple: But I am ignorant.

Swamiji: By sadhana, you get rid of that ignorance. Sadhana means you are cleaning the water, removing the colour and stopping the shaking of the waves. You have made it impure and, again, you are making it pure. It is all in the mind. It is all the mind's play.

Disciple: I still cannot understand why there can be a stop when there is no beginning?

Swamiji: What is that stop? You are not going to die. You are not dying at all.

Disciple: Then there is no stop?

Swamiji: You are not going to die. You are going back to your Source. That is all. Up to now, you are bound. You identify yourself with this

perishing body. In reality, it is only a big dream. All of you are having a similar dream. All of you human beings, as it were, are in a particular vibration. You see the same dream – all of you. When you go to the next stage, you have a second dream — subtler than this. When you go to deep-sleep both the dreams are not there; but still there is ignorance. The seed is there. It is not destroyed. But in Nirvikalpa Samadhi, everything is destroyed — even the seed. There is no more bondage. Then you understand, in reality, you are always there and you will be there. Your own impure mind is the cause of all those things. When the mind becomes pure, you go back to the Source. There are no more questions. There is no more riddle. Then you see your True Nature. Is it clear or almost clear?
Disciple: Almost.
Swamiji: Almost? Not fully? All right. Today you meditate better. I think it will be clear to you.

Reading: Freedom, Peace and Bliss are the three ideals that humanity strives for in this world. There is a feverish hunt for them everywhere but very few know how to achieve them in the true sense.
Swamiji: Any kind of so-called sense attraction, however beautiful the scenery may be, it is only momentary. Suppose you go to a very beautiful spot. The first day you may have so much attraction. You go for the second day, the third day, the fourth day and then it loses all charm. It has no meaning. You want something else. By running after these silly small things, momentary things, you lose the eternal things. That is the harm there. So, you have to discard the unreal and hold the mind to the real. That was the aim of what we were talking about yesterday.

Reading: A vast majority of beings take to the perverted course and begin courting bondage instead of Freedom and misery instead of bliss.
Swamiji: So, every one is struggling to get that real peace and bliss but by taking the wrong course, by devoting the mind to all unnecessary and useless things, you are courting misery and bondage instead of Freedom and bliss. That is what is happening. Running after momentary things, you lose sight of the eternal; so, you have to pay very

heavily. You think you will be happy finding beauty but that happiness is momentary. The mind changes and wants something else. You are fooled; so, it is better to control it.

Reading: *But the world is mad after sense-pleasures. No day passes but new things are discovered or invented for the gratification of our unruly mind and the senses. In their mad search for peace and happiness, ninety-nine percent of people perish by taking to the wrong path.*
Swamiji: So they have found out that LSD and hash make people immediately mad. So miserable it is. So many are suffering; but still, they want it. Every one wants to have a taste of it. When once they get it — gone. So many cases are coming to my kutir almost every day. That is a miserable state; so, all these things will not make a man happy.

Reading: *There can be no enjoyment without concentration of the mind. The two go together.*
Swamiji: So also suffering, both. The more the mind gets concentrated on pain there is intense pain. If there is no concentration, there is no pain also. So, also in happiness, the more you are happy, the more you are concentrated on the object of happiness. So in both cases the mind is the cause. You understand it?
Disciple: I do not. How can insects have mind-control?
Swamiji: Also, in insects there is concentration of mind. That is called automatic concentration. A sadhaka tries to cultivate concentration of mind at will but, in the vast majority of the people, there is automatic concentration. I have divided concentration into more than a hundred ways.
Disciple: But a baby or child?
Swamiji: There is also concentration. We are not asking a child or an animal to control the mind. They have automatic concentration. When a child feels happy, it may be laughing by itself or when it is hungry, it will weep or if there is pain, it will weep. Concentration is there.
Disciple: It is good that the child is a child by nature.
Swamiji: Yes, you become a child now.
Disciple: Yes.

Swamiji: That is all right, if you can, to become like a child. That means you must forget all those things – no responsibility, nothing whatsoever. Go back to that Source. There is no ego also with the child. Get rid of that ego. If there is ego, you are gone. So, a child has nothing. If there are a hundred thousand kroner with the child and a robber comes and takes it, the child has nothing to do with the kroner. The child will be happy. So, become like that then. Get rid of your ego. That is the distinction between you and the child. Your ego center is so strong. In a child, it is not developed.
Disciple: You say to put the mind on any object. Why not choose a beautiful object then?
Swamiji: Put it. You have to put it always on a beautiful object. What is that beautiful object? God is the most beautiful object you can ever have.
Disciples: It is all small reflections.
Swamiji: It is all the same thing. Come to the highest beauty then. Catch it. That is what is wanted. We have no objection to it. Put it.
Disciple: I also like very much reflecting on the sun.
Swamiji: All right, slowly proceed then. Concentrate on the small beauty and go to the higher beauty and then go to the highest, all right.
Disciple: Even when it is painted?
Swamiji: Painted, all right. We don't deny it. That is also one of the ways. Go on. Proceed slowly. You have to go further from the lower to the higher. Go to the last point.

Reading: Whenever there is interest there is also concentration of the mind. As a matter of fact, interest, happiness and enjoyment go with the concentration of the mind.
Swamiji: It is there the more you get interested. That means automatic concentration is already there. It is not that you are concentrated at will. Something else is making you concentrate and that concentration may become deeper and deeper. There are so many people who have that deep concentration – many of the scientists. Perhaps your Edison, he has made so many inventions. He used to be deeply absorbed in his thoughts and often he did not know what was happening around him he was so deeply concentrated. On one occasion, he was at the dining table with his wife and the wife was putting some questions. He was

somewhere else. He did not know what was going on. It was an insult to her and she took a basin of dirty water and poured it on him, but he did not know what was happening. In that way, he was deeply concentrated so he could detect many things. I think the electric bulb is due to him and your gramophone. It is his invention. Whatever object he would take, he would dive deeply into that. He could have taken up yoga. He would have become a great yogi but he took it in the other direction — the material side. So, concentration is there. But what is wanted is concentration of mind at will on any point and then take it to the last point. That is Samadhi state. Going to that state, you solve the riddle of life and you go back to your Source.

Reading: *It requires herculean efforts. It is to be developed slowly but steadily by regular and systematic practices spread over months and even years. And only human beings full of zest, patience and sincerity of purpose can achieve it.*
Swamiji: That is necessary. Regular and systematic practice, slowly. It is not gained in a day. Many people lose hope. They think half an hour they sit in the morning, half an hour in the evening, out of twenty-four hours, one hour's work, and they want Samadhi within no time. They have no patience. Then they say, "I have been working for forty years," but they don't consider how much they have worked — half an hour in the morning, that also in a hasty way and half an hour in the evening. If you take these hours one by one, it will not come to even two years; but, they say forty years. You are doing some sort of sadhana for one hour. All the other time, you are wasting in many other ways. So, how can you make progress? Only human beings full of zest, patience and sincerity of purpose achieve it.

Yes, hard work must be there. One must have an ideal in front always: "I must attain it. I must get it." Accordingly, one has to adjust and find time to work also. Then only can it be. It is not mere tidbits if you want to attain the highest.

When you come to a high pitch of concentration of mind and when you go back to the Source, then you say there is nothing. You see the play of a dream — mere play. Nothing can bind you. That is the secret there. Before that, all these varieties torment you like anything. A little praise and you become so happy. And if someone criticizes you, you become so mad at that person. Why? What business has he to criticize me? Why should he do that thing? So, you want to take revenge upon him. When you come to a high pitch of evolution and mind-control, you see the fun. Nothing can disturb you. You will have perfect balance of mind. That is what we want. That is what is meant by yoga.

June 5, 1973
Swamiji: Outside it is very cold. How do people manage? Is there difficulty in the camp?
Disciple: No, we are quite all right.
Swamiji: Inform all that while meditating, one should press the tongue up to the palate so that the water coming can be stopped to a great extent. And then secondly, when you take water, that saliva, swallow in this way without making any noise in the throat. That all mediating people must learn. Not only meditating people but all sadhakas. You must take it very slowly. Not all of a sudden. It will disturb so many people. And you disturb your own meditation also. Do you follow me all of you?
Disciple: Yes.
Swamiji: It is the starting point. One has to learn everything. To become a yogi is not mere closing the eyes and sitting. One will not become a yogi.

Once I was in Rishikesh. There was a conference with all the best scientists of the world in Delhi. Some of the people, four or five, went to Rishikesh by car and they wanted to learn yoga in five minutes. One of my disciples, a German lady, was coming to visit me. Seeing the foreigner, they stopped their car to inquire. They wanted to know yoga in five minutes. She hesitated where to take them. She was afraid of bringing them to me. Anyway, she brought them there and I made them sit and they were asking all sorts of questions just like babies. They asked, "What is meant by yoga – in a nutshell?" "Yoga means unity between the lower and the higher Self or, in other words, deep concentration. Further, to attain Nirvikalpa Samadhi is the aim of Yoga." Then one asked, "Can I become a yoga?" not a 'yogi', but he said 'yoga'. "Yes, you can. If you practice mind-control, you can become a yogi." In that way, there were three or four questions and they were content. Five minutes over and they left. So, in that way, in five minutes you can become a 'yoga'. So, our work is very difficult. It is a life long struggle. Many Gurus make yoga teachers within three months. They become Gurus rather and they are spreading their yoga everywhere. Here, it is not in that way. You have to work hard for years together. The foundation must be strong. Here come the rules of yama and niyama. Without that there is no yoga at all.

Reading: *How very miserable do people become when they are tormented by explosive desires and emotions such as love, lust, greed, anger, hatred, pride, jealousy, sorrow, etc.*
Swamiji: These are some of the emotions that are working in human beings.

Reading: *How many people can compose their minds when such emotions manifest themselves in a violent form? Under the impulse of these strong desires and emotions what heinous acts are not being everyday perpetrated? What sins are not being committed in the name of revenge and for the satisfaction of the worldly desires and emotional feelings? And is not incalculable injury being caused to the world and humanity at large everyday through numerous and multifarious wicked desires, thoughts and acts?*
Swamiji: So, the whole secret is when there is a very strong emotion working in your system, it starts a sort of reaction and brings poisoning of the blood. Many of the red corpuscles get destroyed and that becomes the cause of your disease. Many of the diseases are of your own making. When you do not check all the emotions and control them, you become prey to a variety of diseases. The so-called cancer and diabetes are all mental worries. When there are too many worries mentally, you get these diseases easily. They create a sort of poison in the blood, all these emotions. So, by mind-control, you can control all these things. That is why many of the big hospitals nowadays have psychiatry apart from medicine just to help the people mentally. That is a great help. So, by knowingly controlling the mind and emotions, you can save yourself from a variety of diseases and sufferings. That is the secret there.

Reading: *It is a gloomy picture, indeed, resulting from the mad and unscrupulous enjoyment of the senses as their slaves.*
Swamiji: Yes, that is what is going on nowadays. Madness is an easy thing now. A strong emotion, when it is not fulfilled, you go mad immediately. What a terrible thing. How helpless you are. So, it is working just like a master and you are a slave. This so-called Freedom means you are actually running towards bondage. It is not Freedom. By going to satisfy your sense-pleasures or your emotions, you are not a free man. You are a slave there — a slave of your mind and senses. Every one wants to become a master. The funniest thing is that unknowingly you are running after so-called Freedom but you are going to destruction and you have become mere slaves of your mind and senses. It is a terrible thing. Even modern science and modern education have not detected that so far. In this way, everything is going in the wrong direction.

Reading: *Is not then an exercise of control over the mind and the senses desirable?*
Swamiji: The word control is unknown to the modern world. They have entirely forgotten that thing.
Disciple: The word control has a negative sound.
Swamiji: The man who says control, they will laugh at him. "Why control?" they will say, that is all. When they laugh at such things, we also laugh very nicely when they suffer. The outcome of this is madness.
Disciple: What is bhakti-yoga then?
Swamiji: That is another thing. That is not in this way. Bhakti-Yoga is not becoming a slave to emotions in that way. Here you are devoting all your love to God.
Disciple: But still in that devotional love, doesn't one also get the opposite of that, like sorrow and pain?
Swamiji: Not in that way. There is a difference between an ordinary man's emotion and bhakti-yoga. Here you weep for God and do everything for the sake of God. You have given Him your whole life.
Disciple: That is a struggle to attain.
Swamiji: Yes, it is. You have to go in that direction. You are devoting all your energy towards that aim. That is quite different from the

ordinary man. He does not know anything. He wants only the sense-enjoyments. That is all. But bhakti-yoga is not like that.

Reading: *How can mastery over the mind and senses be otherwise attained?*
Swamiji: One of the means to control the emotions is to take up bhakti-yoga to control the mind. Here, there is also concentration of the mind at will. You are consciously devoting your emotions to God. It is not so with ordinary emotions. There you are controlled by the emotions. That is the difference.

Reading: *It is for lack of proper guidance and true leadership that so much of misery is rampant in the world.*
Swamiji: But they will tell a lie. Population is increasing so there is lack of food and other things. There is enough and more but it is all mismanaged everywhere. In olden days, kings had some dignity behind them at least. The modern so-called leaders come without any character, without any backbone. They can do anything and everything. But it was not so with the king and the dynasty. People had some nobility behind them. They couldn't go down as low as these people. Now, every one is a leader. They become big people and they destroy the nations. On one side, they will say we want peace – peace everywhere, world peace. Externally they will be setting people to quarrel with each other so their armaments will have sales and much more money. That is how exploitation is going on

Reading: *If human beings had been men and women of character and if all leaders had been persons with perfect mastery over the mind and the senses, there would not have been so much of troubles and tribulations in this world.*
Swamiji: Not even leaders, but all people. Every religion includes rules of yama and niyama: Be good, be kind, be noble, be charitable, be simple, and don't steal. All the religions say the same and if every one followed it, then there is no need for police or courts. Every one can be in peace. You can make this very earth a heaven but nobody wants it. Only in tall talk they want everything. They don't want it actually. That is the fashion to talk in that way. But there is no action, so we suffer.

Reading: *A perfect man with perfect control over his mind and senses can forget everything, can drive away all desires, thoughts or emotions at any time* at will *and can make his mind free of everything.*
Swamiji: And any of its stages also. When it isn't developed or in an advanced state, whatever we may call it, it is a starting point. If you want it, you can control it. It cannot disturb you in any way. So, that is a great treasure to have such a kind of mind, such a kind of control over the mind and senses, and that is a necessity.
Disciple: If Nirvikalpa is so wonderful, why then has God created this universe?
Swamiji: He has not created anything. You have created it yourself.
Disciple: There is only One Thing you say.
Swamiji: There is only One actually. When you get there, there is no more world. The question has no meaning there.
Disciple: But God must be the starting point of the universe?
Swamiji: If you can find out the starting point, there is no more God. That God has also become limited. If we take human life as a starting point, you must have a birth, and a thing that has a birth is not called God. So, God and the universe coexist, as it were, just to make an explanation for ordinary people how it has become many. It is still One. It is just like the sun and the light. The sun has no meaning without light and light cannot exist without the sun. That is the relationship between the world and God. So, God and the world coexist. There is no time limit when it was created. When you go to the state of Nirvikalpa Samadhi, this question does not arise at all. That One Thing is always One Thing. It has not become many. By the ignorance of your own mind, you have created all these things. Your mind is responsible. When the mind is impure, you see so many things. When the mind is pure and you go back to your Source, then there is only One Thing.
Disciple: But how can my mind be separate from God's mind then?
Swamiji: That is just an image. It appears as separate for the time being. The light is there. There is a mirror. The same light is reflected there. In that way, you are only a reflected thing. The mind borrows the so-called light and life from the Self or from God.
Disciple: We come from Brahman and therefore we have to go back to Brahman.

Swamiji: Yes. Coming and going. All those things are only your creation. In Samadhi state you have no idea. You have not come from anything and you are not going back to anything. In reality, the light is real. The reflection is unreal. But still, it has an appearance. It exists for the time being. Samadhi means taking back this ray of light to the Source. There is only One Thing. You have never separated yourself there. There is only One. Your True Nature is Brahman. It is not that you are not Brahman or that you are becoming Brahman, it is absurd to say in that way. You are already That. If you had not been Brahman, you could never become Brahman. The mind is playing mischief by externalizing through the five senses. You have to go to the last point. It is only a question of time. It may be today, tomorrow or the day after or after millions of years. You have to go back.

Disciple: All these desires. Why do they come when we actually understand?

Swamiji: It is from your chitta, mind-stuff. You have given some wrong impressions. It is all in the chitta as in a storehouse. It is coming up.

Disciple: I mean that we are not ignorant because we understand what is in the books.

Swamiji: Still, it is there. You have trained the mind in a wrong direction; so, it is deceiving you. That is the cause of fickle-mindedness. Everything is from the chitta. There are so many wrong impressions you have given and they are coming up now. So chitta must be purified. Then you have your True Nature.

June 6, 1973

Reading: Moral Code of Conduct: *Truthfulness, non-killing, non-injury, chastity, forbearance, non-stealing, contentment, purity, unselfishness, generosity, charity, service unto the sick, helpless and poor and unto one's elders and unto one's teacher, obedience, control of speech, loving all living creatures, and keeping the mind free from* *the clutches of lust, anger, greed, infatuation, pride, hatred, etc., comprise the code of moral or ethical conduct.*

Swamiji: These things are common to each and every religion. Every religion says: Be kind, be good, be gentle, be noble, never steal, never tell lies, observe celibacy and very few follow it. They have forgotten that celibacy now. Why should it be? They may ask that question. What is the first thing?

Disciple: Truthfulness.

Swamiji: Truthfulness. If you tell lies and swindle others, the man who is swindled resents it afterwards and that attacks the person. Then again, a man who tells lies has a bad conscience, however strong he may be. Even a thief also prays secretly but still he is tempted and steals. If you want to be a true sadhaka, be truthful. With a guilty conscience you cannot have peace of mind. The second one?

Disciple: Non-killing.

Swamiji: Non-killing. That is non-injury. It should be in thought, word and deed. If you go on injuring so many creatures unnecessarily, it is very bad. That will also affect you. You will also have pain in return. You can't have peace of mind. Then?

Disciple: Chastity.

Swamiji: Brahmacharya is the foundation upon which the whole structure of religion rests. Nirvikalpa Samadhi and knowledge of the Self or Brahma-Jnana always go side by side. So long as the kundalini shakti remains in the lowest center, three things predominate in the career of a person – that is food, sleep and sex. The whole world is merged in these three things. The vast majority of people are eaten away by these three things. Then again, the sex-energy travels in two directions – upward and downward. The easiest way is with the sex joys, it goes out. When it is controlled, it takes the upward course. So long as the kundalini shakti remains in the lowest center, it is impossible to make any progress in the spiritual world. When the shakti goes above the heart center, sex joy is impossible. One can never carry out sex functions. That is another secret. So, until and unless the shakti goes up to the last point – sahasrara, head center – there cannot be Nirvikalpa Samadhi.

The connection between brahmacharya and kundalini shakti cannot be proven by your research. If at all you want to find out something, there must be mind-control. You have to make the mind as an instrument. That is the only way. Without making the mind pure, subtle and one-pointed, it is impossible to know the existence of the shakti even. Medical science knows the existence of nerve currents but it doesn't know the center or the dynamo of the nerve-currents yet. So, the dynamo is the muladhara chakra in an ordinary person. That is the chakra from where the shakti works and circulates nerve-energy all twenty-four hours. So long as the shakti works in the lowest center, the mind will remain dull and stupid. All sorts of evils will be there with your mind. When the shakti rises above the heart center, the angle of vision of this universe changes completely. To have any result in the spiritual realm, the shakti must rise up. That is the secret there. Brahmacharya is the greatest thing among all the rules. If at all you want to make any progress in this line, celibacy must be observed. If you want to be a true sadhaka, there must be no compromise. Be strong, be strict, follow the rules, and control it, we say. That is a necessity. Then?

Disciple: Non-stealing.

Swamiji: That we told you already. That gives pain. It may even be an insignificant man; but, when he constantly resents his loss, that is a sort of prayer to God and such things will also attack the person who does the mischief.

Disciple: Contentment.

Swamiji: Contentment is a thing we have to learn. You see, always keeping so many things as desires, you have no peace. Planning brings restlessness of the mind. Be content with what you have. Work hard and, at the same time, whatever comes to you, take it in a good light – have contentment. Some people go to India. They don't keep money also. They say they will go just like beggars. They go to temples. They go and eat and say, "Whenever I feel hungry, God gives me food." That is an easy way. That is not the proper way. Work hard and at the same time be content with it. Then?

Disciple: Purity.

Swamiji: One is external purity – keeping the body neat. Put on clean clothes, pure air, pure food, pure water and pure living place. By keeping all these things pure, the mind also gains purity. Then comes

the internal purity – to have good thoughts. By taking the mantra, while doing all kinds of work that will help you in keeping purity of thought.
Disciple: Unselfishness.
Swamiji: If a man is without anything, help him if possible. If you have got extra money and there is a beggar, a poor, helpless man, if possible, give something. You are passing by and you see a man suffering, if you neglect it, the scene will haunt you when you go home. "I could have done that work." Poor man, you feel miserable yourself and it will drag you down. When you do unselfish work for some others that will also be a sort of sadhana. It helps you.
Disciple: Generosity and charity.
Swamiji: That all comes under the same heading – a little difference that is all.
Disciple: Control of speech.
Swamiji: That is a necessity. Control of speech means that the more you speak, the more fickle-minded you become. You feel miserable. Speech is also a great force going out of your body. Always speak sweet words, kind and useful words and don't unnecessarily waste your energy for nothing. Control speech in that way.
Disciple: Loving all living creatures.
Swamiji: Yes, there comes ahimsa. It does not mean you allow the flies to eat you up when they are disturbing you. There you have to use your common sense. When people are disturbing, a little hissing is necessary. First try to drive them away: "Don't come and disturb the whole house and meditation." Then, it is better to go away from such people or else you will be eaten up by the world. You can't survive. You must know how to apply and where to apply. In some cases, they have been asking, "Is it not a sin to kill?" All right, it is a sin.

Suppose you are in charge of some hundred cows at a dairy farm and a tiger is coming. You have a gun. You have to protect the cows and kill the tiger. So also, by telling one single lie, one can save the whole nation also. In that case, you must see what is profitable. You are not to tell lies but by doing a small sin, you help so many people. That is not a sin in that way. If you have any doubt, come forward. If not, we will pass on. Then?

There are six enemies of man. Kama means lust. That is the worst sort of enemy. Then krodha means anger. That brings a sort of poison, a

chemical change in the blood, and that becomes the cause of disease. Then lobha, that is greed. Control it. Don't be attached to anything in that way. Then moha, that is infatuation. Then mada, that is pride. Then matsarya, that is jealousy.
Disciple: Pride
Swamiji: Pride (mada), that is also egoism. That pride comes in a variety of ways. If a man is a great scholar and some people praise him then he thinks he is a great scholar. Or a woman is very beautiful. Some will praise her calling her "very beautiful," then that is gone. Then there are a variety of things which bind a man. They drag a man. So, egoism is the cause of all this misery in the world. So, one has to give it up.

Yes, it is common. Almost all these things are common to each and every religion. They say the same thing but very few follow it. That is why there is so much misery in this world. If all were to follow the ethical or moral codes of good conduct, we would live in heaven or we would make this world really a heaven. But very few do it. So, the suffering is there.

Reading: *The aim and end of ethics or morality is to make man pure, holy, peaceful and happy. Moral code is the very foundation upon which rests the entire structure of religion, government and civilization.*
Swamiji: So, all governments are aiming to make their subjects peaceful, prosperous and happy. The aim of religion and education must also have the same basis but they have all missed it. One is fighting with another. They have a common basis and are struggling to have an ideal state, an ideal religion and an ideal education but now no one cares for it.

Reading: *A dishonest, wicked or immoral man cannot make headway in religion.*
Swamiji: Yes, in the worldly sphere, one can make progress. If a man is dishonest, if he can tell lies, he can be a good politician. I wrote a letter to one of the Prime Ministers some years back. I started the letter like this: "Politics is a foul game played by international gangsters." For what? They want money and power. Unlike this, in religion, thought, word and deed must go in parallel for a sadhaka. But in politics, you

think one thing, you say another thing and act in a third way. So, it is three different things. It is politics. But in religion, unlike that, thought, word and deed must go side by side and only such a man can make progress.

Reading: *And naturally, religion has degenerated. Many of the religious leaders and priests have become mere propagandists. They hanker after name and fame.*

Swamiji: That is a terrible thing. A man, a sadhaka, working towards this line can control kama and kanchana, that means lust and gold, but the vast majority of people are caught by the desire for name and fame. That is a hidden trap and they are bound like anything. So, in 1938, I wanted to see the facts and figures behind the so-called men of name and fame. It was a terrible thing. I was greatly disappointed. Then lastly, I have written in some of the books that there are three kinds of fools in this world. One is the born fool. They remain as fools – stupid and idiotical. The second grade is rich fools because of their money. The third grade is the educated fools. Because of their wrong education, they are made fools. They may be scholars but they are still fools. Owing to the folly of these three grades of fools, the so-called play of the world goes on eternally. I concluded and ended there. I made up my mind that hereafter I will never see any man of name and fame and I kept it. So, name and fame are terrible things. The vast majority of people are caught in that way and they are guided by false propaganda.

Reading: *In spite of these numerous peace movements and organizations, world-peace and world-happiness are a mere dream with a third world war almost threatening. If we closely search for the causes of the failures of these organizations, it will be found that the founders and the leaders of these organizations are not men of character. They have not established themselves in morality.*

Swamiji: If at all you want to make any progress in this direction, the whole education must change. That is the secret. The current generation is rotten. You can't mend it. But the coming, future generations can be mended if they take proper care and mend the so-called education all over the world. That is the only way, the easiest and most efficacious way of uplifting the nations. If at all they want any progress, they have to tackle education and that must come from infancy. Nowadays, there is no room for it so parents cannot mend their children and the teachers cannot mend the children; so, they must grow in their own way. It is going in the wrong direction everywhere, not only here, but also all over the world. With much difficulty, it can be mended. Character building and education must be there and that is lacking.

In olden days you see, suppose something happened in Copenhagen, it would take you one or two months before you got the news. Now you know immediately what is going on. What is happening in America, you know here immediately. In this respect, you have made some progress in science. It is all right, but so many other ways have degenerated. What is the aim of all this education? There is only one aim. If you go deeper and think carefully, you come to the conclusion that you want Freedom. How to get it? That is the question now. We are externalizing all these things. You are searching. You have gone in so many ways and still it is confusing. You don't know what you want. Education has no aim. In a haphazard way, it is going in whatever direction it likes. There is no meaning in it. By making all sorts of inventions, that does not mean progress.

Somebody asked me the question in Rungsted, "If you were the Prime Minister of the world of education, what would you suggest?" I said, "In the first place, I would bring all the religions into one-fold and take all the best things from every religion and make a book and teach the facts and truth to each and every child as a common basis. Then take up all the good things in whichever department you have, in whatever science you have — it may be political, it may be medical or it may be some other science. Take the best thing from everything and give credit to them. In that way you make a new thing. There would be a common understanding for all. It must be implemented completely. We want a common thing — a good understanding, a real understanding. After all, there is only one God. There can never be two. Teach that subject to them. Character building should be compulsory. If a boy or girl has no character, however bright they may be, don't give them the degree. They should not be allowed to pass. Make it a compulsory thing and mend them."

Yes, children must be given Freedom but not in every respect. Give them love and at the same time guide them. When they go in the wrong direction, mend them immediately. That is the duty of the parents. Then again, the teacher must have power also there to mend them. If children get whatever they want, they will be ruined. Generally, a child can pick up wrong things more easily than good things. Then again there are intelligent children who pick up things easily and there are some you have to tell once, twice or five times even, then they will learn. Then there are some idiots. Even if it is said a hundred times, they will not hear. They don't want to learn; so, we have to grade them. In America, they have got an intelligence test and they grade the children in different categories. Give them Freedom. That is all right. At the same time, they have to build up their character. Meditation must be one of the things they are taught and thereby they will not lose anything. They will be happy their whole life. The best period for meditating and for character building is from the age of ten to thirty. Whatever habits you build up in that time will continue to the end of this life.

Reading: *For, one who is a slave to his mind and senses, who is motivated by the desire for name and fame and is selfish can never lead others.*

Swamiji: And then again, it is a very difficult thing to digest power. Often it is like a rich dish to a dyspeptic patient. The patient wants to eat the rich dish. It is very tempting but if it is taken, it is poison. It will be misused by almost every man. The man who handles power as a slave, he is a great hero. Really, he is a hero. He who has power, every moment is a temptation. He can do anything, all sorts of mischief. So easily do they succumb to this low propensity of the mind and they go to pieces.

Disciple: Swamiji, when you see in society that all these people want power, will it not be very difficult then to get a completely new line when every one is educated from the kindergarten for this power game?

Swamiji: I am telling, you have somehow to manage yourself disinterestedly. Do your duty and keep quiet. What else can you do there? If you want to put a new thing, you will be killed. Nobody wants you. Suppose you become a leader and you are the only man and you want to put forward some new thing, the real thing, and nobody wants it. Immediately, you will be shot dead or they will give you poison and kill you. That is what is happening. So, if you can do it, you have to go slowly and carefully and save your life. Somehow or other you have to adjust. If you want at least to get your daily bread and a little butter you can manage. If you want to have an independent opinion, then, of course, you should not have anything in the world. You must become a monk and remain in the forest under a tree. Then it is all right. There will be nobody to bother you. But worldly life means a little adjustment is necessary. Don't interfere with other matters. You pray to God. Tell him, "Oh Lord, what shall I do. I have to work it out. I have to get a little money just to satisfy my hunger and keep myself a bit warm. I require a little money for this thing. What shall I do?" In that way, put it to God and work it out. Then you have no sin. You want to do it. But it is not possible. It is everywhere. It is a terrible thing and if a man is very honest, they take him to be a fool who cannot take bribes, this side and that. He is considered a fool. In India, some of my disciples say it is terrible how the state of affairs in the whole world has become; but we have to manage somehow.

June 8, 1973
Reading: *A warrior in ancient India would never use his weapon against a woman or a child. A chivalrous Kshatriya would rather die than perpetrate such a heinous and shameful act.*
Swamiji: Kshatriya means fighting man. That is a practical fighting class. It is called kshatriya. They have four main castes. One is the Brahmin Caste. A priest's duty is always to learn the Vedas, Upanishads and to meditate – the spiritual life. The second is kshatriya. His duty is to protect the country. All soldiers come from that class. The third class is the traders. They must keep the country rich. Whatever possible production is by that caste. The fourth are sudras. They are for hard work. It was scientific, in olden times, at a particular stage of evolution, to divide the people into four main groups. Suppose a father has four children and they have four tendencies of mind. One may have a religious bent of mind. A second may be a good wrestler, he must be rajasic. A third may be trading, purchasing for the house. And the

fourth, he wants to work in the fields from morning to evening. In this way, four people have four categories. If they go for a married life, they will have the same kind of wives, also with similar tendency. Now these four couple have their own children and find it difficult to mix with one another. Similarly, at a particular stage of evolution, they found out that it was a necessity for higher research to group people into four main categories. Caste was not rigid in olden times. Afterwards, the caste system became by birth and they lost sight of the original scientific meaning and then it degenerated.

Disciple: The sudra power is everywhere.

Swamiji: All right, the sudra power is going on. That means Russia has started the so-called socialism and it is destroying everything, equalizing a donkey and an elephant or even a monkey or whatever. All must be equal now. A man who is highly intelligent and a man who is an idiot, how can they both be equal? Generally, he will have no chance. He will not worry. Why should he work where there is equality? Only food is necessary. Every one will get food. So, the initiative to develop will be going back. That will be a drawback. When sudra power comes, it will eat up all culture. All good things will be destroyed. It is going on. It is happening. But how long your so-called socialism will be going on, that we have to see. It has no backbone – no background. It is easy for vulgar sorts of people. They find it easy because they can easily rob others and then justify it. They find it easy. But it has no principle behind it.

Disciple: Swamiji, is it wrong to think of people as equal?

Swamiji: It is another thing. You are one of a kind but not in degree. You are one with insects. You are one with human beings everywhere, even with animals. That life is there. There are differences in evolution. How can you equalize them?

Disciple: No, but I think it should be an ideological basis of socialism.

Swamiji: It has no meaning there. Then why should you kill a rich man? What harm has he done?

Disciple: But they have also done many bad things.

Swamiji: Whatever the vulgar people say, many rich people are very good. They have not done anything wrong. Then how can you blame only one side?

Disciple: They have been suppressed for many years?

Swamiji: Who?

Disciple: Actually, when industrialism came, they put all the poor people into the factories. They took away the humanity from it.

Swamiji: You see, suppose you don't want industry, all right. What do you want to do? You don't want any human beings also? They have found some resources. On one side, they have done some good. They may be a bit selfish. It is all right; but there is a way to mend it. That is why you have got the tax system. Keeping rich people in a country is just like keeping big reservoirs for storage of water. It is just like that. In the hour of need, it will be a necessity also. You can't make everything equal. It is just like when there is a drought. Then there is no water. All will die. There must be some rich people also. There is a way according to dharma. A portion of money must go for charity. That was practiced in many countries also in olden times. There are charitable institutions where they give free board and lodging to poor students. It is still going on in India. In that way, there are so many ways it can be turned. We have got the highest kind of socialism in every religion. No religion says: Be selfish, be unkind. Nobody says in that way. Every one says: Be kind, be gentle, be noble, and serve the poor and needy.

June 9, 1973

Reading: *The gruesome and tragic events (from the partition of India in 1947) show to what lengths unscrupulous leaders and statesmen are prepared to go to satisfy their personal or national interests, goaded by malice and ill-will towards opponents and in utter disregard of all canons of ethics and morality. And truly, "man is worse than an animal when he is an animal."*

Disciple: Swamiji, all these cruel and horrible things we have heard about, isn't that due to past karma for the people who have been involved?

Swamiji: Then there is no need for anything if you think that way. How do you take life? Is life only karma or something else?

Disciple: Well, it is a mixture between karma and free will. Say if a man is in a crowd and they shoot at this crowd and he is dying?

Swamiji: That you may take as karma. But why should he go to the crowd? That means the crowd is rowdy. They are against the government's order. Why should you go to the crowd then? You have taken a fresh effort and then comes the bullet. There are thousands of people. The bullet strikes you. That may be your past karma. So, both are there.

Disciple: Swamiji, in Copenhagen during the Second World War, there was a school with nuns and children which was bombed. They dropped a bomb in the wrong place and it fell on the school.

Swamiji: Then you can take it as past karma. There you can apply fate. Is it clear?

Disciple: Almost.

Swamiji: In some places, suddenly a thing happens which you don't want, that you can call fate. Fate is nothing but your past effort giving fruit now. It is your own past actions. If they are good, you have good effects. You will have success. If they are bad, you have failure. Some misery is there.

Disciple: So, the children in the school, they had it somewhere in their karma?

Swamiji: In a past life, they have done something.

Disciple: How long does it take for past karma to ripen?

Swamiji: There is no limit for it. There are three ways that may be mild, middle or intense in kind. If the karma is very mild, it may pass away in a dream. If it is middle in kind, it may ripen in the next birth, and if it is intense in kind, you may expect some fruit in this very life.

Disciple: But is it possible that one man is doing something bad and in the next minute he gets karma for it?

Swamiji: It is not possible in that way. Of course, if he puts the finger in a fire, if it is too intense it may come in that way.

Disciple: You mentioned karma with a dream. Do we have free will in dreams then?

Swamiji: Slightly. Some people know they are dreaming. In some dreams, it is as real as anything. In some dreams, you see the future. Some people get enlightened in dream. They are called svapnasiddhas. Svapna means dream. So, they are becoming siddhas and becoming perfect in dream. So, part of your karma, if it is a mild one, it goes away in the form of a dream. So, the vast majority of people, they have at least one third of their life spent in dream. So, how can you neglect that life existence? So, in dream also, you have fear. You have success, you have failure — everything.

Disciple: Some people remember their dreams very clearly when they wake up. Others don't remember at all. What is the difference?

Swamiji: If the dreaming man goes to deep-sleep after the dream, then he doesn't remember it. Generally, he forgets it. If a man sleeps first and then dreams, he remembers it. Some people have their dreams as soon as they sleep and they forget the dream completely. Sometimes you dream just before waking up in the morning. Such dreams you remember easily. Have you noticed that?

Disciple: Not exactly.

Swamiji: You watch it tonight and see.

Disciple: Swamiji, sometimes people get up and do something while dreaming?

Swamiji: It may be a devil catching you. There was a case of a judge who was going to give judgment and he was thinking of the case and went to bed. In the dead of night, he got up and wrote an eighty-page judgment for an important case. Then he slept. And in the morning, he went to the court and asked for the file as he wanted to give judgment. Then he saw everything written down and he was wondering who wrote this thing. He did not know what he had done. Some people do that when they wake in a dream. It is not a dream. It must be some double-dealing. Someone else is entering them and the real man is somewhere else. He is suppressed. It is just like a medium is possessing him. He will do the work and then forget it.

Disciple: But his mind is also working?

Swamiji: It must be some devil – some medium working. It is possessing you rather. You don't know what you are doing. When you get up, you don't remember anything that you have done. There are so many cases of this kind. They walk and open the door and go away and travel some miles together, come back and then sleep. In the morning, if you tell them, they don't know what happened. Some people go to the graveyard, dig the grave and then bring the bones and they keep them in the house. There are so many funny things. But, they don't admit to devils. You can say there must be something like a medium possessing them — some sort of evil spirit or good spirit. Whatever it may be. They go there and do the thing, come back and they have no idea. When they wake up, they don't know what happened in the night.

Disciple: The real people?

Swamiji: The body was working. Another man entered your body. You were double but you have no idea. You are sleeping and someone else entered your body and it carries you and makes you work. Your body, mind, brain, everything is working through him. Is it just like a medium working? It is possible in that way.

Disciple: Isn't there a way to safeguard oneself from such things?

Swamiji: Yes, if you are strong in your mantra, nothing can come. What is it? What do you want?

Disciple: I mean can somebody enter your body if you are not sleeping?

Swamiji: Yes. They can if you are weak. If you are strong, you will digest him. You will make him a prisoner. You will not allow it also. They enter the weak person only. You are controlled. You are a slave. You have no voice. You can't say anything but that thing speaks through you. We see so many people in that way in the waking-state also.

Disciple: How can you know that it is going on?

Swamiji: A sort of force is entering you. You can't speak. You can understand people but you have no power to speak.

Disciple: Then you know something is coming?

Swamiji: Yes, they understand it. The body and everything shakes when it enters.

Disciple: Can one help if you see that someone is possessed and you are nearby? Can you do anything there?

Swamiji: If you have got mantra and other things, you can help also.

Disciple: By using the mantra?

Swamiji: Yes.

Disciple: Then it will disappear?

Swamiji: Yes. Some people catch hold of those who are experts in tantra and make them slaves. They can send them to any person to do mischief. They will frighten a man while sleeping, like magic people. That is disgusting and not worth having. Suppose a man is possessed.

If you put a hand on that person then go on repeating your own mantra, it cannot stand there. It has no power to stand.

Disciple: But is it not dangerous for you to do it?

Swamiji: Not in that way. But don't go for that thing. Generally, don't do it, I am telling. Don't go for all those tests. It is a curiosity. If the thing is very powerful on the person it has entered, it will work against you; but, if it is a weak one, it may run. If you are an expert in mantra, which means you have been doing your sadhana for a long time, more power is manifested in you. With that power, even with the very sight, it may run away also. If you are weak, it will disturb you. So, don't play with it as it is. It is better to avoid it.

Disciple: What will they have the person do when they enter then?

Swamiji: There are certain desires. By entering the body of a person, they say that they want to drink tea or brandy. "I want to eat pig," they will say. So many varieties they demand. It may be they had an accidental death. Such people remain in that way. They have certain desires unfulfilled and they have to get them fulfilled through the body of some other person and then they have their joys like that.

Disciple: But you said that a ghost also has the power to manifest in the gross body if they like?

Swamiji: Yes, they can.

Disciple: But why do they use others then?

Swamiji: Why should they go to such trouble? The easiest way is to enter.

Disciple: Who gets the karma for that?

Swamiji: The ghost will take the karma.

Disciple: But it is using my body.

Swamiji: Yes, your mind is not working there; so, you are merely in the hands of the ghost there. So, karma will go to the ghost, not to you.

Disciple: But Swamiji, if the ghost, through me, eats a big meal, then I will get the stomach pain later?

Swamiji: Yes, when the ghost goes away, you will feel heavy and you have to vomit.

Disciple: The ghost or ?

Swamiji: The ghost has eaten and it has gone away but your stomach contains the fish, the big fish. So, you have to vomit the fish now. Is it clear?

Disciple: Then the ghost is not taking the karma?
Swamiji: It has taken the karma. It has eaten. You have nothing to do.
Disciple: But you have the pain.
Swamiji: So you vomit. Put the finger and vomit. It comes up and goes away. Then you have no more karma.
Disciple: Why is the ghost so afraid of the mantra?
Swamiji: Mantra has power. Mantra is God. It must be afraid of that thing naturally. A ghost is an evil spirit and it cannot stand God's name.
Disciple: But Swamiji, there are also good ghosts?
Swamiji: Yes, there are some who meditate also. Some people have experiences of that kind. When they meditate, the ghosts also sit and meditate. They also count beads exactly like you. There are some good ghosts and they continue the meditation. Some of the animals have the same thing. In the past life, they were men and afterwards there must be some attachment to some animal and they become that animal. Because of their past karma, they remembered their past birth and they took up meditation.

There was a great Saint by the name of Jadabharata. First Bharat was a great emperor in India known as Bharata-varsha (India = Bharata-varsha). He retired according to their olden system at the age of fifty. He gave up his kingdom to his children and went to the forest for meditation, for higher life. One morning he was at the bank of the Ganges when a pregnant deer was going to drink water. From behind, a tiger was roaring and out of fear, the deer made a sudden jump into the water and gave birth to a young one and the mother died. When the monk saw the baby deer, he took pity on it. It was still alive. The mother had died; so, he became the mother to this baby deer and he took it home and fed it. They got very much attached to each other and when he became aged and was going to die, it was crying mercilessly for its "mother." And the Saint was thinking about what will happen to the deer and was concentrating on that point in his last moments. The Saint died and in the next birth he became a deer and though he was born as a deer, he knew his past life merits. He understood his folly and he was not living like a deer. And he used to meditate also.

After some years, he died and took birth in a family as a Brahmin. By birth, he was a Jnani and had wisdom. The father tried to teach him so he pretended he knew nothing. He did not even learn the alphabet.

From the very beginning, he wanted to cut off all attachments. He did not speak. He was taking precautions. By and by, they understood he was a great man. His name was also spreading but the householders, they treated him like a fool. He was told to sleep in the field, to watch the wheat crop. He was happy with it. In the morning, he was there, still sleeping.

The king of the palace had heard about the glory of this man so he wanted to have his darshan. In olden days, there were no cars so they had four men to carry him on a palanquin. Coming to the adjoining village, one of the men fell sick so they went in search of a man to help carry the king. Some of the people saw the man sleeping in the field and they caught him. He did not say a word. He was a robust and healthy man. He can carry a king. Then they went and the king looked at him and the king was happy to see him because he was a healthy young man. While carrying the king, he walked straight. The other people were bent out of fear; so, he was upsetting the balance. Then the king said, "Why, what is wrong with you?" The king got so much pain and was disturbed like anything. The young man did not speak a word. Again, they were going. The king was so much annoyed. He had a cane and beat him. Then the young man spoke. He spoke words of wisdom. The king said, "What is wrong, what happened?" The king was going to have his darshan but the man was made to carry the king. So, the king fell at his feet to excuse himself and he was pardoned. Then he gave what the king wanted — advice for higher development. So, if you get attached to animals, you have to take birth as an animal. Take care. Never do it.

June 10, 1973
Reading: *Brahmacharya is an important item in the code of ethical conduct. It is the most vital and the most efficacious instrument of mind-control.*

Swamiji: So here lies the point. Many people, the so-called yogis, come to foreign countries and preach against the subject easily. If they want to prove it, it is very difficult for them. They cannot face the world. They neglect completely the very topic or subject. So, we are preaching it boldly now. We want to face the world and prove to the world that it is necessary.

Disciple: Is it possible to have mind-control without celibacy?

Swamiji: It is impossible to control the mind without it. Some people say: Watch the mind. Never control it. Remain as a witness. To watch the mind constantly means you are controlling it. It is not easy there. So, it is all merely stupid ideas, wrong views making people confused. That is all.

Where is the need for brahmacharya? The American women are fooled like anything. They say there is nothing in all this brahmacharya. It is a common thing. It is just like passing urine going to the toilet. What is there in sex? They have made it so easy. It is only ignorance. The other thing they say is that women don't lose any semen by sex so there is no need for women to observe celibacy. How they are deceived, poor women. Every one might have seen people coming with a haggard-looking face. When they observe celibacy, even for fifteen days or one month, what a tremendous change there is. There is so much beauty. Everything increases within a few days when they really observe celibacy and live a pure and simple life. The same people, when they have no restraint, when they go to sexual life, they look so haggard. You don't like to look at their ugly faces – so ugly and stupid and dirty they look. By every sexual enjoyment, you are losing so much energy. The whole body is squeezed out of nerve energy. That is common for both boys and girls. When there is something wrong with the nervous system, they have no medicine for it. They cannot recover it. The memory becomes very dull and the health also. A real brahmachari can cure any disease easier than other worldly-minded people. That is why it is said that when one is established in brahmacharya, three-fourths of the sadhana is over. For such a man, there is only one fourth left. He can attain Samadhi easily.

Real brahmacharya — that means in thought, word and deed — can be had only when the shakti rises above the heart center and then the energy will easily be converted to great mental power or ojas shakti. The more power you have within your body, your health and everything increases.

Disciple: Is it blissful to observe brahmacharya as long as you can't convert the energy to semen?

Swamiji: It goes on automatically. Don't worry about it. There is a thing called suppression and a thing called control. When a desire or thought comes in that way, discriminate, see its ins and outs, what is good and what is bad. If you do it, don't yield suddenly and say, "Oh, I am suppressing the thing." That is a wrong idea. A struggle is there. You must struggle. If you do it constantly, it will easily be converted.

So, brahmacharya's first stage is not to have any sex and then not to speak of it. These two things can easily be done by every sadhaka. Then comes the third thing – by thought. Maybe you have not controlled the thought function so it may take a little time. It does not matter. First take care of these two things and whenever such a thought or desire comes, convert it. Cut it into pieces by discriminating. In this way, you have to proceed. If you are afraid of what the doctors say, it should not be suppressed, you want both – gone. Such a man can never make any progress. Immediately, he has a fall. Struggle must be there. Thereby, you don't get any kind of disease as they foolishly say. Many people get frightened. That is a wrong idea.

Disciple: The doctors think mostly of the physical side, of how much hydrogen there is in the blood.

Swamiji: In that way, we are not going to convince them also. They will come to their senses later on. That is all.

Disciple: Some of the doctors say one could not live without a sexual life. I told them my grandmother had lived twenty years without a sexual life. Then the discussion stopped.

Swamiji: So, you defeated them. That is good.

Disciple: What is meant by suppression?

Swamiji: When the desire is for that thing, you have cultivated the habit, sexual habit. Now suddenly, if you want to stop it you can't stop it and it will find its outlet during wet dreams. In so many ways, it goes out. That is the secret. Do you understand?

Disciple: Yes.

Swamiji: Even when you struggle hard and take precautions, you don't want to lose it but you have wet dreams occasionally. Then you understand the difficulty. But with all those things, go on and continue the work. You can control it – take precautions. Regulate your food, eating and drinking and your society also. You must apply it constantly. A hard struggle is necessary here.

Disciple: When a man has very hard work, he doesn't feel the craving for sex.

Swamiji: Yes, many people go to India. Many of the hippies, they will be starving. They have no money. One boy was telling me, "Oh, I have controlled it completely," he said. I was laughing at him. He said, "I have no more sex. No more idea at all. I have complete control over it." "All right," I said. After that thing, he came to Copenhagen. As soon as he came to Copenhagen, he wanted his wife and she was hiding somewhere. He went in search of her for sex. Then last year he came again here: "Why were you talking in that way? What happened to you?" "Yes. I can control it in India but not in Copenhagen." "What a horrible creature you are. You told me that you had control over it completely, then where are you now?" Now he had no voice.

In that way, they speak some nonsense without knowing anything. It is not easy also but with all that, it is not impossible. If some slight tidbits fall in the form of wet dreams, don't get discouraged. Continue the work. There are so many ways to get it. I have given the rules for brahmacharya. You observe it. That is not a problem. People who take too much butter and milk; it is very bad as it produces sex instincts. Too much hot coffee and tea is also very bad. If you are a slave of your tongue, you become easily a slave to sex also. That is a secret. There is a close connection between the sex organs and tongue. First, take care of your eating. Side by side, keep up your sadhana, mantra-jap and meditation daily. Then you get more and more strength and you can kick out all these silly things easily. Then you come to a higher pitch. Then the world is nothing but a dream to you. Nothing can drag you down. Nothing can make you impure also. You have crossed the dangerous zone. Until then, you must take precautions. It is a struggle with the mind.

Disciple: Swamiji, it is very difficult to know sometimes how much to eat and how little.

Swamiji: So, if you have the desire to eat one more plantain or some other thing, stop it there, you understand? The best way to eat food is to fill half the stomach with whatever you eat, one fourth with water and the remaining one fourth must be kept free for the passage of air. You should not feel drowsy. You must feel alert. In that state, stop it. Even if you take a bit too heavy mid-day meal, it does not matter. But your night meal must always be very light. There you have to exercise control. Never suppress the urine before going to bed or while sleeping. Many do it out of laziness. When they feel the urge for urination, they stop it. That is very bad. The urine comes up to the seminal storage for men, not for women, and then it becomes discharge. That is the secret. Whenever you feel the urge, go immediately. A life of brahmacharya means alertness. You must be alert. When you taste a thing, it is very beautiful. All right, reduce the thing. Don't eat more. There you are exercising control. You know it is a very delicious thing, very nicely prepared. Don't eat more. Only one spoonful — let the tongue starve. That is a punishment for it. In that way, there are so many ways to control it.

Disciple: Why do you write that one should fast on a day one has had wet dreams?

Swamiji: As a punishment, you are taking the self-punishment. There is no government to punish you but you are repenting as a punishment for your system. Whenever you lose something in that way, in the form of wet dreams, keep a fast. Then that will also give you fear if you have to fast. So, you will be careful, not lazy.

Disciple: There have been so many funny things at the hospital.

Swamiji: What fun?

Disciple: One day they sat telling a bad story when I entered and they said, "Don't you think it is a very good story?" Then I said, "If virtue will win, then I think it is a good story." They said, "Then there is no story." Then I said, "It would also be better if there is no story." Then they ran away. Next coffee time when I came in, the doctor said, "I have very much respect for you." Now they don't come with such stories any more.

Swamiji: You have tamed the doctors so they are afraid of you. That is very good.

Any more questions or we will sit for meditation.

Reading: But one cannot escape the loss of one's physical and mental energy which follows almost immediately if one commits adultery or self-abuse even covertly.

Swamiji: Sex joy means immediately you have a loss. Just like putting a finger in a burning fire. It burns you. Immediately there is a fall. But in all other things, you may tell lies and escape punishment for the time being or you may steal something. For some time, you can escape. In all other things, you can escape for a certain time. There is reaction for it also, but here the punishment comes immediately.

Reading: *For those who aspire to attain perfection in yoga and those who wish to gain higher concentration of the mind, observance of strict brahmacharya is a necessity.*
Swamiji: Yoga means here, higher attainments not merely putting the head down and putting the legs up. Many people take it as yoga. There are so many yogis nowadays. They go to America; but, it is only hatha yoga. They don't put the word hatha, only "yoga." So, all are big yogis. The main thing is forgotten. They only teach some exercises. Every one can do it, that kind of yoga. That is not yoga. But they go to America and all over the world. Even in Germany and Switzerland, there are so many yogis and they make their fortune.

Reading: *Mind-control and control of sex energy go together.*
Swamiji: So that is a necessity. To control the mind completely there must be brahmacharya. Brahmacharya and mind-control always go side by side. It is the so-called demarcation – apparent division of shiva and shakti. In the starting point of evolving this microcosm, as an example, if you take a chicken egg, which has been spoiled half way before hatching, you can see a line coming from the head to the tail. That is the sushumna. It is already formed there and from that, all other things go on growing. So, in evolving this body, the starting point is sahasrara. It is the static center and one by one the six centers are formed. When it comes to the last center, muladhara chakra, it remains there in its grossest form. The shakti is very subtle and cannot be detected by man-made instruments yet. That is why modern medical science cannot understand it. It is impossible. From there, all the twenty-four hours, it circulates nerve energy — that is the dynamo. Now, in every sexual act, a portion of that accumulated, generated energy goes out so there will be a lack of nerve energy for the different functions of the body. That is why after sex one feels so heavy. The brain

center becomes very dull. You cannot work properly. The whole energy has been squeezed out. Shiva and shakti, in its grossest form, is the unity between man and woman. That is sex joy. The same thing is when it is controlled and goes back to the last point. Their unity there is called Nirvikalpa Samadhi. So, without brahmacharya, it is impossible to take the shakti back to the Source and without taking the shakti to the brain center, Brahma-Jnana or knowledge of the Self is quite impossible. Many people think jnana means reading books or making big lectures. It has nothing to do with that. Jnana means wisdom or knowing your True Nature.

Disciple: I want to ask if in one state bhakti-yoga meets with jnana-yoga?

Swamiji: When you go to Samadhi, the last point, all these things fall away. In bhakti-yoga, you see the form of your Ishta-Devata face to face. Many stop there. They don't want to go beyond but even that, also, you have to cross by discrimination. When you go to the last point, even by devotion, you forget the form.

Disciple: And then it is jnana-yoga?

Swamiji: In jnana-yoga, there is no form — nothing whatsoever. The thing is by itself. You go back to your Source. When you see two things, there is dwaita. That is two. In Nirvikalpa, there is nothing — only One Thing. You see, many people want to eat chocolate but they don't want to become chocolate. It is rather a weakness but they are content.

Disciple: But Swamiji, even in bhakti-yoga and karma-yoga, if there is real self-surrender, must it go to Nirvikalpa Samadhi?

Swamiji: There are stages even in surrender. In the initial stages, it is too rough and tough and you forget the thing.

Disciple: Yes.

Swamiji: By practice you go on surrendering. You may fail when there is something successful and some people praise you. Then you think, "I have done that thing." That "I" comes secretly. Outwardly you say, "It is all God's will. He has done it". "I am working for God," you may say, but the "I" is still there like a thief hiding behind. It says, "Oh, I have done that thing." The "I" is there you see. So, there you have to find the thief and catch the nose by a rope. "I don't want to be a slave to you." In that way, go on slowly. There are stages also in that.

Disciple: But the last stage of surrender?

Swamiji: Last stage, there is nothing to surrender at all. Whom to surrender to? You are that Thing. "I am Brahman. I am that Thing." But don't make a confusion of these two stages. In the beginning, you have to discriminate between good and bad, pain and pleasure. All are there. When you come to a certain point of evolution, you understand that what you call good has a portion bad too. There is not a single thing in the universe which you can call absolutely good or absolutely bad. But if you take this idea in the beginning stages, you will miss the point.

Disciple: But how can one stop after attaining Savikalpa Samadhi?

Swamiji: Because you are enchanted. You are satisfied with it. You are already tired. The whole life long you have been working. "Now," you think, "Let me rest. Why should I work more?" That is the tendency there. Apart from that, there are so many people who see a little light, some sort of flashing. They say that they have seen God and they become Gurus. There are so many Gurus of that kind.

Disciple: Can one become a victim of one's own delusion?

Swamiji: It is nothing. He does not worry about it. It was what happened once. I was writing the big book. "The Mysteries of Man, Mind and Mind Funtions". I was in a secluded place. One Guru, she was a big Guru, she wanted to see me. First, she asked, "Why did you become a monk?" I understood her motive, so instead of giving her a reply I said, "Why have you become a nun? If you can explain that to me, I will tell you my story." She was caught. Now she thought, suppose if you put an ordinary question to any one of you like why have you become a monk, you will say, "I have to realize God or to attain Nirvikalpa Samadhi." Then the other question will come immediately, "You are already that Thing. Then what is the need for Nirvikalpa Samadhi?" In this way, she wanted to catch me. She wanted to become a so-called Guru. So, I did not give her a direct reply. I said, "Why have you become a Guru? You are also in this line." So, she was caught now. She tried her best. So, I put the question first. "You will have to answer me." "No, no, there is nothing." Then I said, "Yes, it is very easy. One can read some books. Here and there get some sort of knowledge and become a big Guru. But the actual side is quite different." And I explained the whole thing. Then she understood her mistake and began saying, "Yes, that is the state with me."

She had read some of the books — Upanishads, Bhagavad Gita and other books. Now, there were so many disciples. She had enough money so she had a luxurious life. Afterwards, the division of Pakistan and Hindustan came. She was in a Muslim country. The whole property was robbed by Muslims and some of her disciples were massacred and she had to run away for her life. Coming to Rishikesh, the devil malaria caught her. She had no place to live, nothing to eat. Now she understood who she was. "It is all mere false things. I have not gained anything." She understood now. Up to now she thought she was a big Guru, she explained, that was the state of her mind. "Yes, that is why I told you, one may talk so many things, all sorts of nonsense. It is all right, but to become a real Guru is quite different." She understood and went away. In this way, there are so many false Gurus.

Disciple: You say you have to observe yama and niyama to attain the highest, but isn't it so that you cannot observe yama and niyama absolutely before you have attained the highest? For example, how can one be content?

Swamiji: You can observe all the rules in word and deed but to do it in thought, that can be gained only after Nirvikalpa Samadhi or at least the shakti should come above the heart center. Then you can control your thoughts. This is the most important subject. You have to guard yourself. You have to argue. Some false people may argue against you.

Disciple: In bhakti-yoga, it can be very difficult to have the feeling of love always.

Swamiji: There are different grades of love, you see.

Disciple: But if there is no love because you feel tired and have reaction?

Swamiji: All right, force it. Even if it is too dry, force it. Go on with the mantra.

Disciple: By what nature is this love? How is it manifested?

Swamiji: That is an emotion that cannot be explained. You can feel it. Love, lust, hatred and other feelings cannot be explained as to what they actually are. Can you explain anger?

Disciple: No, I cannot explain it.

Swamiji: So, it cannot be explained. But, when a man is angry, he will make some gestures, his eyes become red, and then you understand that he is annoyed. When you are overly joyful, you begin laughing and laughing but you cannot explain what it is. So, emotions cannot be explained in that way.

Disciple: One has to wait to get this bhakti.

Swamiji: When you go on with mantra-jap and meditation, automatically devotion will develop. You want to go to higher and higher pitches. You have that intense love. Again, the word "love" comes there. You cannot explain it, but you feel it. You think that your whole heart will burst. You want only that thing, nothing else. You understand?

Disciple: Yes.

Swamiji: The same thing happens when a man becomes annoyed. He forgets the whole world and then he wants to kill the man, whatever he has done. When one is too much annoyed, one goes mad. There is only one object. Similarly, when love increases, you want to reach it at any cost. You want to give the whole life for it. There is only one thought. The mind gets concentrated in intense love. So, to increase the love, you have to live a pure life, do mantra-jap and meditation. Slowly you will increase the love. If you live a dirty life, a stupid life that also gets hidden, you cannot have pure love. That love will disappear and you will become dry. On the other hand, you will try to find happiness in all worldly things – in stealing and robbing or in some other mischievous things you will find pleasure. You lose sight of the real thing. That is what is happening. Is it clear or no?

Disciple: When the mind gets this feeling of love, why does all that very often come again?

Swamiji: It will come because it is mixed — good and bad. When the mind gets purified, you always get that pure love. It may be owing to your past karma or it may be some lack of your daily discipline in all the daily work. There may be so many causes. When the stomach is too heavy, you eat more, then also you lose sight of the pure love and then you take pleasure in sleeping. That love is gone. In that way, ups and downs there will be. With all that, you must have patience and perseverance. Then, it will come. When the mind is especially working, you feel so much happiness even in your work. And, during the time of reaction, you don't want to do anything. You feel, "Who wants this God? Let it go to hell." "Damn," you will say. You get annoyed there. Then comes reaction and you have a fall.

Disciple: But how does love then lead to adwaita?
Swamiji: With love you have to come to Savikalpa Samadhi. Then you become one with it later on. The love, lover and the Beloved, all the three things become only One Thing. There comes Nirvikalpa Samadhi. There is perfect unity. There is no more trinity. That is subject, object and knowledge. These three things blend into one — the subject by itself. That is Nirvikalpa. That is the last point.
Disciple: Swamiji, when love during sadhana increases, will reaction also increase?
Swamiji: Not in that way. You can control the reaction. In the initial stages, reaction becomes very strong. Sometimes it may be often. But in the advanced stages, you can't have such a reaction. There you know how to control it. It comes sometimes in a very terrible form.

I was just preparing myself. I had no Guru, no one to guide me. I was young. I was preparing to renounce the world. I used to have four times meditation. Nobody guided me. I was regulating my diet. In the morning, take a cup of milk and one or two plantains, midday light meal and evening also. No tea – nothing whatsoever. I was not taking anything. Then, the thing came double. Four times I used to meditate – morning, midday, evening and midnight. Then the reaction came. I did not know anything. It was so horrible. It lasted like anything for nine or ten days. That is an unknown sorrow. There is no reason for it. You cannot sleep. I could not speak with friends. Some of my friends used to come and sing devotional songs. I was shedding tears. There was no consolation. It was too terrible and for nine or eleven days, something like that, it continued. That was the longest period I have ever witnessed. After that, I renounced the world. I left hearth and home and I never carried a single penny with me. I distributed all my few things, all I had to poor people. I left without even a blanket to cover me.

Then I was to travel. Now came the difficulty of putting on a strange cloth with nobody to guide me and nothing to eat or anything. Now it came, the reaction. "Oh, you fool, why did you become a monk, where to go now." It was too horrible. I forced myself to never look back and to go ahead. I was going in search of a Guru somewhere. I don't know, thousands of miles somewhere, and sometimes I had to walk and I was fasting. Such reaction I had for a day or half a day. Then, I took my sadhana very seriously. I could control it. Whenever there was reaction, even for a few minutes, when it came, I knew it was reaction.

Go on, change the center of the kundalini and immediately you can control it. In that way, you understand the reaction. It has come all right. It does not matter. You change it and you forget it completely. In the beginning it comes and in advanced stages, you know you can control it at any stage and so, also, your emotions. If you know the function of your mind and the working of the kundalini, you can change it at any state of any emotion without allowing it to develop further.

In this way, I had no book learning. I never went to a scholar to learn anything and I had no Guru to teach me also. Many of the things I have given are original contributions to psychology. I don't think even the Vedas and Vedanta, give you details about the mind-functions in this way — thought functions especially. In Vedanta, I think they give six causes for how a thought arises in the mind. Western psychology has given only one cause. Senses coming in touch with sense objects. That is the only thing they learn. I have given sixteen causes for it. It is the first time you will get the history of the spiritual world, in that way. Nobody taught me. For twenty years I was living away from all the din and bustle of the world. I remained hidden. I never cared to see anyone.

Then, also the books, I never wanted to write. After the partition of Indi in 1947, seeing the difficulties of the people, then only I took up writing. That is a big story. Even that writing, I did not spend much time. When I wrote, I wrote for half an hour daily then I forgot the point and left it there. I was busy with other things. Next day, I took up from where I stopped and continued writing. I had nothing, no books. People who write usually have a big library behind them. They will write ten pages here, ten pages there, join it and make a book. Then came the problem of how to publish them. I had no money so I had to face so many difficulties. Still, they were published. There are so many other things I had to face. All right, that is a good thing. That made me strong or else I would have been a stupid fool somewhere. Twenty years back, they also wanted me in America. They were prepared to pay all my expenses. They wanted me there after seeing my books. I said goodbye, I will not go. Anyway, Denmark caught me lastly. Denmark has brought me here. All right that is also good. Any other points?

Then sit for meditation.

June 12, 1973

Disciple: When I sit for meditation, I get disturbed by other people. What can I do?

Swamiji: Put some cotton in your ears. After a few days, you will get accustomed. You can get some plastic plugs from the doctor. They may also help.

Reading: *But he who establishes himself in brahmacharya in thought, word and deed shines like the midday sun, and displays great powers.*

Swamiji: It can easily be seen. Those who have excess of sex lose all sorts of charm – mentally, morally, physically and spiritually. They degenerate slowly and they pave their way to so-called death. Even in leading a normal life, a well-regulated sexual life is absolutely necessary. When there is excess of sex, they go to pieces. Many of those who have excess of sex in a hot climate like India, they get terrible diseases called gonorrhoea or syphilis. In a cold climate, you may escape to a certain extent. The man going to such a woman and uniting sexually will be gone. He will also get the same disease. If a man suffering from that disease is sitting in one corner, he will be stinking like a dead animal — such a horrible disease. But normally, we don't ask every one to observe strict brahmacharya. Those who want sex, all right. Marry and have a legal sexual life but control it, restrict it, don't go freely.

Even animals have a better understanding in this matter than human beings. Animals, especially females, have no sex apart from the season. When there is pregnancy, they never mate. But, the human brute is worse than that. We have no restraint for it. It is a most pitiable thing. Not only the animals, even the insects, they have their mating. In that season only, they mate. Off-season, they never mate.

Ordinarily, we grade people into three groups. One is an animal man, one is called man, and the third is called superman. For animal man, we don't speak about brahmacharya at all. We ask him to beget as much as possible — eat, drink, beget. The vast majority want these three things. They want food, sleep and sex. If you want at least to call yourself a human being, we say regulate your sexual life. There also we don't say absolute brahmacharya. The olden system was that they had sex until they begot one or two children to keep up the line of heritage. Then they used to observe celibacy and meditate and evolve to higher pitches. Lastly, there is the superman, there must be brahmacharya and that is the subject here.

Disciple: I want to know how to concentrate on the Self?

Swamiji: That is a subtle object. How can you go to that formless aspect of the Self? You can't go. It is better to go with certain forms. Taking the form, you learn how to concentrate and then slowly, slowly you have to go forward. If you take up the method of concentrating on the formless aspect, it is very difficult. You can't make progress. You understand?

Disciple: Yes.

Swamiji: All are not fit to take up jnana-yoga. First, you put the question, "Who am I?" "Then, am I the body?" "No." Why? The body is changing. Then he asks, "Am I the senses?" "No." "Am I the mind?" "No." So, in this way, he goes on discarding everything. Then he comes to, "Who am I?" "I am that Self, that Sat-Chit-Ananda, Existence, Knowledge and Bliss Absolute. I am that Thing." The Self has no birth, no growth, no decay, no disease, no death, and no sex; so, all these things are false. In that way, you have to hold the mind to the last point.

It is a difficult thing. It is better to begin with a gross object, take mantra and Ishta-Devata and concentrate on that. Then you can go to subtler and subtler things. Don't take up the last point suddenly. You can't make any progress. You will be confused. Only the ego grows there. Many people make that mistake.

Disciple: Where to concentrate in yourself?

Swamiji: Start with the heart center. Concentration there slowly makes the mind steady. It is not so easy. The mind wanders here and there but again and again bring it to the point. After some time, you will feel it and still there will be disturbing thoughts. Again, you make use of the mantra and control those thoughts. After some time or some months, you get accustomed to it. Then the mind gets easily

concentrated on the form. When it goes deeper and deeper, the form also disappears. Then you may see a sort of divine light, an all-pervading silvery light even, concentrate on that. Focus the mind and it will take you to the last point – formless aspect. That takes time, but you must proceed with the form. Don't go for the formless aspect. You will miss the point. Clear?
Disciple: Yes.

Disciple: Has God always got the same form?
Swamiji: There is nothing like that. As you think, He will appear. That is the subjective form, not the objective. You give a particular form and then you go on thinking on the same thing. Then you will see that that is a subjective vision, not objective. Sometimes, one may have the objective vision also. Both are there. Without thinking of any form, something may appear before you. It may be God. It may be a ghost. It may be a devil. So, it is possible.

Disciple: Is man the only creature in the universe that can attain Samadhi or are there other creatures?
Swamiji: As it is, man is highly evolved. He has his intellect which is more highly developed than other creatures. It is also developed in lower creatures but not so highly. So, it is possible only through man. Then, there are some cock-and-bull-stories where they say, some, even the crows, have attained the highest. They say he was a man previously. He had a curse and then he became a crow or a frog or an elephant. They have made all such stories but, anyway, the last point is to evolve as a human being.

Disciple: I want to know if all beings are born again, reincarnated, on earth or on other planets?
Swamiji: It is possible in so many ways. Both are possible. Those who think of heaven or other planets, they may go there after death also. Those who find heaven and hell on this very earth, they will find it here. It is all mind's creation. Your effects of karma, what you have done, good or bad, that also counts here. Anything else?
Disciple: No.

June 13, 1973
Swamiji: So, what is your program now?
Disciple: First discussion.
Swamiji: So, on what point?
Disciple: Now we should see whether there are some questions from this winter.
Swamiji: All right, see.
Disciple: We had discussions here every week but it seems that many of the questions have run away.
Swamiji: Run away, how?
Disciple: It is just like shadows. They disappear when the sun comes.
Swamiji: In that way. Let me know, what are the doubts? Come forward.
Disciple: We were dealing with the subject of creation in the big book, "The Mysteries of Man, Mind and Mind Functions".
Swamiji: That creation is just a sort of explanation.
Disciple: But it is there.
Swamiji: It is there but when you go deeper and deeper and take a higher and higher point of view, there is nothing then. This worldly point of view is just a sort of explanation.
Disciple: But still, it is dealing with so many things there.
Swamiji: What are those?
Disciple: It is said that the Supreme Spirit, when it is reflected in Maya Shakti, is called Ishwara. And when it is reflected in Avidya Shakti, it is called Jiva. We want to know the difference between Maya Shakti and Avidya Shakti?
Swamiji: Avidya means ignorance and Maya is without ignorance. Suppose you have got so many microbes or cells living in the body and over that body you have a ruling monarch – Jiva. You understand? Similarly, in the universe, the Jiva can be considered as that Ishwara. So, Ishwara and Jiva are just like your Self and the so-called microbes or cells living in the body. It is somewhat similar when you go to the highest point of view. It has no meaning there. Jiva, Shiva, and Brahma, are only one. It can never be two things. As it is, we find so many things. So, we put all sorts of explanations just to explain as a sort of story for ignorant people.
Disciple: There must be some facts in it.

Swamiji: It is a fact. Seen in that way, you cannot deny the Self in the body. When the Self leaves the body, the whole body dies. So, the cell lives are also owing to the Jiva in this respect only.

Disciple: Is the Ishwara the same as the Saguna Brahman?

Swamiji: That is Saguna. When you to go Nirguna, there is only One Thing.

Disciple: So Savikalpa Samadhi means?

Swamiji: There are, in this part, different versions. There is Ishta-Devata and other things.

Disciple: Is that the same as Ishwara?

Swamiji: It is similar to that.

Disciple: But does it have a form itself?

Swamiji: You are giving a form. That is all. And that form, it can appear. When you constantly think of a particular form, that form appears to be real to you, and then knowledge dawns. That form disappears and you go back to the Source. So, taking that point of view, there is no creation. There is no Ishwara. Everything is eaten up completely. So, don't be afraid of that Ishwara there.

Disciple: Do all minds give the same form?

Swamiji: They do not. Suppose you are now seeing a particular form. You say God has that particular form. Some others may have a different form of the same thing. In a different way, they may think. You understand the scene. God can be taken in different forms in that way. There may be some energy working on the same thing in different forms and they are given different names. They are so-called Gods and Goddesses ruling the universe, as it were. But that rulership goes to pieces with the highest knowledge. There you don't admit anything. You don't give room to anything.

Disciple: Do all these things have only a so-called reality when we live in dualism?

Swamiji: That is all, that much only. Now science will tell you so many things. Take the five elements. They have divided those elements into ninety elements, something like that. There is reality in that way but when you go further, the elements will disappear. Lastly, they come to atoms and that atom also disappears and now they say there is only force. But if you still go further, there will be nothing — only One Thing.

They must come to that. I have called it "The Ocean of Consciousness by Itself." From that, all these things appear to have existence.

Suppose you take vapour. It is there, but we don't perceive it. It is very subtle. When the vapour becomes cooler, it becomes grosser. First it takes the form of cloud. Further, when it becomes cool, it takes the form of water. And further cooled, it becomes ice. Now it has got a form. It has a name. It has a reality. When you heat the ice, making an experiment, it will go back to the vapour state again. In the same way, is this so-called evolution. In reality, there is only One Thing. That is vapour in the causal state. Similarly in duality, there is only One Thing. That is God. So, from that state, all other things come. You go on dividing and making all these forms. Then there is a creator and then there is a preserver and then there is a destroyer. In this way, you divide – that is the trinity. The last state is what you call Jnana.

Disciple: Swamiji, when you start meditating on a certain form of God and until you go beyond the Saguna aspect is it the same form all the time just getting more subtle?

Swamiji: For your concentration, use the same form. When you go with the same form and get concentrated on the form first, later on the form will disappear and you go to the last point. That is the state of Nirvikalpa Samadhi. That is Nirakara – the formless aspect.

Disciple: Isn't it so that when one comes to those higher states, one perceives that everything is mental, pure mental?

Swamiji: You will understand it. Everything is in the mind only. It is all mind's creation. That is why it is said, "The universe is only a projection of your own mind." All the experiences, your pain, pleasure, whatever you call it. It is all the mind's creation, nothing else. In one word – mind. Now your struggle is to control it. So, we say again and again, mind-control is a necessity. The force of pain entirely depends on how you discriminate and decide the value of the thing, how you understand it. Suppose a man is dead. You hear the death news of your neighbour. You know the person but you are not concerned. You feel, "Poor man. He was so very young and a good man." That is all. There ends the matter. Now, other news comes to you, say one of your friends has died, not so close friend, but friend. There, you feel more pain. Now the third news comes, an intimate friend has died. He was a good man. He was your very closest friend. Immediately you begin to weep. Tears come out. So the news is the same. How much value you give it depends upon your mind. So, everything is in the mind, how you discriminate and decide the value.

Disciple: But after having attained the highest, is it possible to have any tears?

Swamiji: Tears may come sometimes. Just to play with you people, He may weep also.

Disciple: Without playing, then there is nothing, no sorrow?

Swamiji: If you want to make a show, be sympathetic.

Disciple: But if He doesn't want to make a show?

Swamiji: That is possible, you can control it. So, to play the drama, one must pretend. He may weep loudly also just to make you understand.

Disciple: Swamiji, before going to Nirvikalpa Samadhi, is there perception of the Jiva?

Swamiji: You can have the understanding in the right side of the chest, just before Samadhi. You see the concentrated form. That is the Consciousness coming, as it were, from a small point and spreading abruptly all over. You see it in the right side of the chest, that is the seat of Jiva.

Disciple: Is there any idea of an object?

Swamiji: In that state, you have a little idea. The Jiva is there. Your object is there. You have not yet merged. You are just in the process of going. That is only a preparation to go to the sea.

Disciple: So, the subject is the object?

Swamiji: Everything is there — subject, object and knowledge. Without that, how can you understand Jiva? So, mind is there. Shakti is there. Jiva is there. Then all this comes to one point and when you enter that great void, everything is eaten up. Even your breathing stops completely there.

Disciple: In the process of evolution, when the shakti rises and reaches one center after another, then the energy working at the particular center stops working.

Swamiji: The shakti does not work in that particular center; but there are subtle energies working from different centers. They are very subtle or in a causal state, you can say. They stop working. With all that, the shakti must go up. It goes on working different other centers when it goes to higher pitches and from there it circulates nerve energy to the whole body.

Disciple: So, it takes these powers, these energies with it?

Swamiji: It is there. The lower energy, which is binding, that is gone. Now it takes higher forms. The mind is on a higher level, a purified state, and the lower things which were disturbing up to now, they are no more. A man has good vibrations, good thoughts. All things develop in him more and more and the angle of vision of this world, which was binding him up to now, all those things die. He has some other idea. He finds it all useless. It has no meaning. Nothing can bind him. There, sattva guna predominates. His taste and tendency will be for a secluded life for sadhana, for higher attainments. Nothing can drag him down.

Disciple: How can you misuse the mantra?

Swamiji: Why should you misuse it? There are so many ways. You go on praying and using the mantra. You are praying for someone. It may be some of your friends who are suffering or doing something to help others and that is a sort of misuse there. There are so many ways how you can misuse it.

June 14, 1973

Reading: *In leading a sexual life, the vast majority of human beings are reckless in sharp contrast to the animals in general.*

Swamiji: Generally, when children are too young or even grown up, when they have no sexual life, they have so much energy. When once they begin a sexual life, the whole energy is gone. Even to go to higher study will be difficult. That you might have noticed among students. It is a common thing.

Disciple: It is a great change.

Swamiji: So much change, but they have neglected the thing all over the world. It has become a kind of disease. In India, it has gone from bad to worse, sinking every day. It is following the West. So many people don't know what is meant by brahmacharya. When I was writing the book, one college student asked, "What is meant by brahmacharya?" The word was a new thing to a grown boy in India. Then what about the western world? If you watch carefully, you will see the change. When they take the sexual life, their whole energy is gone. For higher research or growth or study, there will be lack of energy, both for boys and girls. They will suffer.

Reading: *To sum up, to gain real intuition one must observe strict brahmacharya.*
Swamiji: There is a distinction between real intuition and so-called intuition the western world talks about. Here, man perceives a certain object he knows, without knowing why and how, he follows certain things. They call that intuition. It is not real intuition. Intuition means seeing a thing face to face. It may be past, it may be present, and it may be future. Intuition can work only after the attainment of Nirvikalpa Samadhi, not before. That is the secret. They don't actually know what it is, what is meant by intuition. So, to gain that intuition, there must be brahmacharya. One has to go to the last point and merge the kundalini shakti there. When coming back, intuition works. That is known as the Superconscious plane.

Reading: *Without it, one can never attain Samadhi and gain Brahma-Jnana (knowledge of the Self). To bring into action the enormous hidden and creative powers of the mind, the observance of brahmacharya is essential.*
Swamiji: So, it is not easy to control the shakti. It is an enormous power. You cannot imagine what that power is. A little neglect of the subject means it is gone. It goes down immediately. The orgasm takes place. Orgasm means a portion of the shakti goes down and it is a misfortune for a sadhaka especially. There must be perfect brahmacharya. Then only, the shakti will rise up fully or else it will be partial.

There are some people, after drinking, will have a partial rising. When the shakti comes to the brain center, there one may feel a sort of inspiration. So, inspired people, many of them are of this kind. To raise the shakti fully, there must be three-fold purity — purity of the body, purity of the nadis and purity of the mind. Without this three-fold purity, one can never take the shakti up fully to the brain center or sahasrara.

Reading: *Food and drink play a very important part in mind-control.*
Swamiji: You are the best doctor yourself. You must know what suits you and what does not suit you. Many people have no idea about it; so, they make a big confusion. They blindly follow some rules some man has said, like vegetarian diet is necessary. Many of the great founders of religion are non-vegetarian. You take, for example, Jesus and Buddha. If you go to Tibet, they have to take raw meat and in Burma, they even take snakes raw. They purchase one and eat it as you eat radish raw. The head is cut off. Then they go on eating it raw, horrible. The very idea is horrible. So, who is right and who is wrong? You can't blame anyone.

June 15, 1973
Reading: *In Tibet, the people live at a very high altitude. No corn grows there except in the low-lying valleys and it is too insufficient to support the whole land.*
Swamiji: The same thing, why do you go so far. You can understand your own difficulty. Here, in winter, nothing grows. So, you have to dry the vegetables and keep them for winter. That is a simple thing. If you don't keep stock for the winter, you can't eat anything. Then, if you prescribe only one sort of food for all, it will be a complete failure. Man must die or religion must die or God must die. Everything must go to pieces. So, you must have common sense in all these things. If you think it should be all dry vegetables, it is very bad, injurious, unhealthy, unwholesome — all these things are silly things. It has no meaning. If you want to survive you have to yield to the available things. Even by keeping the things in cold storage, that is also not very good but you can't help it. Still, something is better than nothing. You have to survive. Then again, all this tinned food, preserved, that may survive for long.

That is also not very good. Still, we cannot manage without all those things. So, necessity is the mother of invention.

If you want to live, you have to manage. So, we can't make any hard and fast rules on these things. The absolutely necessary thing is while eating you must take care of how much you eat. Always fill half the stomach with food, one-fourth with water and leave the remaining one fourth empty. That is healthy. Then you escape many of the diseases. Even if you take raw food and overload the stomach, then you get disease. So, you must adjust. You must know what suits you and what does not suit you and avoid the things which are not suiting you, however good they may be. With many people, milk diet suits. They can take two or three kilos of milk with some fruits also. But the same thing may not suit another man. It may produce a lot of wind and other troubles. With some, it may be fish. They can digest easily half a kilo or one kilo even of meat. It works well for them and the same man cannot take even one kilo of milk, then they have loose motion or so many other troubles. If you think milk diet is the best one, that is what people say, that is nothing but ignorance to say in that way. No doubt milk has all the good nutritious qualities but still, if it does not suit you, it has no meaning there.

Then again, people who make a big claim that a vegetarian diet is the necessary thing for attainment, then comes the question: What about milk? That is also blood of the cow in white form. That is all. What becomes of the milk if you don't milk the cow? It will become blood. Is there any difference there? Little difference, I think. Then you don't take meat. Take only soup. All right, it is also better. Boil it and extract the juice only and take it — that is called soup. So, they should not have any objection for it. It is nothing but blind arguments. If you minutely watch it, some of the sayings have no meaning. Thereby, don't misunderstand me that I am asking everyone to take meat. Many people conclude in that way. It is the bare facts I am saying. I am not supporting any kind of thing. You must know that. I don't ask anyone to take either milk or meat, whatever it may be. I give the choice to every one. Adjust yourself. That will be the best thing.

Disciple: Swamiji, can you do pranayama on a meat diet?

Swamiji: If you know how to eat it, you can also do it. There is no harm if your digestion is powerful, if there is no disturbance in the stomach.

What about your cabbage and cauliflower? After eating, there is so much wind in the stomach. What kind of pranayama can you do there? The climate is such here that there is so much wind. Every one suffers. It is a cold climate which is a natural thing here. So, you have to adjust somehow.

Suppose you take a lot of black coffee or black tea. In a cold climate, it is necessary. But if you take black coffee or tea in India, in a day or two you will have blood dysentery. You will go to hell. It is so terrible. In summer, it is so hot you can't sit inside a room. All the walls become so hot you can't even touch them. It is just like sitting near an open fire, so hot it becomes. If you open the tap water, you will get hot water, such terrible heat. So, a man eating in India will prescribe the food as chapatti and green dhal. You must eat these only, no rice, nothing whatsoever. The man coming here, without knowing this difficulty, will prescribe the food from India. It has no meaning. So, you have to make adjustments. That is one word. You have to learn all these things.

Reading: *If religion forbids fish and meat-eating as sin and limits its followers to vegetable diet alone, were these great men non-religious?*
Swamiji: Then again comes the question is it not a sin to kill? If you go deeply, life means at the cost of another life. The higher one eats the lower one. Living means at the cost of another one. Even the vegetables have got so much of life — poor creatures. We like chewing them like anything. Insects have got more Freedom and when you come to animal life, you feel more. When you see a big whale or elephant being shot dead, you feel so unhappy. You feel life so big there. You feel it. Somebody was telling me they went to see hunting of whales, the big ones. Oh, it was a terrible task, they were telling. It takes several hours to kill it. It is running here and there for life. It is painful, they were telling. But actually, to live means to kill some other things. It may be a vegetable, it may be meat, or it may be fish. You survive at the cost of other lives.

When you go to higher pitches, according to Jnana, there the life is not destroyed. Your science also will tell you, the atom is not destroyed. So, there is no death also. "Death to whom?" becomes the question. The Self does not die. So, there is no death also. So, to solve that thing, we say, "Be kind, be good, be gentle." In that state take precautions. Don't go and disturb unnecessarily. What is necessary, that you have to do. Adjust according to this. Don't be bigots.

Disciple: Swamiji, how is it that religious people always are so stiff and unkind?
Swamiji: They should be. If they are kind, they will be eaten up.
Disciple: Who will believe them? I cannot understand these religious people. I am disgusted.
Swamiji: They will be eaten up by every one; so, they must make a show of anger even if they are not annoyed. What is the difficulty?
Disciple: Many difficulties. They want to meditate and meditate but who should take care of them in the night?
Swamiji: No one. They need not be taken care of. They are not afraid of anything.
Disciple: Oh, they are so scared of things. The more religious, the more scared they are. They are so stupid.
Swamiji: They are not afraid of anything. They may be in their own mood when they are deeply absorbed in some thoughts. When you are observing certain thoughts, you don't want to speak to others. When you are annoyed, how much will you speak with others? You will be in your own mood and if somebody speaks to you, you will eat them up. So, it is similar there. When they are in their own mood, it is natural.
Disciple: But how to get the work done then?
Swamiji: Oh, you are worried about your work?
Disciple: No, I am worried about their worries.
Swamiji: He is cutting jokes, all right. That is all right in a way.

Reading: Lord Buddha with his followers attends a dinner given by the King Singa Senapathy. Therein in reply to a query on meat-eating, Lord Buddha says thus — "Oh Bikkhus, you should not eat any fish or meat which has been specially prepared for your dinner. Any body eating such a thing will be guilty of the sin called "Dukkat". But I order that you may eat such fish and meat, as, you are sure, has not been killed for you."
Disciple: I don't understand.
Swamiji: What is it you don't understand?
Disciple: A fisherman catches fish to sell them.

Swamiji: He gets the sin. But, you purchase the fish and you cook it for yourself for eating, then a part of the sin goes to you. Now you have cooked and I go to your house. I want to eat something and you give me the fish. I will not get any sin. You understand?

Disciple: Is it better to buy fish in the shop than to take a fresh fish?

Swamiji: Yes, it is better. Don't kill fish. You will have the sin. He has already killed. Go and purchase and eat. It will not give you that so-called sin. That is what they say.

Disciple: Swamiji, then again, does it depend upon the attitude of the fisherman if he is aware of dharma?

Swamiji: He has to do his duty, terrible duty. That is all right. He is also free from the karma.

Disciple: Like the butcher in the story?

Swamiji: Yes, the ego must not be there. Doing his duty in such a way, he was not attached to anything.

Disciple: But then he must be an extraordinary fisherman. He must be high above the normal?

Swamiji: Yes, he must have mind-control also. It is not easy. When he gets a big fish, he will be proud of his big fish. "I have got a big one today," he will say. And next day, when there is no fish, "I did not get any fish today." The "I" is there. In all these respects, the "I" must be controlled. The aim of karma-yoga means, whatever work you do, it is not the work that dignifies a man, but it is the man who dignifies the work. In that way, you do the work.

Suppose the man is doing the cleaning work of your toilets and another man is cleaning this hall. The man who is here, he is proud. He says, "I am here while all are meditating." In a half way, he will be sweeping one side, here another side and the middle will be left. He will finish in a way and he will have meditation. But the other man who is working on the toilet, he takes it all as God's work. "I do it with pure love." Every little bit is cleanly done. Out of these two people, who is the best one? The man who does the toilet work is the better man than he who does the work here. So, you dignify the work. It is not the work that dignifies the man. The mental attitude, how to take the work, whatever work you may do, you take it as God-sent work. It is God's will. "God has given me this work". Let me do it correctly, whatever it may be. It may be good work. It may be bad work. It is not your concern.

When a man completely self-surrenders, he has no will of his own and whatever work comes his way, he takes it in a good light and does it whole-heartedly not half-heartedly, not in a lukewarm way. He takes it with full concentration, thinking that it is His work, a sort of worship. Such work will not bind you. On the other hand, when you make a selection, your ego is working there, the dirty ego. You want the good ones, not the bad ones. What is good? Everything is sent by God. It is His work. You have no choice. When you work, put your whole heart into the work, whatever work it may be and it has the highest kind of result. That is the secret. Even while eating and drinking, offer it mentally to God. Make a sort of prasad. Don't think, "I am eating." Offer it whole-heartedly. "It is for you Lord — take it. This body is meant for you. Everything is for your sake." So where is that "I"? That "I" must die. You may be a karma-yogi or bhakti-yogi or jnana-yogi or raja-yogi. Whatever yoga you take, that dirty ego must be given up. If the ego escapes you, then you are bound. You will have the karma-phala. If the ego is absent, whatever work you do, it has no effect on you. That is what the Bhagavad Gita also preaches. So, give up both, don't take either good or bad. Give up all the things. Surrender to God completely. That is the only way to escape Karma-Phala — fruits of action.

June 16, 1973

Reading: *Jainism stands on the bed-rock of ahimsa (non-killing or non-injury). No religion has given so much importance to ahimsa as Jainism has done.*

Swamiji: It is not possible in that way. From the highest point of view, when you go deeply, you will find real ahimsa. All this perfection can be had only in Nirvikalpa Samadhi. There, you are not breathing, you are not eating or drinking. So, there is ahimsa. Apart from that place, as I told you yesterday, life means at the cost of another life. And moreover, this Ahimsa Theory, which you have propounded rather recently, they make a big hubbub about it all over the world. It is impractical. It can never work. It is impossible. You cannot apply it in this world. Even in a family consisting of father and mother and one or two children, there also you cannot observe it. It is quite impossible. With all those things, one must be kind, gentle, don't injure others. All these moral codes have to be kept. It can never be applied to the kingdom of politics. One will be eaten up.

So, in India, some of the leaders wanted to carry this out to the last point, as it were. When they came to power, they wanted to take up Gandhi's idealism, so-called ahimsa. More than twenty arms factories were left by the British and those people foolishly converted all those arms factories into glass factories for drinking water, cold water. What happened then? China made a so-called ethics conference and said, "We are all brothers. We support one another." And China was preparing herself from behind. So, suddenly they took all of Tibet and the Dalai Lama had to run away for his life. So, he fled from Tibet and came to India and that was taken as an offense by the Chinese people. So, the enmity began and they began conquering India also. India had not even a gun. They had no arms, nothing whatsoever. That was a great shock to the so-called leader and thus he became almost mad with that shock and died. This is politics. Now the philosophy of Gandhi is no more. No one wants it. In that way, it made the country wake up that China stabbed from the back.

Reading: *To give practical guidance in this matter, injury to others has been classified under four heads; viz., 1. accidental, 2. occupational, 3. protective, and 4. intentional.*
Swamiji: It is all mere patchwork. If a householder has some farming, how can you carry on with your so-called Ahimsa Theory? Jainism has gone to such a stupid extent, absurd and terrible. They never wash their clothes. It is against their dharma. There were some rich people, Jains who kept a big wooden cot that was made with rope and with millions of bed bugs in that thing. If the hippies go and sleep there, they would be a good dinner for the bugs. What a horrible thing it is. You can't imagine. Such stupid things are going on in the world in the name of God and dharma. It is ruining the body. You want to live in the house, what is the use of destroying it? You have to keep it properly. That idea is completely gone there. If a man can fast, the more he fasts, the greater he will become a great saint there. If he can fast fifty-sixty or even eighty

days, such ideas they have got. So horrible it is. There are so many horrible customs, so superstitious and horrible in that way.

We want the rational side. It must be appealing to one and all. It should not be bigotry or some other foolish ideas. There will be hundreds to follow it blindly. That should not be. You have to adapt to the modern world. Everything must be scientific. It must be reasonable. It should appeal to reason. If not, nobody will follow. So, religion and philosophy must withstand the acid test of reasoning or logic. Whatever you may call it, reasoning or logic must be there. If you can't give reasonable things, then they will kick it out. They are not afraid of hell and they are not anxious to go to heaven also. That is all man-made — heaven and hell. So, they know all those things and are not afraid of anything. So, if it is reasonable, all right, they will come. They have to come in that way.

Reading: *In conclusion, and in considering what food and drink a sadhaka should take, it should be seen what particular food and drink would suit him best.*
Swamiji: See, in that way, you must understand that it is a thing ascribed to the Indian climate, but here, if you say Swamiji has written in that way, it should not be eaten, then it would be a dangerous thing for you people. In a terrible, cold climate like this, make use of your common sense.
Disciple: Yes, you cannot transfer it.
Swamiji: No, you can't make it. It is only meant for the Indian climate. Many of the books were written in olden times. It was meant for India, but not for this climate. In that way, you have to make certain adjustments. If you take honey in Delhi, it has a very bad effect. In hot season, generally, they don't touch it. It is so heat-producing there. Here it is a necessity. Mustard seed may help you in a cold climate like this. In a hot climate, there is no need for it. In this way, some adjustments must be there. Don't be blunt on that point.

Reading: *Some things are harmful in as much as they produce lethargy and are not conducive to concentration.*
Swamiji: But the same thing may help you in a cold climate, I am telling you. To kill your so-called wind in the stomach, garlic can also

help. Don't take a large quantity. In seasoning the food, put one or two. Certain vegetables, they require it. Don't use more. It is bad. It produces abnormal heat, so also onion. Onion is good for the stomach.

Disciple: Some people use garlic for curing diseases.

Swamiji: Yes, it is good for so many other things. If there are ringworms, they put a little water in the earth and then make a paste with the garlic and then they give a coating. It gets burned. The ringworm is gone. So, these are old medicines for the people. Garlic is the best medicine for snakebite which the doctors have not understood. Even the most deadly poisonous cobra, if there is a bite, immediately take garlic, grind it nicely and mix it with one glass of milk and after half an hour take one more for three or four days. The poison cannot affect the person. The doctors cannot understand it until and unless you produce the snake that has bitten you. There are two varieties of poison. One kind of snake bite makes the whole blood clot and with another type, it becomes liquid. So, now the doctors use poison from the snake which makes the blood clot for the man who has been bitten by a cobra which made the blood liquid. So, poison is the medicine for poison. Apart from this, there are some people also who can cure it by mantra. He will not give any injection, nothing whatsoever. There are certain mantras with which he removes the whole poison. How do you explain it scientifically? There is no explanation for it. As medicine acts, so also the mantra acts.

Disciple: Certain vibration?

Swamiji: No, it is a formula. Mantra produces a power just to kill the poison. It is just like you can't see electricity. It is a subtle thing. Still, it can produce power and it can give a certain push also. There are mantras for heat also. One man in Nepal some years back was demonstrating certain mantras. He would go and sit in the burning fire. The fire was not burning him. Others can walk on burning cinders just like coal and it does not burn them. So, by mantra, they make the fire not effective and that is possible for cold also.

Disciple: Is it how sadhus live in cold climate without clothes?

Swamiji: Some get accustomed to very cold climates. They live in caves. But don't imitate in Sweden. Don't do in that way. Have enough clothes.

Disciple: In Tibet, they are used to living in the cold. They can sweat through blankets full of ice.

Swamiji: There are certain pranayamas they keep up. And some people keep a lot of hay. They never use blankets but they sit and cover the whole body with so much straw. It has no meaning. Don't go to such an extent. Don't get attached to the body. At the same time, don't destroy it also. Take the middle course. That is the best thing.

Often, in denial, in extreme cases, they get so attached to small things that the main thing is forgotten. You are fighting with unnecessary things and necessary things. They remain as they are. So, what is necessary is mind-control. For that thing, you have to keep the body healthy. That is only the means, not the end. So, take precautions. What is necessary, give it without attachment. For higher things, mind-control, the body and everything must work in a proper way. If not, you can't control the mind.

Reading: *Those who live in very hot climates should take cool drinks and cold-producing food.*

Swamiji: It is a natural thing. When you are in a hot climate, you can't take heat-producing things. When you are in a cold climate, generally you want some heat-producing things. Now, your climate is such that you require substantial food. You can't take liquid diet. You will be undone. In India, many of you fall sick. You think, "Oh, in Denmark we are eating so much." Here, it is very poor food. You can't take it. You take one, two, three days. The third day you will have diarrhoea and you go to pieces.

Here (in Denmark) you require sweaters and not even that is enough. You require a big sweater just to protect you. Over that there will be a coat and other things. Without that, you can't go out. It is so terribly cold. But if you put on the same thing in India, you will sweat and sweat and die, it is so hot. So terrible it is. Many of the Indians coming to Europe, they live here for six months or one year for studying. When they go back, they want to imitate. They want to sleep up to seven in the morning. It is terrible there. At five, they want bedtime coffee. Here, without coffee in bed, you can't get up. It is so dull and hard here. It is necessary. And that fellow stupidly said he wants to imitate. "Oh, I have been in America." It is disgusting rather. Many are fools. They follow it in that way. It has no meaning.

All right. Sit for meditation.

June 17, 1973
Reading: *But wherever one may live and practise mind-control, one must be very regular in taking food at fixed hours.*
Swamiji: They make a big hubbub over this. Sometimes it may fail also. A little adjustment is necessary. It is said to make you strong. A habit is created in that way. Know the spirit. But, sometimes there may be lapses. "I did not take my food so I got a disease." Don't make a jump all of a sudden and make a hubbub over it. A little adjustment is necessary everywhere.

Reading: *During the sadhana period even one morsel of food more or less, will prove injurious and will upset the mind.*
Swamiji: Put stress on this point that no one wants. They will eat like gluttons when they are hungry. And then they will say, "I did not take my meal in time, so I got sick." They will avoid the point. They will blame the book for that point.
Disciple: Yes.
Swamiji: He does not say he took more. He won't make that point. That is weakness, put stress on that point. It is more important. It is a necessary thing also to control. If you take less, you feel a sort of uneasiness. There is a desire and if you eat more, there will be dullness and drowsiness. You want to sleep. Here you must know how much you require and accordingly regulate it. This is an important point to catch and much stress must be put on this point. When there is a good and delicious dish, you will think, "Let me have a little more." Now, regulate it. You have to control it. That will upset you really. When you come to a certain pitch, when the mind and body are gaining purity, you will feel a little less or more will upset you. So, you must know your requirements exactly. There comes the difficulty with many people.

Reading: *For a sadhaka, to become a slave of the palate is an unpardonable sin. It brings on a great fall also in mind-control and concentration.*
Swamiji: You have to put stress on all these words. If you at want to be successful, pay attention to it. If you are careful about eating, you will overcome lust also. When there is lack of control in eating and drinking, there will always be temptation.

Reading: *The desire for and hankering after any particular kind of food or drink must be scrupulously checked.*
Swamiji: That is slavery. Don't crave for anything. You have to fill up your stomach; but, don't get attached to any particular kind of food. It is very bad. That means you are a slave of certain things. That will make you fall.
Disciple: But sometimes you want a thing because the body requires it.
Swamiji: That is not necessary in that way. If you think the body requires everything, whether it is your desire or something else, that must be known. There is a little truth in what you say also. I have been telling the same; but still, see whether your body requires it every day or sometimes. If it is only sometimes, that is all right. That cannot be avoided. But if you want a delicious dish every day, then it is not the body which wants it. Your mind is deceiving you there. You must make a distinction. Is it clear or not?

So, it is all weakness. The mind wants to escape. You may say, "Swamiji told when a desire comes, there will be a particular need for a certain thing, so the desire comes." Then, with the desire, there is a thing called habit. See that thing whether you actually want it or whether it is some dirty habit the mind wants to have. There you catch hold of it. Make a distinction. It is not easy. You will have to watch the mind constantly. Don't be a slave to it. That is sadhana.

Reading: *Food and drink should be made pure and holy by mentally offering them to God before using them. This mental offering, in full faith, removes all their impurities.*

Swamiji: That is all right. That is another way. You have to make it as an offering then you get rid of many sins. In India, the orthodox families observe it even now. Every household has a deity. Kula Devata, it is called. First, they offer it to the God or Goddess which they daily worship. Then a portion is kept for begging people. They used to offer with all kindness. Whoever came in time for eating, they treated him like a God. That idea they had behind. Then a portion was kept for feeding the lower animals such as dogs and cows. After giving to all other people, then only the household would eat. The wife would not eat first as a glutton. She would feed all the children, honourable people and all others and lastly, she would take. That was the custom in olden times. That was not to degrade women. They divide their lives in such a beautiful way; rather, I appreciate all.

Disciple: Swamiji, why are God incarnations always men?

Swamiji: That you ask them now. They will say, "Man has made them." I don't admit incarnations, then?

Disciple: No. I say men will not obey a woman God.

Swamiji: A woman Goddess. The Goddesses are all women. There is Durga, there is Kali, there is Lakshmi, there are so many. They are world mothers.

Disciple: We don't see them as incarnations.

Swamiji: Make some. You understand now? They don't admit your incarnations. Then what is it for? There is no "why" then. You understand or no?

Disciple: They will not admit that there are incarnations of men at all.

Swamiji: Our philosophy does not give room for all these so-called incarnations, Gods. There is only One Thing.

Disciple: It is also often forgotten that the whole responsibility for education lies with women.

Swamiji: Yes, it is a fact. There you have got the highest place. In India, the olden system was that the mother was given the highest place, not the father. And the whole future education of a child entirely depended upon the mother. The child had to be constantly with the mother; so, the mother influenced the child more than the father. Not only education, even dharma and religion also. There you have got so much responsibility; so, I am not degrading anybody. I am giving the highest place now; so, men have been defeated now.

Disciple: I remember that some have asked why women have not realized God. And once Swamiji said, "How could we know the names of all the saints?" And that we should not degrade ourselves by thinking we are inferior to men.

Disciple: I want to know why a woman must have so much menses during her life? I think it is so heavy when you can't meditate.

Swamiji: That you ask your God. Why he has made all these things. If it had not been so, women would have eaten men like anything. So, in order to pull her down, just to check her, it has come. Men would have run away to the forest.

Disciple: The problem probably arose when all the machines took the work from women; so, they have nothing to do at home now.

Swamiji: Not in that way. Machines came recently, but not before all the movements began. With all that, have you made any progress by getting all this so-called Freedom? There is no peace. What is progress? You have lost the aim of life. So, it has no meaning then.

Disciple: Swamiji, do sadhakas have any special responsibility to their aged parents?

Swamiji: When they have taken up sannyas, what kind of responsibility?

Disciple: Today, is it not so that the eldest son has to take care of the parents?

Swamiji: There is nothing in that way. Here the system is quite different. Even if the father has enough and more money, he will not give to the children. Children have to work and they have to survive. They have to make their own arrangements.

Disciple: And when aged parents are put into an old people's home?

Swamiji: You see the parent and child relationship is not working here. They are independent. The state is taking care of them. At the age of sixty-seven, there is a pension and there is a house for them. What responsibility can a sadhaka have? If a man were to live in the world, he himself would not worry. A man who has a wife and children, he will not go to serve the old parents. He will let them go there (to the state-run house). When you have become a sadhaka, it is much less. You have no responsibility at all. Now you have chosen a life. You must stick to it.

Reading: *Food and drink become impure under the following conditions and these should be avoided at all costs: cooked food left over for three hours or more should not be taken by a sadhaka. If taken, it will produce wind and stomach disorders.*
Swamiji: It is not so in cold climate like this. You have to take as an exception on this point. Some of you are making some confusion. In a cold country like here, you can keep even ordinary milk for two or three days. In winter, it will not get spoiled and there is no need for boiling. But, if you take the milk and keep it without boiling for half an hour in India, it will get spoiled immediately. You can't take raw milk.
Disciple: Does that mean that when the meal has been cooked and you have not eaten it all, you can heat it up later?
Swamiji: It can be done a little. Here in a cold climate like this, it is necessary.

Reading: *When dust, hair and flies fall in food, it should not be taken. This is rational even from the hygienic point of view.*
Swamiji: Nobody cares for that item. There you have to pay particular attention. Last year when I came, some thousands of flies were in the kitchen. It was so horrible. Flies go and sit on a variety of dirty things outside. If there are some people who have got some bad disease, it may be TB or other things, and they have spit carelessly somewhere or you have thrown some bad things in the dustbin, there also, flies survive. From there they come. So, it makes the food impure, so also dust. Then again, food offered in the name of a dead person should not be eaten.

Reading: *Food should not be taken from the hands of an impure and wicked person nor from one who earns his livelihood illicitly.*
Swamiji: They made a confusion again. How to know who is wicked? If you actually know a person who is not living a pure life, don't take the food. But don't suspect that from everything, you get some disorder. "Oh, it is due to that man who came. He had a very bad vibration." It has become a terrible thing, the so-called vibration. "He or she has got a very bad vibration, so I got stomach pain." Poor man, he has eaten as a glutton and disorder is there. He gets the pain and he puts the blame on the person who came. That is a dangerous game. Many have that stupid idea. That is all foolishly applied. One must have common sense

in all those things. But the thing is there. When you know actually a person is not living a pure life, the earning is not good and such a person wants to give you something, don't take it. That is all right. But don't suspect every one in that way. That is bad. Taking food from hotels is not good. It is impure food in a way. While cooking, they will lick the spoon and they may go on eating. It is tempting for them to eat the same thing they serve you. It is better to avoid such things. If you are travelling, you are compelled to eat sometimes. All these things are there. Some of the points are important. Every one has to observe them. There is no compromise with it. Utilize your common sense.

June 18, 1973

Reading: *Discrimination and dispassion (viveka and vairagya) always go together. Real discrimination is always followed by genuine dispassion.*

Swamiji: The so-called western philosophy is speculative. It leaves the other side out. It has no meaning. It makes man miserable. Many of the students who take up philosophy have this dilemma. They are good for nothing, so they make life very miserable. When you say a thing is unreal, then how can you cling to it? That is the most pitiable thing. You say it is a filthy thing, that it is dirty and not good. Then, at the same time, how can you eat it? That is impossible. So, when you say the world is unreal, then comes the question, "What is real?" And then you have to discriminate. In this way, come to the Real Thing. The real thing is Atman or God – whatever you may call it. That is the Ultimate Truth. You have to keep the mind always on that One Thing and forget the evanescence that is a very fleeting, momentary pleasures and all those things. Those are not real. So that is real discrimination and dispassion, viveka and vairagya. These always go side by side. It is a fashion nowadays to discriminate all those things – "Why? When? Where?" Such people, if you ask them to meditate, then comes "Why? When? Where?" During meditation, you are nowhere. It is all ridiculous things.

One philosopher, a girl from Denmark, wrote to me. It appears she observed her dog was looking at something strange and she wanted that I might give a reply from India. She wrote, "What was my dog thinking?" What a horrible thing, crazy and stupid. It has no meaning. A devil or some great-grandfather might have come to see her. So, it was seeing that thing and she wanted a reply for it, such a ridiculous thing. They never make any progress. The ego grows there. "So, I am a philosopher. I will become bigger and bigger." Unconsciously, that dirty ego will grow. So, they miss the point. That is the most pitiable thing.

I narrated the story of a doctor last year. He was doing the duty of post-mortem. All the dead bodies from accidents, he was cutting open and stitching. All those things he was doing. Then he retired. So, now he proclaimed to the world: "I have been cutting thousands and thousands of bodies but I never came across a soul; so, there is no soul." Such is the so-called speculative philosophy. It takes you nowhere. You are wasting time for nothing. So, be practical. We want the practical side. When you know it is unreal, cut it out, kick it out, leave it forever and come to the real thing. Then only it has meaning, that is viveka and vairagya. So, these two things always go side by side with a sadhaka. Is it clear or any doubts?

Disciple: Anyway, there will be slow progress.

Swamiji: What is that progress? You know that it is fire and that the fire is burning but at the same time, you want to put your finger there. What is the progress there? If you put your finger there again and again in the burning fire, what is your progress there? When you know it is burning, don't put it. Then there is progress. Knowingly, you put it again and again. It is mere stupidity. It only shows the man is block-headed and has some screw loose. You will not call a man wise who does all this constantly. He is a stupid fool, rather.

Disciple: No, I was meaning process. I am sorry.

Swamiji: Process is quite different. You will put the question, "Who am I?" Then you say, "I am not the body, not this ego, not the senses, not this mind, not this intellect – none of these things. Then, who am I? I am Sat-Chit-Ananda (Existence, Knowledge and Bliss Absolute). I am that. I am Brahman." This is the process, the jnana marga. You understand? That is sadhana. You are giving every moment that impression. Even when you are walking or doing work in the garden, you are putting the idea that it is all false. You see, that is the process.

But speculative philosophy is not in that way. That is the fashion. Always they ask, "Why? How? When? Where?" They want to argue. They want to defeat their opponent by argument. Their brain must be sharp. They want reasoning, but they don't want to act. They think they are intelligent men. They think they are above the level of ordinary people. Such people will laugh at them. "Why all that devotion? Why meditate and do all these things?" Some will tell you, "Have you done so much sin to meditate daily four times?" In that way, they put the question. Then what will you answer? There are people who put it in that way. It is all merely egoistic. It has no meaning. They don't believe in the Atman. That is the thing.

Reading: *The idea of "I" and "Mine" is the cause of bondage. This idea is verily the hell. It is due to this idea that man suffers terribly.*

Swamiji: You understand there? By reasoning, you don't come to this point. It is merely keeping that ego, that puny ego "I" idea that goes on growing and growing. According to many Indian philosophers, desires are the cause of bondage and misery. But I go further. I say, "Desires keep up the mind when there is the ego idea." When there is no ego, when the "I" is no more, then you have no more desires. So, the starting point of all desires is the ego, that puny "I" and that is to be rooted out. Keeping up that "I", you have all other desires, and desires are the cause of bondage and misery in this world. That is the secret. So, the starting point is "I". In that "I", there are two "I's" – the real "I" and the puny, the small, stupid "I". And that stupid "I" is "I am so-and-so." "I am Mr. so-and-so," you see? All those things creep up, keeping that "I". You want a house, a bungalow, or you want a car. All these worldly things come with that "I". When this "I" is conquered, you have solved all the problems. That "I" is one of the functions of your own mind only. When the mind identifies with the body and senses, it is called ego. When it discriminates and decides, it is called intellect or buddhi. These are different functions of the mind.

Disciple: The tantrics stay with the corpse and meditate in order to root out the body idea.

Swamiji: They go in the dead of night and dig up the buried person. They have certain formulas and then they sit on that corpse and meditate. The corpse will open the mouth and you have to feed it. Some people go mad with fear and some may become successful. They have to gain courage.

Disciple: What is the gain of this?

Swamiji: They have some certain siddhis, not the real Jnana. They get some supernatural powers. That is all. It is a kind of black magic.

Reading: Therefore, one must, at first, discriminate between good and evil and discard all evil desires and thoughts and, in their place, fill one's mind with good and noble desires and thoughts.

Swamiji: So, you understand now what is to be done. This is to be done. All silly things must go. Have pure ideas, high things, noble things and stick to the Self, not to the body. That is what is meant by discrimination and dispassion.

Reading: At a later stage, one should learn to discard even these good desires and thoughts to attain perfect concentration of the mind. For, both good and evil desires and thoughts bind a man and act as hindrances in the way of the highest concentration of the mind.

Swamiji: So, don't give up at this stage. There is good. There is bad. Always stick to good, not bad. When you come to a certain pitch, then even this also has no meaning. What you call good has a portion bad too. Every thought and every desire is a mixture of these two – good and bad. So, when you come to a high pitch, you have to go beyond these two. Then nothing is binding you. To reach Nirvikalpa Samadhi, all those things must disappear, good and bad, even the desire for Moksha must be given up. Automatically, it falls. There is nothing binding. Then it goes directly in Samadhi state. You solve the problem. Then you have a long rest, you understand? Until then, you have no rest, no holidays. When you come to that pitch, you have long holidays. You are free. Any questions?

Disciple: When did you start taking disciples?

Swamiji: It is nothing. There were no disciples at all. I was keeping aloof. I was discarding all. I was living away from all those things. For twenty years I was away and afterwards, slowly, slowly some people came, in that way. So, what was your difficulty? What was your question? I had some I told you. It may be not much.

Disciple: Even if the Guru doesn't like you, can you still go on with the mantra for the sake of liberation?

Swamiji: I don't know whether you have the Guru idea? One man went to a Guru and he said, "I want to become a disciple." The Guru said, "My dear gentleman, it is very hard to become a disciple." Then the disciple asked, "What is the work of the Guru?" "He will sit quiet, straight and then he will command: Do this, do that, all those things — fetch water, wash cloth, sweep the room." "Then what is the disciple's work?" "He has to obey." "Oh, I don't want to become a disciple, I will become your Guru!" That is your idea. He said, "I will become your Guru, not a disciple." That is your tendency there. You will always talk and talk for nothing and waste your time and what is told to you, you don't want to do. Whether the mantra is to be taken up, it is left to you. Nobody will compel you. It is not the duty of a Guru or anybody else. It is left to you whether to abuse it or use it properly.

Swamiji: So much rain today. How do you people manage in the camp?

Disciple: It is all right. We are accustomed.

Swamiji: Now, it is the rainy season — June, July, August, and September — for three or four months also in Coorg, South India they have heavy rainfall. They get about two hundred inches. That is too terrible. You can't go out. Everything gets drenched. If you wash your clothes and dry them, even after eight days, it will still not be dry, so bad. On the white cloth, there will be spots but it will not become dry. You have to keep some sort of fire just to dry the cloth.

Disciple: It will be like that here also in winter.

Swamiji: Similarly, your winter here is terrible, like the rain is so terrible. In Rishikesh, we have got seventy-eight or eighty inches, something like that, not so much. In Delhi, it is much less. Some days, it is full of water. Drains, roads, everything is filled up with water. Your winter is the severest with long nights, so horrible it is. In winter many people are eaten away. All sort of failures and falls come. They are eaten up, poor creatures, and then they wake up in Spring.

Disciple: Then you will come here.

Swamiji: I will come. All right now, wake up. That is all right. Make the best use of the thing. Don't waste your time, every one of you. You must become heroes. That is what we want. With mere long and tall talks, all right we make you laugh but side by side there is a serious thing going on continuously. Catch it. All right, I want you to laugh also. We don't want to be morose and always in a serious mood. Have relaxation side by side. Catch the thing. Every one of you in the camp should not waste a single minute. Make use of your time for a higher purpose. All of you have come with a sacrificing spirit. You are all young people. It is a noble idea, a noble idea indeed. It is very hard even to think of religion or God or meditation. It is very hard in a terrible world like this. With all sorts of attractions, so horrible it is, you can't imagine.

Once I went for the first time to a big city in India. I was just a young boy. Seeing the terrible noise and other things, I thought, "Is it possible to think of God in such an environment?" I was putting the question. I got headache in the evening. Even after a few hours I got a headache, so horrible it was. I wanted to run away from that place. So, actually living in all these horrible things and even to think of this side is very difficult for ordinary people. All who have come to this line might have had some great samskaras, past merits, so you could come. It is not easy. Now you have come to this line. Face it. Don't be worried about so-called failures. Rise up again and again. Work and it will come. Success must come. That is the thing. Keep this idea always in mind. Don't get discouraged. Work it out. It must come. It is a question of time. So, when will you go?
Disciple: Next Monday.
Swamiji: So, how do you find the camp?
Disciple: Very nice. I like it.
Swamiji: You like it. All right, come next year also. They are working very hard. They have taken it up in a right spirit, in a very right and noble way. That we have to appreciate. So, all of you must rise up now. There is no easy-going way. As I told you, when you reach the point, then you have got very good and long holidays. It will be coming, when you don't want it. And when you want it, it will run away from you. When you want a thing, it will not come to you. If you don't want it, "Take," it will say. Then you don't want it. In that way, kick off all those

things. Then everything will become your slave. That is the secret. Have that thing, work it out. Don't be bothered by anything.

I remember when I was young, just like you people, working and doing sadhana, if anybody would give me one minute or one hundred thousand kroners, I would kick out those kroners and use that one minute for meditation. I had no time to waste. In that way, take the spirit. Devote your time. It is all right to do some useful work and then, if you have that spirit, everything becomes easy. Don't waste time unnecessarily in gossip and other things. You have to repent for it. You pay for it very heavily. There is no play with it. All right, build up these three or four months at least, in the camp life. It is good to have discipline. Take up as much as possible. All right.

June 19, 1973
Swamiji: When you come to that point, automatically the so-called discrimination falls away. There is no need for discrimination. That is another secret. And the mind, with difficulty, goes on concentrating, discarding the bad and the good follow them as a starting point. But when you go on with that idea, you come to a certain pitch and automatically it will fall away. There is no more discrimination there. When you come to that pitch, allow the mind to go further and don't draw the mind back to discrimination or any other things. It is a natural state, then allow it. Focus the whole force in such a way. It is just like a flash light. You are focusing on it and coming to one point. Go on. If you allow that point, it is just like seeing a gap, then a sort of light, by going further and further you get completely merged in that and go on to the last point.

So, coming to that point, many people search for supernatural powers also. When they come to that pitch, they want to see whether they have gained any powers or other things. That is a foolish idea. Immediately they fall down.

Some people want to help others. In doing sadhana and doing meditation, they have gained concentration and a sort of ego comes there – let me help the world. That also pulls them down immediately. Then you have to weep and weep. So many will do that silly mistake. That is a temptation, too, for an ordinary man when he gains all those things. For many, there is a little burning sensation. They think of kundalini shakti. Then they say, "My kundalini has woken up." They will write to me also. Instead of a burning sensation, it may be due to indigestion also. A little burning sensation is there. Then they want an explanation. Then they watch it and lose concentration. Always when your mind goes to watching the shakti – gone. You waste your time in that way. So, the mind and ego play a dirty game in so many ways. One must be very careful. Moreover, in the sadhana period, it is better not to tackle that thing. Leave it. When you gain three-fold purity — purity of the body, nadis, and mind — automatically the shakti will rise up safely. That is a wise thing. Never watch it. Many people, by doing hard pranayama more and more, they want to rise up at any cost. There will be partial rising. With the partial rising, you are increasing your misery like anything. It will be very difficult to control. It is a wrong idea altogether. Thereby, be wise. The thing will come. It must come. But the only thing is to take care of your meditation and mantra-jap. Go on with it easily. Don't watch the shakti at all. Leave it. It will work by itself. Many people want, in a hurry, to wake it up. A temptation is there. "How long am I to wait? Let me wake it up." And that waking up is then partial. It is a very terrible game.

Disciple: Somewhere else in the same book, you write about the Mother (kundalini shakti) rising?

Swamiji: She will not rise up so easily.

Disciple: No, but isn't it an attempt to tackle it?

Swamiji: That is a temptation. That is why I am warning you now. Take the warning. Don't go for that thing. That process is given. In a later stage, it is all right. In the beginning stages, never do it. The worst sort of enemy here will be the partial rising. When the shakti rises up partly, you have some sort of emotions. Many people shed tears. Some roll like this. Some dance. Then what happens is little tidbits. Just like a baby given one spoonful of brandy, it gets intoxicated. It is just like that. It is a stupid idea. It goes to the eyes and they start weeping. Afterwards, it comes down immediately to the lowest center, muladhara. The first and foremost thing one feels is abnormal sexual cravings. There you are ruined. That is why I am telling it is a dangerous game to wake it up partially. Many of the intellectuals, they have it. And many of them also, are immoral. With many writers and orators, for example, there is partial rising. Then they are intellectuals in the worldly sense for the worldly people. They may be above their level. It is all right, but above all they are not men of character. There are so many cases of that kind.

So, don't go for that. Don't wake up the Mother there. Ask her, "Mother sleep for the time. I don't want you now." Tell her. When you come to that pitch after making some sort of advance, then only ask the Mother, "Now wake up." For the time being, let her sleep.

Disciple: If a person feels tempted by, for example, supernatural powers?

Swamiji: Then you have to control it.

Disciple: There must be a conscious telling of this to take care of it.

Swamiji: Yes, yes. You have to tell it. You have to warn yourself. You say "No," with a stern "No" when that desire comes. Many people are tempted there. They make a display of their little tidbits of power and they lose everything.

Disciple: So, there is a choice. You have the choice to say "No" or "Yes." Have you always the choice?

Swamiji: Yes, you always have the choice. Train the mind in such a way from the beginning. Don't run after supernatural powers or people who make a display. Avoid such people from a long distance. Bid goodbye from a long distance. Never hear or see such stupid people. We hate them like anything. We have no tolerance. That is why when some people come and praise me like anything, I only laugh. I don't make a show. And some people criticize also. Then I say, "Both are fools." I keep quiet. You have to digest. You have to control it. It is all a great temptation. At every step of your evolution, you must be careful. Don't be duped by all these worldly things. Remember that it is all false. There is only One Thing.

Supernatural powers are just jugglery. They catch hold of some spirits. They go to the burial ground and catch hold of them and with that, they make some sort of black magic. For that, you have to pay very heavily in the long run. The man worshipping and doing all those things is always miserable. Evil spirits, they are always miserable. With their very sight, you will understand there is something wrong. The vibration is so bad. It is so unhappy, that it is not worth having or even to look at. So, avoid all these things and stick to the ideal thing. You must be strong.

Disciple: It is not a common thing here, this tantric.

Swamiji: It is black magic. It is going on everywhere. I hear every day complaints from different people. It may be their own imaginary thing.

Disciple: It may be their imagination.

Swamiji: They may do some mischief also. They have been doing so. I have been hearing complaints about it. It is all over everywhere. It is a dirty thing. For black magic, there is another magic that is just an antidote for it. There are people that fight each other. Two black magic people and one fights the other. He destroys the other man's wife or children and that man returns again to kill. There are cases I have seen.

Reading: *To eradicate the ego idea and to gain desirelessness of the mind, people adopt various methods. Some of these are: raja-yoga, bhakti-yoga, karma-yoga and jnana-yoga. People in whom the gathering faculty of the mind predominates take up raja-yoga and they find it easy to control the mind through pranayama and meditation and thus eradicate the ego idea by attaining Samadhi (Transcendental State).*

Swamiji: Thereby, never take up pranayama suddenly. One must proceed with it slowly and carefully. There must be an expert Guru also to guide you in pranayama. Many people go on increasing pranayama without knowing anything. It is very dangerous. One may go mad also. There may be abnormal heat in the brain center. If you cannot control it, it develops first into insomnia (sleeplessness) and if it further continues, then one goes mad. It destroys the brain center where the discriminating faculty works. Many people are suffering in this way; so, one must be careful. The same thing happens in deep sorrow. Every deep thinking means you are attacking that shakti. Then there will be partial rising. That is a very dangerous game.

Reading: *People in whom the willing faculty of the mind predominates, find it easy to take up karma-yoga and gain the purity* *of the mind and heart through selfless work, and thus attain Samadhi and go beyond the ego idea.*

Swamiji: With all that, the yogas are mixed. Concentration of mind is necessary in all the yogas. In the course of a day, you can see it if you watch your mind. In the morning as soon as you get up, you have the tendency to sit for meditation. Raja-Yoga is there. Afterwards, you go for work in the garden. There comes karma-yoga. And then you want a sort of devotional side. That comes side by side. You go on changing the mind in the course of a day. Sometimes you want to read some philosophy or other things. There, jnana-yoga comes. In this way, all the yogas go side by side.

Disciple: Why should one give the fruits of one's actions to God? I mean that everything is God. I have to do the work because I need food in my stomach.

Swamiji: You do it and don't worry about God. Don't expect anything in return. Do the work for work's sake. Then you have satisfaction. You have done the work with full heart, with full concentration of the mind and then leave it. Don't expect some reward. Then you have peace of mind. On the other hand, if you expect something, and the person comes and does not reward you, then you have pain. That is the secret of karma-yoga. By doing karma-yoga without expecting anything, you have done your duty. What the wage gives you, take it and you go away. There ends the matter. But, if you have some expectations, "I have done such nice work. He must give me some reward." But if he does not want to give you some reward, you have pain. That is what is meant by not expecting the fruits of the action.

Disciple: Should one try to force the ego aside and imagine one is God and try to suppress it?

Swamiji: Suppression has come now. You have to control it. Conquer it. If you suppress, then it will have more children. The ego will grow more. When you go on controlling, discriminating and discarding, the ego should not grow. It may grow in so many varieties and that should be conquered. Don't give room for such things. Control it. When somebody praises you, don't say, "I am successful. I am so-and-so." It should not come. Be humble there. You might have done some extraordinarily good work and some people may praise you. Don't get elevated by it. So, "I have done nothing," put it. Control it in that way.

Similarly, some people, out of enmity may criticize you, abuse you and say, "He is a silly man. He is mad." Don't give way to such things at all. Keep the balance. That is also ego. Degenerating is also part of ego playing. There also keep above it. It is nothing. A devotee surrenders to God. He will take all pain and pleasure, success and failure — all the pairs of opposites in equipoise.

Disciple: How can one surrender to pain? That I don't understand.

Swamiji: Whatever comes, you take it, tolerate it. If you have got severe colic pain, take it. God has given, all right, have it. That balance of mind must be there. There is intense bliss. Then also take it. It is God's will. Don't be elevated by it. That is keeping the mind in balance. It may be good. It may be bad. It may be pain. It may be pleasure. Keep the mind in balance in all the pairs of opposites. Then you have control. You have come to the point of yoga.

What I mean is, a man who surrenders to God has no choice of his own. Whatever comes on its own, without you willing it, you will take in an easy way. That is what I mean. If pain comes, that is all right. It is His will. If pleasure comes, it is His will. In both things, he will see the divine hand and divine purpose. A devotee's attitude will be, "It is His. It has come from Him." The devotee has no choice. "It has come, all right. Let me take it easily." So, in that way, keep the balance of mind.

Disciple: Why should I then not be content?

Swamiji: You are coming to that point, only if you are content. Be content with both. Don't make any choice. If you have choice, there is discontent. You can't be there. If you want to be content, don't have choice. Take things as they come. There is no "but".

Disciple: Swamiji, when contentment is there, I need to say "I".

Swamiji: You have finished everything when contentment is done. You have crossed the horrible, jumping of the hurdle and reached the point, the last point. Everything is burned, so you are free now. If you have the idea of good, bad will be there. If you give up both, then you are free. That is the secret. You have to give up both. You give everything to God and whatever comes, take it. "God has sent it to me; so, let me have it." That is the easy way of taking it. You have nothing to grumble about. You must have contentment there. If there is success, that is all right. It is His will. You don't say there, "I am successful." That "I" must die. And when there is failure, then you don't say, "I have failure." Both things you overlook.

All right, close it.

June 20, 1973
Disciple: Will you explain the difference between black magic and white magic?
Swamiji: Black magic means you are misusing the thing to injure a person. They catch hold of ghosts and then make use of them for some evil purpose. That is black magic.
Disciple: And white magic?
Swamiji: To cure a person, to help people who have been possessed by devils or ghosts. By mantra, they get rid of it. That is white magic. To make use of this mantra, that is tantra. There are certain diagrams that are called yantras and then the mantras dealing with them are called tantras and to make use of them for a good purpose is called white magic. The same mantra will become black magic when it is misused. Really, there is nothing called white magic but anyway, it is a good one. On one side, you help people and, on the other side, you injure people. Some people get possession of some evil spirits that go and enter the body of another and it makes them dance and sing and do all those things. They are fooled. They can't do anything. They have no power. They are suppressed. In such cases, the people who know the yantra, mantra can help. They can stop the spirit. That is a big subject. They have got so many formulas, so many mantras. They have got mantra siddhis. That means they must go and meditate on a particular mantra and then they have a sort of siddhi. Then they make use of it for other purposes. So, these are very dangerous things. It is better not to interfere with such things. But yet, it is a curiosity too to make use of them.

I think that Paul Brunton has written a book. He was making secret research here and there. He wrote about a man who was practising black magic. He was a Brahmin and with that black magic, he was catching hold of a ghost and with it would do some miraculous work. But, in the long run, the Brahmin got disgusted with the ghost. He did not know what to do. It is not easy. If you do something, your life will be in danger.

So, the Brahmin went to the King of Nepal. It must be about thirty years ago this incident happened. He was there. Paul Brunton was wandering here and there. The Brahmin told the king, "I have a ghost and I will give it to you. You can make use of it in ruling your kingdom. It may help you in so many ways." The king was a wise man. He said, "I don't want the ghost. Get out." Anyway, it was a full moon day, a particular day they have to worship these devils. If you want a human being to be caught and offered to the devil ghost, he has to be given also. All these things are horrible. So anyway, on that night, the Brahmin performed his puja (worship), then he said, "Now, hereafter, you must go to the king." Though the king had refused, the Brahmin was sending the ghost by force. "You must go to the king. Hereafter, I don't want you." Then the ghost left him and went away.

The king was sleeping. It was the dead of night, at twelve, and he felt so bad — suffocating and everything. He was about to die and suddenly he had his Guru mantra that mantra suddenly came. The ghost had no power to withstand the mantra and it ran away. After that, the ghost ran back to the Brahmin and said, "You have sent me to the king, he has not accepted me. He has abused me. By the coming full moon day, on that day, I will kill you." It actually happened. Next day, the Brahmin went to the king and told the whole thing and the king said, "I don't want your devil." And then the Brahmin actually died. This is the story.

Disciple: How did the ghost kill him?

Swamiji: They have got certain powers. They can misuse them. They can kill a man and he will also become a ghost. He will become his brother. He will become a Brahmin ghost or he will become his disciple, the ghost disciple. So, don't play with ghosts or black magic.

There are so many cases. Another, I think, was in Benares. There is a big tank where four Gods are made in different directions. One particular God might have drowned there; so, no one can take bath there. They were telling me the incident of one man who was a Hindu doing mantra-jap and he thought it was all cock-and-bull stories that the mantra had no power. He became an Arya Samajist. That is a new sect. They don't like this going to temples worshipping. They have some other stupid ideas that are good for nothing.

He was going to take bath on that particular ghat only. Somebody told him, "Please don't go there." "Why," he said. "There is a ghost. You can't take a bath there." "Let me see your ghost. I will see to it." He was proud and he was proceeding. Just as he was going near, a voice said, "Don't come here." There was nobody. He turned, but a voice said, "Don't come here." He did not care. It must be hallucinations, he thought. Then he removed his cloth and he took one dip and was caught there. He was not able to rise up and suddenly that old habit of the mantra came. He began. It must have been a powerful mantra, Durga or Kali. With that thing, they can't stand there. All these evil spirits and black magic, nothing can come against the mantra and immediately, he was let loose. Then this fellow understood that there is power in mantra. It saved his life and he became a Hindu again, not an Arya Samajist.

There are innumerable instances of this kind. We have seen it. In certain places at night, you can't travel. I was told by one of the boys, when I was at the Coorg Ashram last year, that a man was taking his cows to the forest. There is, about three miles from my ashram, a big forest, a very thick natural forest. While he was going, there was an elephant with a big tusk. Suddenly it came running towards him and he was caught. It rolled him and killed him and threw him into the forest. Some twenty or thirty people went out searching with lanterns. There was no trace of him. They couldn't find him. Next day, his death was found out. Even now, he makes a loud noise at night, even in daytime sometimes. One of the boys from the ashram was going there. He heard the noise. He got afraid and ran away.

There was another instance. Close by my ashram, there is a government bee farm where they are cultivating a lot of wild bees. They teach people how to keep small boxes and collect them. There, one boy committed suicide last year and at night now they can't sleep in that area. The whole night there will be a disturbance. So, the people who are in charge of the bee agriculture center were telling me that they don't sleep there. So, how to make an account of it in a scientific way when they don't admit there is rebirth, reincarnation or anything, but still, it is there. It is all a dangerous game to play with such things. It is better not to play.

Another man was telling me, there is a certain kind of abscess that they can get rid of by certain mantras but not by operation. By a certain process, they wipe it off. He had this done when he was a small boy. The man was my disciple. He died last year. He told me the story of a monk who got rid of the abscess of another man through the earth. The monk was removing it from the body of the person who had the disease. Then the boy said, "What are you doing?" He was cutting jokes with that monk and that man said, "You come here." "What can you do?" the boy said. He went there and the monk slowly transferred it to the boy and he immediately got the disease. He ran home in such terrible pain, weeping and crying. He told his mother. Then the mother asked, "What did you do this for you rascal? Why did you do all those things? Go and beg the monk's pardon and ask him to get rid of it and follow what he tells you." The boy went there and the monk removed it immediately. When the disciple told me this incident, he was an old man. Only last year he died in Delhi. In this way, mantra has power. Certain mantras, they can do miracles. In this way, it can be used for a good purpose or for a bad purpose also.

Once there were two boys, two students. One boy had faith in the reincarnation theory and ghosts. The other boy said, "Oh, there is nothing. That is all foolishness. There are no ghosts. How can it be?" They were working in the general hospital and he made a trick, that fellow. The dead bodies, in daytime before the cremation, are preserved in some private rooms in different coffins. He made a plan. "You see, we will make some laddus and see if there are any ghosts. Let us see if any of the dead people open their mouth when you go on giving laddus. If there is a ghost, he will open his mouth and eat the laddu. If there is no ghost, no one will eat." So, that fellow made a bed and pretended to be a dead man. And the other one went on giving a laddu to each one — nobody took. They were all dead. And then one, the boy pretending to be dead, opened his mouth. The boy giving laddus got frightened. He died immediately. Like that, he knew that there was a ghost. He got frightened so suddenly that he had to give up his life.

Disciple: All those ghost incarnations, are they not only a sort of suffering to get rid of some bad Karma?

Swamiji: They have some bad karma. A man with good karma cannot become a ghost. People who commit suicide or have a sudden or accidental death or some other misfortune, only such people become ghosts. And those who are very sinful, who do all sorts of sins and wicked things, such people also become ghosts. Among these ghosts, there are some that are good and gentle ones.

Disciple: But is a ghost just a man in the subtle body?

Swamiji: Yes, the mind is there, subtle body is there. They have certain powers and they can manifest that power.

Disciple: Swamiji, in olden times, people always prayed and satisfied their father's spirit or their forefather's spirit.

Swamiji: That custom is still present. That is why in India every day, morning and evening, they do Sandhya. There is a certain process. They send good thoughts and good vibrations to those departed people. With a well-concentrated mind, you can kill a man by bad or injurious thoughts or you can help a man. They may be living anywhere. That does not make a difference. Both are possible.

Disciple: Swamiji, what about astrology?

Swamiji: Why then? Are your planets greater than God?

Disciple: No, they are not greater than God.

Swamiji: Before God, there is nothing. All these things cannot disturb you. That is why you take your mantra. When you take your mantra and meditation, nothing can disturb you. When you are weak, if you forget it, only then can all those things come and disturb you. So, the best thing is instead of wasting your time with all those things, use your mantra. It has all the powers to help you and save you, to take you to the last point. Be strong and firm in that idea. There is only that much to do. Neither ghosts nor devils nor astrology nor astronomy, whatever you may call it, nothing can injure you, if you are strong in that one thing. If you are weak in that way, all other things will come — black magic, tantra, yantra, all those things will come. Be strong there. Have no compromise with it. Go on and it can change your life. Even your fate, everything it can change. That is the secret. That is the best remedy.

Disciple: Swamiji, the mind has the faculty to receive and reject. What does reject mean?

Swamiji: Rejecting means kicking off.

Disciple: Isn't that discrimination?

Swamiji: There is no discrimination. It has not yet come. Suppose you are not taking, you are busy somewhere else, not taking it. What is the difficulty?

Disciple: The difficulty is when a thing is received; then, the mind is in action. But, a thing that is not received?

Swamiji: The sound has come. You have received it. Then if it has not come into knowledge at all, it is not received. The mind does not want it. Now it has come to the brain center. It has come but it is not received. A man has given a blow, given a slap. It has come but you have been somewhere else; so, it has been received. The mind has received but the further action now is it goes down immediately to chitta. There it makes a stir of what it means by slap. Then it reacts. Now it has become something. What is meant by discrimination takes place now.

Disciple: Yes.

Swamiji: Now comes the second stage. You discriminate. What does it mean when the slap comes? "Oh, he has given me a slap, a good blow." In that way it comes. Now, discrimination has worked. Your intellect or buddhi is working. You understand?

Disciple: Yes.

     Disciple: What is gossip?

Swamiji: This is gossip, then?

Disciple: That we should avoid?

Swamiji: There are so many ways of gossip. You know what it is?

Disciple: Yes, I know.

Swamiji: There was a wise man, a Jnani. One day he wanted to take bath and his wife brought some oil. She was rubbing his head and she wanted to say some gossip. He said, "Yes, there was one sin left and you got it." Then she got afraid. What is that sin, she wanted to know?

The whole story was as follows. They had an understanding: Yama, the ruler of death, and his private secretary who was writing all the good and bad things in a book. That was their understanding. The secretary used to keep a record of all those things. Now, there was a man who never cared for God but he was devoted to that secretary. So, one day the secretary was reading the whole book. There was not a single good thing about that man. Everything was bad, bad, bad. So, the secretary took pity, "How to save this man?" He called the man and told him, "There is not a single one of your acts which can be called good.

Everything is bad, bad, bad for you." The man got frightened, so he said, "I never pray to God or anything. I have prayed to you only. You must save me."

"All right," the secretary said. The man had a grown daughter. "From tomorrow you do this. You pretend you are having some sex or lustful love with your daughter, but don't keep anything in mind, only pretend." As, he already had this fear, next day he pretended in that way. People saw it and they began to say, "Oh, this Kali-Yuga, horrible father dealing with his own daughter as a wife, horrible thing." So, the gossip went on. Old women and some of the narcotic addicts are especially fond of gossip. It went on and on. Whenever somebody went on talking about this, one of the man's sins went off and, in this way, the sins were distributed. Lastly, there was only one sin left. The wife of the wise man told him the world is such and such. Then he said, "There was only one sin left and you got it on your head now."

Gossip means there is something you are talking about whether you know it is a fact or not. It is some nonsense and you believe it. You take part in it and you get the sins. That is gossip. But we don't call this thing (satsang) gossip when I make fun with you people. I call this thing gossip but it is another thing, it is not gossip. Gossip actually means dealing with others sins and other bad things and you go on talking and talking for nothing, wasting your time. When your mind is not occupied, you go into all dirty things. That is the evil. That is not a good thing. So, by talking ill of others' affairs, you take the sin. You take part in their affairs. That is bad.

Disciple: That is very good. Then there are so many who can share the sins there.

Swamiji: Yes, there are. But a sadhaka must avoid all those things. One should not waste time in that way.

Now start your music.

June 21, 1973

Reading: *All things mundane are false. They are impermanent and ever changing. A man takes his birth in this world all alone and all alone does he depart after death. What follows him like a shadow is his good and bad effects of karma (work).*

Swamiji: So, generally that word "karma" is very weakly or very badly used: karma, my karma and other things. The word should be karma-phala which is the effects of past Karma. When you say karma, it is a Sanskrit word which means "work." Karma-Phala means effects of work or every work is followed by an effect. It has that result and that is called karma-phala. So, this world of suffering is owing to all this attachment to one's so-called kith and kin, body, senses, mind, all this wealth, everything. So that idea must die if you want real peace. Some may think, "Oh, I am peaceful" by having little tidbits of success and by fulfilling the so-called desires. Or one may think, "I am successful, I am happy." But it is only momentary things. After some days, that happiness changes. You are in need of something else. So, your desires go. By going to fulfil one desire, you create so many hundreds of desires. Still there is no end of desires. They will go on multiplying, increasing like anything and you are fooled in the end. There must be discrimination and dispassion when all these momentary pleasures and attractive things in the world come. Is it absolutely necessary for me to have all those things? Why should I be a slave to it? Why should I not kick it out? In this way, create dispassion. The more you do it, the more the mind will be steady. No desire can then drag you out and you will have peace. Real peace can be had only by controlling the mind. Complete control is Samadhi. It takes a long time. But until then, don't crave for unnecessary things. When the mind craves it, give a check.

Disciple: Compassion and dispassion, how to combine them?
Swamiji: So, you have compassion to whom, to a suffering person, and then?
Disciple: And then it occupies the mind very much.
Swamiji: You have to cut it off. You have dispassion and at the same time, do the work also. If somebody is doing the work, you have to carry out the law. You may have sympathy. You may have it, but you are bound to carry out the law and order or else you will be hanged. So, what is the difficulty there? You understand?

Disciple: Yes, but still, it is difficult.
Swamiji: Why is it difficult? Do you want to stick to your job or what do you want to do? If you want to do karma-yoga, you have to do your duty. A soldier's duty is, if you say fire, he will fire at whomever it may be. The man who gives the order, it is his responsibility. The duty of the soldier is to obey; so, by not firing, he has destroyed his duty. The result, whatever it may be, the man who gave the order is responsible for it. You understand?
Disciple: Yes.
Swamiji: The same question arose with Arjuna. He became a coward. He forgot his dharma. Then it comes that he is pretending as if he is giving compassion to his grandfather, Guru and other people. He forgot his dharma. You understand there?
Disciple: Yes.
Swamiji: So, it is a mere weakness to think of compassion there. The first thing is your duty. The duty that has been entrusted to you, do it, then let us see the compassion. So, you have been doing the work and other people have been screaming and they have been abusing you. That is all right. That is not your duty. That is all right.
Disciple: But Swamiji, when we do our duty, there is not much left for love and peace. It is always kicking people.
Swamiji: Not in that way. If there is no government, it will not work. If the police are not doing their duty, then everything will be eaten up. The whole thing will be in chaos. Now you are managing the camp, some discipline is there. All have come with the same purpose. They want to meditate and they want to improve. Another man is a fool or a madcap. He comes and disturbs the whole camp. Instead of disturbing hundreds of people, it is better to keep the man away from the camp. That is your duty.
Disciple: When I have done my duty, where is then the place for love and peace?
Swamiji: Love is also there. Out of love, you are doing that work. Out of love for hundreds of people, one man you have to kick out. That is all right, kicking out a disturbing element. That is a greater love. You are doing a greater service to hundreds and thousands of people. So, it is a better service.
Disciple: Oh, then I will kick very much.

Swamiji: Thereby you don't commit any sin. For the sake of hundreds of people, we kick one silly rascal, whoever it may be, kick. So, you see, that is dharma. If you don't do that, it is impossible to carry on the camp. You have to take the interest of the majority of people. So, what is your problem?

Disciple: Every day I have new problems.

Swamiji: We will give solutions also, every day new methods. I am not tired of giving new methods. Whatever problem you have, I will solve it within a second. I will give a new suggestion every day if you want. So, don't be anxious about it. Go on and do your duty.

Disciple: Every day when the sun shines, I think today I will have rest.

Swamiji: So, today you are given good poison. He has given freely. (The neighbouring famer was spraying pesticides from an airplane.) Many are having headache. It was burning me like anything, nose, throat and other things. I also have a headache today. So, I laugh at it. It is all right. So, this is the world. Then what other problems, come?

Reading: Friends and relatives, kith and kin, etc., are like the friends one makes on a railway journey. People going to different places meet one another in a railway compartment for the time being and become close friends for a while. But when their different destinations arrive, they alight one by one, bid good-bye to one another and depart.

Swamiji: That is the connection here with all these worldly things. You come alone and you go alone, there is nobody to follow. And what follows is your own karma. What you have done, either good or bad, follows you. So always be good, be kind, be gentle and cultivate all those things. Meditate and control your mind and senses. You will be helped in that way. No other things can help you. Instead of giving the children money they will squander away, give them a proper education. That will help them lifelong. The highest kind of education you can give is spiritual knowledge. You help a person here and hereafter. That is the highest kind of dharma. They are saved for their whole life. So, a father and mother who have left a fortune to the children have not done anything good for them. If the children are good and wise, they can make a fortune themselves. If they are stupid and vulgar, they squander everything. So, it is. We see it every day.

Reading: *But, then, are all the people to renounce the world and become monks?*

Swamiji: We don't say in that way. Many people say, "If all were to become monks and nuns, what will become of the world?" That is a weak idea, stupid idea altogether. It is cowardice. That is out of fear. They cannot conquer anything. Just to put a question of that kind. Many people have been asking me this question. "If all were to become monks and nuns, what will become of the world?" It is a great problem for them. They are stupid fools. They cannot control anything. They are attached to all those things, so they put this question as though it is so easy to become a monk. All cannot become monks and nuns. Such a question has no meaning.

Reading: *What is required is only a change of heart and a change in one's conception of the world which is really nothing but a projection of one's own mind.*

Swamiji: There you understand the thing. Don't get attached. Live in the world as it is said: "A lotus flower lives in the water but it is not soiled by water." In that way, you have to live in the world. Don't get attached to your duty. That is also one of the ways. All are not to renounce the world. We have put this new type of sannyas, we are not depending on anyone. In India they say, "What are monks doing? They are like drones. They are not doing anything. They are living at the cost of the nation." I want to kick off such ideas. We are not disturbing anyone. So, every monk is earning his livelihood. He is standing on his own feet and, at the same time, doing the highest kind of activity. There can never be a nobler life than this. So, a new type of Sannyas I have created for you people. Now, we want to rise up. We are not beggars. We are not depending on anyone. At the same time, we are doing the highest kind of dharma. Really, if you live the life, it is heaven. You are seeing heaven. You cannot see anything higher than this. The world is not separate from God. That is what they conclude. In that way, the monks also can remain if every householder also follows their duty. Many people make a big hubbub and say that the householders think they have no more duty and they find fault with the priests. That is a wrong idea, one-sided view. Every one has got his own dharma. A student has his own dharma and that dharma is now gone.

Householders have their own dharma but they are not following it. They only think they are doing so because the politics, stupid politics, are in the hands of the householders. They think they can criticize other people. It is all stupid ideas. It has no meaning. Dharma is being protected by householders. If every householder really follows the dharma, they can change the thing.

Religion fully rests with the women of the nation. If they are pure, good, kind and gentle, then the children will also be good and prosperous. Children have more influence from their mother than the father. They can change it if they want to. When the females themselves become corrupt, then the whole nation is becoming like that. So, protection is mainly from the householder's life. If that is gone, then the whole nation goes to pieces. They are the protectors of dharma, not the monks. According to the old system, I am telling, the monk has to depend on the householders for everything. Our monks are not in that way. They are free from all those things. If you have kicked out everything, don't depend on anything. Work it out. Stand on your own feet. You have got your own free will. Nobody can challenge you. Nobody can criticize you.

Disciple: Swamiji, karma is the only thing that follows one when one dies. But when a monk dies and gives his karma in that moment to his Guru, will he escape then?
Swamiji: How can he go if the Guru does not take it?
Disciple: He will offer it to the Guru.
Swamiji: Offering, how can he offer?
Disciple: Why should the Guru not have all his duties?
Swamiji: Duties, bad karma and good karma, both?
Disciple: Both.
Swamiji: That is all right. Then you are free. Actually, if you believe in that way, with firm faith then there is nothing. If you come to that pitch, don't take both.

You see, there was a gardener. He made a very beautiful garden and for doing all bad things, he would say, "Indra, God Indra, is responsible." And for doing all good things, he would say, "I am, I am." That "I" was there. One day this went to Lord Indra; so, he went in the form of an old cow. The garden was so beautiful and the cow went and entered and ate the best plants. The gardener got annoyed. He took a stick and gave a beating to the cow and it fell and died. Now the people began to criticize him, "What a horrible man. He is a Brahmin and he has killed a cow by beating." He said, "What am I to do? This hand has done it. The hand of God Indra, Lord Indra, all this he has done." So, now the man wanted to escape.

Next day, Lord Indra came in the form of a Brahmin and he began praising the garden, "What a beautiful garden. Oh, I have never seen a garden of this kind. Who is the gardener?" The gardener was behind him. The Brahmin was pretending he had not seen the gardener and, he was praising in his own way, loudly. "Why," he said, "Why are you here? Who is the gardener? I have never seen a garden so wonderful." The man got so happy. Then the Brahmin said immediately, "And there was a case I had the day before yesterday, a cow was killed, is it you?" The man said, "No, not my hand, that was the God Indra. The God Indra has killed it." The God Indra then explained, "For all good things, you have 'I', you are there. For all bad things, God will take it. But you have to take both." Then the God Indra disappeared.

It is easy to say in that way, "both," but the ego grows there. So, watch it carefully. If you give up both, that is all right, both good and bad, all the pairs of opposites, complete surrender. Whatever comes by its own way, good or bad, accept it and work it out. Then you have no more karma. So, you follow me?

Disciple: I am a follower.

Reading: *Man can live in the world safely by cultivating real internal dispassion. Let there be no attachment to any one or anything.*

Swamiji: So, live in the world. Take whatever work you do and at the same time never get attached to it and you get no sin. You may go into a cave unknown to anyone and live there secretly. But if the mind is thinking of worldly things, you are worse than the man who lives in the world amidst all the sense-pleasures. So, it is the attitude that counts more than the actual work. If the mind is detached from doing all kinds of work, you are free. In this way, by living in a cave and at the same time evolving sense-pleasures, thinking of them and so many other worldly things, you have not done anything good. On the other hand, if you are living in the world and at the same time, you are not attached to it, you have done better than that man. Your progress is speedy. It is the mental attitude that counts more than anything.

Disciple: But Swamiji, I am a little attached to Saraswati.

Swamiji: Why?

Disciple: Because of that bliss, how can I kick out the mother of bliss?

Swamiji: We did not say to kick out such things. You have that attachment. That attachment will take you to the highest bliss. That is not called attachment, in that sense. The Goddess Saraswati, mother of learning, you are attached to her, that is a necessary thing. That attachment will take you and elevate you. It will not drag you down. Your Ishta-Devata is Saraswati. And you are getting attached more and more. And the more you get attached, the better it is. When you go to the last point, all those things disappear and you go back to your source. Until then, that attachment will help you go to that point.

Disciple: I was thinking about people who have never heard about dharma and karma and things like that. Does it depend on their attitude towards their work?

Swamiji: They are creating more and more bondage. They only want the worldly things. They don't know other things though they are suffering. That is why they eat, drink, and beget and do all sorts of things. Their life is no better than animals.

Disciple: I was specifically thinking of people doing bad acts which they don't know are bad because they haven't learned about it and are doing it with detachment, for example?

Swamiji: Whether they know it or not, the thing will come. The result must be there. After all, the Innermost Being is there with you. It must come to light one day or other. A man living in ignorance can never remain in ignorance forever. It is not possible. He has to change. Then, when he changes, it is too late. He becomes old. Then he remembers all his past karma, what he has done, what he has not done. Then he will say, "I have wasted my time. Now, in the evening of my life, oh God, help me, save me." It comes there. So, no one can remain in a stagnant position forever. It must change. You are intelligent, God being within you. That must come to light one day or other. It is only a question of time. Even an ignorant man, in his last days, will be praying to God. Whatever may be his idea of God, he will be praying there. Is it clear or no?

Disciple: Yes. Very clear.

Swamiji: Many of the animals, they know. They also have intelligence though they are not very intelligent. Man does not understand this. Even the rabbits running about say, "Don't come now. They are coming out just now. So, we must hide." They know when all are meditating; so, they will have a good dinner. Just now they were hiding somewhere. So, they are very intelligent. They know the time at four o'clock the monks were chasing them. That's all right. After chasing them the monks go to the hall and they come out again at five-thirty. They are so intelligent. How do you say they are stupid creatures?

Disciple: Yes, in olden times I heard that people thought that they could purify themselves by killing animals. I do not understand that.

Swamiji: Even now they offer sacrifices to some God or Goddess. They make an offering. That custom was even in Europe. Even now when they fall sick, they offer to their local Gods saying, "Oh, God, let me be cured. If I am cured, I will offer a goat to you." Then he gets cured and then he offers a goat.

Disciple: Is that a right understanding?

Swamiji: Right or wrong, they are doing it. So, they promise a cock, sometimes a hen or it may be some eggs. Their God is fond of hens and eggs; so, they offer them and they have satisfaction.

Disciple: Do they have to pay any karma because they have killed the animal?

Swamiji: Karma will be there. The God also will get karma and the man, also, who gives the thing will get karma.

Disciple: So they are progressing by doing that?

Swamiji: He does not know of hell and heaven. He wants to get rid of his disease. They are unknown to him. He does not want all those things. Why all that botheration? He has got some fever or some colic pain, now he wants to get rid of it. So, he offers in that way. There is some response. He feels it. That is all right. What else does he want? This karma and other things, they don't know much about it.

Disciple: Swamiji, in these days, whole species of wild animals have become almost extinct from the earth. There are almost no more tigers left and no whales in the North Sea. Will that not upset the balance?

Swamiji: There are cheetas and tigers still. They might have gone to some other life. Some of the tigers and bears might have become human beings, so they have evolved. It will not upset the balance or anything. It adjusts itself. Ice has melted. It has taken the form of cloud or water. That is all. Then how to upset the balance? The balance is ever the same.

June 22, 1973

Disciple: Swamiji, won't a rich man have the desire to renounce in his next life when he has had so much trouble?

Swamiji: Yes, generally they will renounce. To become a monk means they might have been kings and emperors or rich people. Monks are called Maharajas, great kings they are called, without possessing a single penny. So, who knows? Many of you might have been kings in the past life or else it is not easy to come to this life at a young age. You have had enough and more. You have seen life so you are vomiting from it.

June 23, 1973

Disciple: Swamiji, the world is a projection of your mind. How is it to be understood?

Swamiji: How do you understand it?

Disciple: If you are happy, you see a good world; if you are unhappy, you see an ugly world.

Swamiji: That is one way. A drunkard sees the whole world full of drunkards. A man was lying flat in savasana and he was meditating. One man came by and said, "Oh rascal, he was in the cinema the whole night and now he is sleeping." He gave abuse and went away. Another came by and saw the man lying down and thought, "He must be a thief. He might have robbed last night and is pretending to be in that way, sleeping." The third man came. He was a hash smoker, "Oh rascal, he has taken too much hash and is lying down unconscious." And the fourth man who came had nothing painted in his mind. He was a good man and he knew how to meditate. Then he said, "He is meditating." This is projection. You understand?

Disciple: Yes.

Swamiji: You project your own views. You have some preoccupation in your mind and it is called projection. Or, let us take another example. A beautiful rose is just blooming so beautifully. A devotee sees the flower and thinks; "It is a very good flower to offer to God." His thoughts come in that way. The lover comes, "There is a beautiful flower." The thoughts go in that way. And the third one, he catches the flower. He is enchanted by the beauty of the colour and he goes and plucks it. In this way, you project your scene and that projection is your own painting. Is it clear now?

Disciple: Yes, it is clear.

Swamiji: So, an ordinary man gives value to so many things. Everything is real to him by ignorance. When you go on bringing discrimination and bringing dispassion, as we were talking about yesterday, you see it is all due to your attachments. Then you discriminate, "What is beauty? Where is beauty in all those things? You paint it yourself and give beauty to those things, so they are beautiful." In that way, you go on discriminating and you are not charmed by so-called beauty. When you go to a high pitch of evolution, then you will see it is all false. There is only One Thing. If you remove name and form of the universe, what remains is God and God alone.

You take another incident. In the waking-state, everything is real to you, so many things. From the waking-state, you go to the dream-state. You forget the world completely and when you are dreaming, the dream-state world is as real as anything to you. When you go to deep-sleep-state, these two vanish and you live in your True Nature. There is nothing, no painting there. Then?

Disciple: May I ask one thing? The physical form we have when we come to this earth, is it also, in a way, a projection of our mind?

Swamiji: Not exactly. Karma has produced you. Owing to karma, all these things have taken form. The projection of the universe comes with the mind. All of you are in a particular dream. You see it as real. It is day for you, and for some animals or birds, it may be night. They are in a different vibration. Their understanding of time also differs from that of yours. There may be some small insects. Every hour may be a hundred years for them. They are in a particular dream.

Disciple: This sentence that, "Even the Gods have to become human beings to reach the highest," that I do not understand.

Swamiji: The so-called heaven is full of luxurious things. That is a one-sided view. I don't know where the Gods remain, if at all they can go.

Disciple: Is it just a mental conception?

Swamiji: The thing has been painted in this way because heaven means God lives there. There are always plenty of pleasures, not other things. Who wants this so-called liberation then? Who wants moksha? Who works for it? In that sense it is said.

Disciple: If a man wants Moksha and not heaven?

Swamiji: That is quite different. There is no room for heaven then. Moksha is quite different from heaven where there is always happiness, without the other side, pain. That has no meaning but still people want it.

Disciple: It is very difficult to want when it is beyond happiness even.

Swamiji: Yes, for children, if you say Moksha only, there nobody will work for it. They will run away from it. So, you must have a heaven too, just to drag them. You make them good, kind and gentle. There must be hell, too, or else man will eat man. In order to restrain him, make him good, there is the idea of hell and heaven. But when you think logically, it is impossible to have such a place like heaven or hell. It is all mental creation. With a purified mind, a well-trained mind, you are in heaven. An impure mind means you are in hell. You are suffering hellfire every second. But, if you give that philosophy to ordinary people, who wants all those things? They will not do anything. So, there must be some fear for them. So, religion begins with fear and ends in Moksha. Out of fear he prays to God, "I am a sinner, help me, save me." But after making some progress, if at all they make progress, they come to this line of meditation and mantra-jap. Then you understand your innermost being itself is God. Now you have to realize it. You have to do more and more mantra-jap, purify yourself and then, lastly, go to Samadhi. There, you solve this problem. Is it clear? Any doubt?

Disciple: I find it very difficult to want this Moksha because I don't know what it is.

Swamiji: Every one is searching for it but you have taken a wrong course. You have selected a wrong path. Instead of taking the right course internally, you are externalizing. You think by sense-enjoyments you will be happy, but there is no happiness. Now slowly and steadily, you have to take the mind internally and go to the Source.

Disciple: How can you write in your book, how to please the Guru?

Swamiji: Then, not to please or displease. There is no displeasing and no pleasing also. You have to please and displease your own mind.

Disciple: I understand.

Swamiji: It is with God also. He does not take anything. He does not expect anything. It is only for your purification you have to think of God and meditate on Him. He is not in need of anything. Then again, He is not offended by the doing of any kind of evil. And, he is not pleased by any kind of good you do. It is all for your own sake you do it. As you think, so you become. You are what your past desires, thoughts and acts have made you. The present weal and woe, failure and success are owing to your past. Your future is entirely in your hands. So, you have to mend yourself. Nobody compels you, but if you want to get rid of all sufferings, we say, "Control your mind by meditation and other things." Your whole destiny is being controlled there. That is the secret. It is not that God is pleased or the Guru is displeased. It is for your own benefit you have to do this thing.

June 24, 1973

Reading: *Asana means posture. There are innumerable postures but the yogis consider eighty-four of them to be very useful. These yoga-asanas are meant for preserving good physical, mental and spiritual health. Regular and systematic practice of these asanas makes the body strong, agile, healthy and very elastic. Asanas bring on keen and vigorous appetite, help to control emotions and to retain brahmacharya (celibacy). They also distribute blood equally all over the body, tone up nerve-currents and keep the different organs of the body in sound working order so as to produce mental peace and to help concentration of the mind.*

Swamiji: So, here you have to take into consideration why these asanas came into prominence. Can any of you yoga teachers explain why it is better than the various forms of gymnastics?

Disciple: Gymnastics only prepares the outer physique of the body; whereas, yoga asanas have an effect on the internal organs also.

Swamiji: It is one of the benefits. There may be so many. What about young people and children? What kind of asanas can you give or can you give other exercises?

Disciple: Both.

Swamiji: What about aged people?

Disciple: The aged people can keep their health and vigour with the help of asanas.

Swamiji: Yes, that is necessary to understand. These asanas came into prominence or vogue because after the age of thirty-five people generally cannot go for outdoor games and, in order to preserve good health, the yogis found these asanas. You can teach children. That is all right. But the first and foremost thing for children is to build up their muscles. They must be strong. A weak man may be very intelligent, but he cannot put his ideas into practice. A man who is very strong but has a dull brain, if you once get him to understand, he can put it into practice. He has got the courage and energy to do it. So many people, so-called bookworms, they are intelligent. They come first in the class and other things. On the other side, lifelong they suffer from all kinds of diseases. So, we want both. Children can learn yoga asanas but, side by side, they have to build up their body, that you have to keep in mind. After the age of thirty-five, it is difficult for people to go for outdoor games. Then, yoga asanas will help you immensely just to retain good health. A good physique makes a good brain also. Mind is also connected with it. When it works properly, you can do miraculous work. That is the secret there.

Reading: *Asanas cure diseases of many kinds. Even chronic ones are rooted out completely through regular and systematic practice of asanas.*

Swamiji: Pranayama and asanas combined can have miraculous effects on chronic diseases. Generally, the doctors don't root it out. They give medicine for one symptom and it changes. If there is disease in the stomach, they give medicine for the stomach. It slips away and it comes to the heart and when you give medicine for that, it goes to the head. It is a moving pain. It is very difficult. They can't cure it. It can be eradicated by pranayama and yoga-asanas combined. In this way, you can make the body healthy. That is good. When the body is healthy, your mind-function is also healthy, that is good. So, all work can be done easily. You will have good concentration.

Disciple: Can some of these asanas help in awakening the kundalini shakti?

Swamiji: Yes, there are some, especially sirshasana (head stand) that helps. But, don't do that for half an hour or more, as some do. When people do it, then the kundalini shakti will rise up. But I don't advise you to take that course. It is dangerous. It is just like doing pranayama and raising it up suddenly, don't do it. Last year, I think I told the incident of a disciple making yoga-asanas. He was an expert in doing sirshasana especially. He did it for more than an hour. When he got up, he had double vision. He would see two things. Then, he had to go to the eye specialist to get rid of it. It took some months to get it cleared. So, those are all dangerous things. It can raise up the kundalini shakti suddenly. Then again, you must understand it will not rise up fully. If you want to raise it up fully, three-fold purity is absolutely necessary: purity of the body, nadis and mind. Without that purity, any effort made will only be increasing your misery. There will be partial rising. That is what happens, as I have been telling often, by LSD. They get some sort of results. It is due to abnormal heat that makes the shakti work like a sort of hot current that goes to the head and it keeps you awake. The rajasic will be more rajasic and often you will have some sort of experience. Immediately when it goes down, it goes in a wrong direction. It is a very dangerous game. Never tackle the shakti. Many become mad due to that.

Disciple: Swamiji, in which nadis is the kundalini going if you take these drugs?

Swamiji: All the nadis are depending on the kundalini. All the nadis, they become heated. All work. It rushes up like anything. You cannot control it. You always feel burning. So people who take LSD, they can sit where there is ice without covering. They become so heated.

Reading: *Four of them (asanas) are prescribed for the purpose of (i) doing Mantra-Jap (repeating God's name), (ii). Pranayama, (iii). awakening of the Kundalini Shakti and (iv). for practising concentration. And they are called: Padmasana, Siddhasana, Swastikasana and Sukhasana.*

Swamiji: Padmasana (lotus posture) or any asana you like or can easily sit for a longer time, that asana can be used for these purposes. Always sit erect. Never sit in a bent posture. It will be very injurious for your health both physically and mentally. It will bring disturbance to the nerve-currents. The secret is that when the currents are excessive in any part of the body, that is disease. When there is lack of current in any part of the body, that is also disease. When you sit in a bent posture, you get both. The head does not get enough currents for its work and you feel drowsy. It is just like the electric current. There is some leakage somewhere. It is burning but it is very feeble. On the other hand, the generated energy must be there. Instead of going up, it clogs in the lower abdomen and then you get stomach disorder. So, always sit straight. Without nerve currents, the mind cannot function. What do you mean by tired? When you do physical work or when you go on speaking and speaking for hours together?

Disciple: Lack of nerve currents.

Swamiji: Suppose you have a certain amount of electrical supply to the room. And now you are concentrating only on one side and all the other things suffer due to lack of nerve-currents. So, doing heavy physical labour or doing mental labour means you are using all the fuel to one side, to one sense and all other senses are lacking that current. Generally, you feel tired. You want to go to sleep immediately. In deep-sleep-state nothing is wasted and the whole current is retained. The kundalini shakti is working all the twenty-four hours and its currents are limited. It supplies currents to various functions of the body. That is how, after deep-sleep, you feel rejuvenated. That is the secret. But, a yogi who knows how to make the kundalini shakti work at a high speed at will, he can supply any deficiency. That is the secret. By supplying the deficiency, wherever there is lack, it is owing to this, he overcomes disease. By circulating the nerve-energy equally all over the body, you can control many diseases. Also, pranayama number three can be taken here.

Disciple: Swamiji, can pranayama be used in the evening if you feel very tired?

Swamiji: Yes, pranayama number three will remove drowsiness.

Disciple: But won't it be difficult to sleep afterwards if it is done late in the evening?

Swamiji: That number three can bring sleep when you feel sleeplessness. A few rounds then you feel sleepy. In this way, you can control sleep. That is the best remedy. Those who can practise regularly will feel the effect. This pranayama can help you in so many ways: when you feel tired after heavy work, when overloading the stomach and with heavy drowsiness. At any time, you can do it without any danger, number three especially but not number four. Don't misunderstand one for another and go mad. You must be careful.

One man in New Zealand was having heart trouble due to excess of nerve-currents to the heart region. The doctors did not understand what was the cause. Then he was taken to the hospital and there, for fifteen days, he was treated with all sorts of medicine. There was no cure. Then the doctors said, "You will die. Go home." Poor fellow. What was to be done? He got afraid. Then he wrote to me, "What is to be done?" I told him to go on with this pranayama. He took it up very seriously because of this fear of death. And in fifteen days he was completely cured. Then he went to the same doctor and told him, "Please test my heart" and the doctor was astonished. "How could you cure that incurable disease," the doctor asked? He only laughed at him and left the place. So, it has been effective.

June 25, 1973
Reading: *Ida and Pingala are the two main sympathetics which carry the afferent and efferent nerve-currents.*
Disciple: What is meant by afferent and efferent?
Swamiji: Positive and negative, active and passive. Is it clear?
Disciple: Not fully.
Swamiji: One is taking and one is bringing, in that way. The current, the starting electricity from the dynamo, there is only one kind. Then they divide into two groups, one is negative and the other is positiv. Always there must be a combination of two things to produce a third thing. Some take the sensation to the brain center and some carry the sensation from the brain center. When any of the nadis coming or going are destroyed, it is called paralysis. You have no sensation. By attacking the kundalini shakti, you can create abnormal nerve-currents. When you do pranayama, you increase the heat there and it will work abnormally. And when you do not work it properly, it may work in a subnormal way. That is why many people lack energy for brainwork, even for pumping the blood. For some reason or other, the action of the muladhara is not normal then. That person will have below normal activity and also of the blood circulation. With some, that center remains heated and they will suffer from fickle-mindedness. When the currents going upward are too strong, they feel restless. Both ways it can work. So, everything depends upon the kundalini shakti. When it works abnormally, it is disease and sub-normally, it is also disease. When it works in a normal way, you enjoy good health, good mental and physical health. That is the secret there.
   Disciple: You write that mental work is harder than physical work. I do not understand?

Swamiji: Yes, it is much harder.

Disciple: Why does one have to eat so much more when one is doing physical work?

Swamiji: You have to eat. The fuel is there. It is just like in mental work, you require mental energy. The whole energy, which is in the food, is all converted into mental energy. But in physical labour, the gross thing is immediately wasted. It is in that way. What is your question there?

Disciple: I don't understand why one has to eat so much when one is doing physical work? Which is less work?

Swamiji: With physical work you see immediately that when you eat, you have so much digestion. It takes place and you require more food. But the energy used is still not as much as the energy used in mental work.

Disciple: What kind of energy?

Swamiji: In a subtle form, you get the same energy when food is transformed into subtler and subtler things. The subtle energy is being used, that is ojas shakti, especially in mental work. In physical activity, what you eat and drink is used immediately and you have to eat more when you are doing so much work. If you don't do physical work, it gets converted into subtle energy and that goes to mind function, brain function and other things.

Disciple: So, one is not using the mental energy of the food, the subtle energy of the food when one is doing physical work?

Swamiji: He is using it but less. The energy is used more in mental work.

Disciple: You can see with people who have very demanding, mental work, for example, people who work with children, that is very hard mental work. They are exhausted in another way than people who are working in the field.

Swamiji: They act quickly. The mind is working constantly in this way and that way. In physical work, you only have to take the spade and dig and dance.

Disciple: We have seen in certain schools that the children have such Freedom and so on. The teacher stays at the school for five years, and then he is wasted.

Swamiji: Everything?

Disciple: Yes. He is wasted. He has to go somewhere else.
Swamiji: That is the cause you see. It is natural.
Disciple: Yes.
Disciple: How then to do sadhana?
Swamiji: You have to make a compromise between these two. That is why I see some of them are sleeping, poor men. I have sympathy with it. Many of them have been working hard in the field and doing other work. It is natural for them to feel sleepy while meditating. It is a sort of sadhana. Still, you are sitting there. When you get more comfort and lessen the work, it will be all right.

June 26, 1973
Reading: *For the practice of mantra-jap and meditation, a good place which is lovely, neat, even and picturesque should be selected. If one can obtain a solitary place away from the din and bustle of the world it would be very congenial to the practice. But if one can afford, a separate room should be set apart for the purpose of meditation only.*
Swamiji: If it is not possible, what will you do?
Disciple: Make a meditation box.
Swamiji: Some have no money for a box, then?
Disciple: Just a corner.
Swamiji: Put a curtain or something. We have to make adjustments. That is what I mean. The real thing we are discussing is how it should be. Many people make lame excuses like I have no room. Others say there is no place where I live. It is all lame excuses. There are difficulties everywhere.

Suppose you get a lonely place. Then after some time, you feel disgusted. There is a thing called monotony. You know monotony? When you get the best kind of food daily, then after three or four days, the mind says, that it is a disgusting thing, always having the same thing. So, you want a change. That is called monotony. In the same way, when you are doing mantra-jap and meditation, sometimes when you are working and working after some days the mantra becomes so-called monotonous and then many people make a mistake. "Oh, what can this mantra do for me? It is not for me." Especially all these things come in the time of reaction. Don't be duped by the mind. Make adjustments. Work hard and you must succeed. Success will come. It is only a question of time. The mind plays so many tricks. It can fool you within no time. That is why we have been telling you, a purified mind acts like a very good friend and an impure mind betrays you every step you take. It does not want to have a regulated life. It hates it. It likes to shun work and be easy-going. Why have this "bondage" as they call it? It looks like bondage to them.

If there is a secluded place, that is all right. We have got all the facilities here in this place. We find it very peaceful. Even the birds are not disturbing you. When I am alone, I think there is no world here, no sound. Neither in Delhi nor Coorg, even when you retire into secluded places in India, there are so many birds to disturb you. Here, you have no birds, no crows, nothing whatsoever. You are absolutely in seclusion but you have to make use of your mind. Make the mind work. That is all.

If a secluded place is not available, then make a room, those who can afford it. And if that is also not possible, use the sleeping room, you have to. On the bed itself, you should not sit. The tendency to fall asleep is there. Then comes the question, how to make the place for meditation? The seat should be a bit raised, about thirty centimeters. If it is too hard, then you will get pain in the ankles, so you can put a cushion and cover it with a clean cloth. Some keep a skin and over that they place a small mat they call Kusha grass and then put a blanket or a small neat cloth. Then?

Reading: *The room thus selected must be airy and well-ventilated, free from dust, dirt, flies and other disturbing elements.*

Swamiji: Even your sleeping room, it should be kept well ventilated. There must be fresh air coming and going. When there is smoke and dust, don't do breathing exercises, that will injure your health. Immediately, you will be sneezing and other things. Before doing pranayama, clean your nose, throat and mouth. Wash nicely before sitting for meditation and doing pranayama.

Reading: *This room should not be slept in.*
Swamiji: That we told you. Cleanliness must be kept. Sleeping or not sleeping depends on the circumstances. Keep the room holy always. Don't allow people of different temperaments to come there. They may be friends, but don't allow such people. Keep it separate, if possible. Keep special clothes for meditation purposes and after some time, you will feel a sort of good vibration there. You feel it actually. That is why it is said, man makes temples holy and the temples, in turn, make man holy. Before we came here, it was a cowshed. Last year, it was very difficult to come inside. It was so full of flies, dust and dirt. When we came for the first time, we felt some difficulties and now there is a sort of good vibration. Every one may feel it. Do you people feel it or not?
Disciple: Yes, very much.
Swamiji: Now, instead of a cowshed, you have made a temple. In turn, this temple helps so many people. Those who come in a disturbed state of mind, when they come to the room, they feel a sort of vibration and it has a cooling effect on the mind. Automatically, the mind has peace.

In this way, make the room neat, don't allow any sort of people with bad vibrations to enter. Don't give your bed or blanket to anyone. They may be friends. Don't allow them to sit on it. Even your asana should not be given to each and every one. Keep it only for yourself. If you observe these things carefully, after some days you will give a vibration to the room. And when you go for meditation, you will have easy concentration.

Reading: *No one of a different temperament and taste should be allowed to enter the room. It should be treated as a shrine and it should be entered only with clean clothes on and after a bath.*
Swamiji: It is not necessary. That "after bath" means if it is a very hot climate, then only go for that. You must take the spirit behind. Be neat, that is one word. Even if you cannot take a bath, take a wet towel, squeeze the water out and clean everything so you are clean there. That is also a kind of bath. In that way, you can manage.

Reading: *No evil and wicked thoughts should be entertained inside the room.*

Swamiji: That is not possible. It is only a possibility, I am telling. But anyway, knowingly if you can control it, that is good. One cannot have control over the thoughts in the beginning. It is not possible. Don't make a hubbub over it. Only take precautions not to speak or do other things if it can be avoided.

Reading: *Photos and pictures of Gods, Goddesses, great Saints and of one's Ishta-Devata should be hung and kept inside. Even beautiful flowers in flower vases should be kept, if possible.*
Swamiji: It is just to create a good vibration. All these things help you. When you look this side and that side, you see the photos of Gods and Goddesses or great men and that will give a sort of inspiration. You may think, they have worked very hard, they have realized God and attained Samadhi; so, I must also attain. When you have a good vibration, good sight, flowers and a good scene, the mind calms down and you have a lift there. So, all these things help you in that way.

Reading: *This holy atmosphere always influences one's mind, helps meditation and elevates one spiritually. In due course, the room will so vibrate with serenity that even if one enters it in a disturbed state of mind, one will feel soothed and consoled. It will gain the power to still one's mind and so to influence it that it would be led to higher and nobler things automatically.*
Swamiji: So, that is called thought vibration. Every man or woman has a thought aura and that thought aura is acording to his or her predominating thoughts inside. If a girl or boy is always struggling to repeat the mantra and lives a pure, holy and good life, he or she will be vibrating a good aura. People coming and seeing them by the very sight alone will have a good impression. They have a good vibration and the mind catches it.

On the other hand, a person, it may be a boy or a girl, they are not living a pure life, they are living a dirty life. Their very appearance vibrates that dirtiness. They cannot hide it. The face, the eyes and apart from this, the subtler thought vibrations, the mind catches it automatically. So, by seeing a person, immediately you get disgusted, "Oh horrible creature. From where has he come, so horrible?" So, no one can avoid the vibration. Purity and impurity immediately have an effect there.

Likewise, when you go to a house where there is always quarrelling between the wife and husband, you cannot remain there for five minutes. Your inner voice will tell you, "Let me go, let me go." You don't know why you feel so much impatience. On the other hand, where there is a good understanding, pure love among the family, when you go there, you feel at home. "Let me wait. Let me have a little rest," you may say. You don't want to run away.

Disciple: If one gets the vision of one's Ishta-Devata in the hour of death...
Swamiji: Not before?
Disciple: Yes, I hope so, but what kind of attainment is that?
Swamiji: You will go to Ishta-Devata. Then?
Disciple: Is it a permanent attainment?
Swamiji: It is not a permanent attainment. After some time, your Ishta-Devata may kick you out. He will push you down and you will take birth and become a wise man. Wherever there is name and form, your Ishta-Devata is not permanently there. The permanent thing is only One. That is Brahman.
Disciple: Is it Savikalpa?
Swamiji: It is not exactly a Samadhi state. Even to think of Ishta-Devata is not easy. You must work. Then only you come to that pitch or else all the things which you have been doing during your whole lifetime, while dying, you have those ideas. So, the preparation must be there. To come to that pitch, you require sadhana. If you constantly live in that form, then only you can remember it or else it is not easy. Whatever they have been doing the most, that thing will be there. In order to get a divine vision, that we have explained somewhere in the book, you get it only with the rising of the shakti to the heart center, not before.

So, in Ramakrishna's life there was a story. He had a terrible sort of disciple. He was an intelligent man. He was the founder of a Bengali dramatic theatre. At the same time, he was a great drunkard. Always he would drink. He became a disciple of Ramakrishna. One time he drank and drank the whole night. He did not know where he was. In the morning, he was sleeping somewhere with some girl from the drama, his own companion. He was so sorry; then again he was putting a big bottle in his pocket and went directly to Ramakrishna who asked, "What is it, one bottle? It is all right." The disciple began drinking and drinking and then he began to criticize Ramakrishna, to abuse him. The disciple gave one abuse. Ramakrishna gave two. The disciple became louder than his Guru. For every word, Ramakrishna gave two or three more scoldings. The disciple was bawling out and the Guru was also bawling out. Lastly people came running, "What is wrong?" They used to call Ramakrishna a mad boy. This mad boy was calling out and he has a mad disciple also. And then they were seeing the fun. For every single scolding, Ramakrishna was giving two, three or four. That fellow got defeated. That is what happened.

He prostrated. "You are also a Guru giving scoldings, not only the good matters. In scoldings, you are a Guru to me," and in this way he allowed him. One day he found Ramakrishna almost in Bhava-Samadhi. He thought, "How nice it would be if he takes all my responsibilities, then I will be free." His name was Girish. Ramakrishna said, "Try to take God's name at least in the morning and in the evening." Girish said, "How can I take it? I don't know when I go to sleep. There is no setting. How can I do it?" He thought the Guru would take all the responsibility. That was his motive. "All right, don't do that thing. At least do it once before eating." "That is also not possible for me." Then Ramakrishna said, "All right. Never mind. I will take care of it." Girish was very much relieved. He thought, "I am now free."

After some days Girish came, he was telling something, "I will do it. I will do that work," he said. "Ah what, that "I", where is that "I"? Now, how can it come, "I"? You have given all the responsibility to me. How can the "I" come now?" Girish understood his difficulties. For doing every work, he had to forget himself and put the Guru in front. He was caught. He improved much afterwards. Now he understood the difficulty. He thought he had escaped completely and he was waiting for sympathy. When he said "I", how can that "I" come when it is already dead? So, he understood now. He was caught. In this way, all funny things happen.

Now, all right. We will sit.

June 27, 1973

Disciple: Swamiji, if workers have some repair work to do in the meditation room, how can one avoid that they spoil the vibration?

Swamiji: It does not matter. It does not get impure so soon. It will take some time to kill the vibration. If a man suddenly comes and enters, don't become annoyed and say, "He has come and ruined the whole atmosphere." It happened, one person after smoking hash or something, he went to see his friend and that man got pain due to something else. His friend said, "The vibration was so bad, I got pain immediately." So, he was putting something else on another. Not in that way. It will not change so soon. By mistake, somebody enters the room; don't be nervous and think of it. Actually, you feel you are depressed, that is your own creation. You understand?

Disciple: Yes.

Swamiji: Don't go to such an extent. Somebody was asking, suppose a man was selling something which was not properly earned, and you have to pay and bring it from the shop. If you go into minor details, in that way, you can't get any food anywhere. So, it is not possible to live in that way. So, you have to make adjustments to certain things. You understand or not?

Disciple: Yes.

Swamiji: Now, by chance, one enters the room where you are meditating. Don't jump up and spoil everything completely. "Horrible it is, I don't have concentration today." That was your own making, You have created the wrong vibration. In that way, don't go to extremes. Have tolerance. If there is something needed, a window or something that needs repairing or cleaning. If somebody comes to do it, that is all right. After that, clean the room and burn incense, have a good smell. That is good. Then it changes the vibration.

Reading: When a man desires and thinks, he sets up thought-vibrations of lesser or greater intensity. The force of a thought-

vibration varies according to the purity, sincerity and concentration of the mind.

Swamiji: Even if you go to a graveyard or a cremation ground, automatically you feel a sort of sorrow. You may not know it but the vibration is there, in such a way you feel sorry. The air is full of that thing, weeping and crying for the dying. Likewise, if you go to an old church, you feel a sort of peace there.

Reading: *Whenever one visits an ancient sacred church, temple, mosque, pagoda or monastery, pure, holy and inspiring thoughts begin to surge in one's mind and one feels intense peace and bliss.*

Swamiji: This is one of the ways pilgrimmage helps a person. An ordinary man who cannot do any sadhana finds some value in going from place to place. But higher than this is to sit in one place and devote your time to doing mantra-jap and meditation. The highest kind of sadhana is if you go to the last point and attain Samadhi. But ordinary people get some sort of inspiration by going on pilgrimage.

Reading: *These thought-emanations continue to vibrate in those places till they are changed by stronger and counter thought-waves. It was with this idea that the keeping of shrines holy came into vogue in different religions and this very idea applies to the meditation room also.*

Swamiji: Even in the churches where the image is put near the altar, no one is allowed to go there. People who go there, bend their knees from a distance in the hall but they never go to the altar where the priest is worshipping. It is kept sacred. Everywhere they have that system and to keep it sacred is only for that purpose. If every one with a dirty hand and dirty clothing goes and sits there, that would create a bad vibration. It spoils the sanctity. Nowadays it is said, "What is there? We are all made by God." So, they make a big hubbub without knowing anything. The same thing happened in India. The caste system is based on this principle and that is why one must not touch the other. It may be his own brother and now they destroy the thing completely. Even the sudras have been allowed to enter the temples. Who wants the temple? Nobody cares for it. Without knowing anything, they have spoiled the whole thing.

Reading: *Why should one send out good thoughts and what are the benefits?*

Swamiji: So, when you are sending a particular thought, there are similar thoughts waiting outside. You are giving a particular way for it to enter you and it will disturb you also. If it is a good one, it will help you and if it is a bad one, it will disturb you. So, you are sending some similar thoughts that go out and so many other people have similar thoughts. So, in sending good thoughts, you are helping yourself and you are helping so many others also. Similarly, by sending bad thoughts, you are injuring yourself also. You are not free from it. You will be injuring so many other people also. There is so much loss. Your gain is also immense by sending good thoughts; so, in both ways it works. Once you begin doing something bad, you sink down lower and lower. It is just like dropping a rubber ball from the first step, it doesn't know where it will go and stops. In this way, there are reactions, so one must be very careful.

Disciple: Swamiji, is it possible to remain without thoughts like you describe here, as if you live in a closed room?

Swamiji: You can remain without any thoughts if you want. When you come to higher pitches, especially in the state of Samadhi, or in a trance, there you can do it. You can also remain without any thoughts. That is a practice. By practising every day to make the mind blank from all desires and thoughts, every one can practice a little but it is very difficult. But, it is possible. You can make the mind blank at will.

That is why I have been criticizing the so-called, "I am a sinner, Oh Lord. I am a sinner." The sin of the first man who did that sin is following us to eternal damnation. So, I have been criticizing that way of thinking. It has no meaning. It is degrading oneself, that thought. That is why it is said, "As you think, that you become." You are what your past desires, thoughts and acts have made you. That is all your karma-phala. It is your own making. Nobody else has made it. By thinking wrong and sinful thoughts of your past sins, you are going down and down. You are giving wrong impressions to the mind and chitta. That is very bad. You have done something wrong. Let it go. "I will not do it hereafter. I must do good things." In this way, build up your life. You must have constructive thoughts, "Be brave. Let me rise up." Such people can make progress. There must be life.

Disciple: How do these two people influence each other, the man with good thoughts and the man with bad thoughts, if they open their mind to each other?

Swamiji: The good thought is already vibrating everywhere and that enters you automatically. Bad thoughts are vibrating there and that also enters you. Similarly, the man who is sending some bad thought, it also injures you. Both are there.

Suppose one is sending good thoughts and there are some thoughts waiting outside your mind. You are giving a particular channel for them to work. They enter your brain; thereby, you will be influenced to do good things again. On the other hand, you are sending out bad thoughts and bad thoughts are waiting. They will enter you and they spoil you and so many others also. In that way, it has double action. Good thoughts help you and help so many others. Bad thoughts injure you and injure other people also. In this way, they interact on both sides. Is it clear?

Disciple: Yes.

Disciple: You say there is not a thing you can call absolutely good, that everything is a mixture of good and bad?

Swamiji: Suppose you are helping a poor man with money, say a charity; but, on the other side, you are injuring the person. You are creating a bad habit for that person. He wants to beg and beg. He does not want to work, so in that way it develops. Considering that thing, you have done something wrong also. On one side, you have done good, that is all right. On the other side, you have given some room for bad things. In this way, if you search, every act has got these two sides.

Disciple: What bad is there in trying to attain the highest?

Swamiji: There may be some — your children, babies crying for you. You are not feeding them. Yes, you are trying to attain the highest and they are criticizing you, "Horrible mother you are. Why did she give birth to us? If I had a better mother, she would have given me kisses. She does not care for us." So, in that way, it is a bad thing.

Disciple: But could I give them something better than that?

Swamiji: I am telling, you are doing good. You are going towards God. That is a good act. But, on the other side, they have got grievances

against you. Something bad is there considering the viewpoint of the children. You are doing something wrong to them, they say. In this way, both things are mixed everywhere. You catch it or not?
Disciple: Not quite.
Swamiji: On one side, you are doing a very good thing going towards God; but the children require love and nourishment and so many other things. When you are busy thinking of God, you cannot attend to them properly. You have to neglect some side. They say, "We are suffering. We have no love."
Disciple: Yes.
Swamiji: In that way, somebody is enjoying and somebody is suffering; so, these two things always go side by side. In the thing which is very good, a major portion is good for you so it is called a good act. If you take a bad act, there is also something good. In this way everything is mixed. Is it clear now?
Disciple: Yes.

June 28, 1973

Disciple: Swamiji, what is meant by grace?
Swamiji: What do you understand? What do you want there? The word grace, it might be an act of kindness. A king may be gracious; he may give something, a plot of land to a poor man. That is also a sort of grace. Then if you want to call it Divine Grace, what is it? You see, men who follow jnana-yoga, they do not worry about grace. They depend on their own effort. They don't cry. If good comes, that is all right. If failure comes, that also they will face. They will not worry about anything. They have to stand on their own feet. People who take up bhakti-yoga, they depend on God and Divine Grace, His mercy. All these things they say because they feel weak. They want someone to catch them and guide them. If there is failure, they weep for God, "Oh God, help me, save me, let me have your grace," in this way they put it. Generally, your effort must be there.

It is just like, suppose there are two people, one has a plot of land this side, another this side. One man has struggled very hard. He has ploughed the ground in season and he has put down manure and other things. He has made everything ready. The second man, he has neglected it. He has not done anything. Now rain comes and falls on both plots. On the first plot, there comes a good crop and, on the other, you will have only weeds. So, this rain is called grace. Divine Grace is like this. It is everywhere. Like the sun, it shines on a poor man, a rich man or an ignorant man or it may be a sinful man, whatever it might be. It shines on all equally.

Disciple: So, everything is grace?

Swamiji: Yes, in that way, but you have to make use of it. Without effort you cannot catch it. That is a simple thing. Without hard work on your side, you cannot catch the grace. You understand?

Disciple: Yes.

Disciple: There is right effort and wrong effort but is there effort in wrong effort also?

Swamiji: Then you get a wrong thing.

Disciple: Yes, but you think you are managing in the right way when you work in the field.

Swamiji: But if you don't manage it properly, you don't give proper manure, you get weeds or some insects and they will eat away everything. You will get nothing.

Disciple: But there is effort?

Swamiji: That is wrong effort. You get so many worms instead.

Disciple: But do you think that effort is right?

Swamiji: How can you think that? You may think so many things but it is by the result that you understand. A student may write so much nonsense. He may think, "I have done well, I will get top marks." When the results come, he may fail completely. So that is your result. You get the result. That is the failure. Your working was wrong. Your understanding was wrong, that it clearly proves. When you have a bad result, there is something wrong in your understanding, in your effort.

Say a robber also thinks he is doing the right thing. He also prays to God. Before going to rob, he says to the Lord, "Oh God save me. Send me plenty of money. I must get more and more money. Let me not get caught by the police." He also prays; so, he is also doing right effort.

According to his understanding, he is doing right. But the next day he is caught and he is hanged, so, in that way, he was wrong in his understanding. Is it clear or not?

Disciple: Yes, that is clear.

Disciple: How can it be Swamiji, sometimes by doing good, you get a bad result?

Swamiji: That means in a past life you have done something wrong. It crosses that thing. That also you must understand. If you know the thing, you can withstand it and face it. It is not by running away. You can't help yourself in that way. Many people do that thing. They want to commit suicide when they are caught by everything. They want to become free. That is not the way. By committing suicide, you have to pay very heavily for it. Again, with all possibilities you get in this life, you lose them completely. You become more sinful rather; so, thereby you are not doing anything good for yourself. You have not escaped. Many people think there is only one birth. "By committing suicide let there be an end to this birth." It is terrible. They have to come back again.

Disciple: There is no stop?

Swamiji: They have to go back still further to a worse kind of life. In this life at least, you have a good body, good intellect, but if you don't make use of it in a right way, then you have to go down owing to sin. So, it is very dangerous. You can't escape in that way. You have to face the thing. What you have done, you have to face it. Know the thing when it comes, face it. Work it out. "Face the devil," we say. "Don't run away." By running away from the danger, your difficulty, you don't help yourself. Be prepared for it. That is the only way to get rid of all those things, by paying your debt. That is a punishment you get. You have done something mischievous or sinful so you have to pay in this life. Knowing that, when it comes, face it. At the same time, take the right path. That is the only way. Nobody can escape it.

Disciple: The mantra purifies the chitta. Is that an unconscious process or is it a conscious process?

Swamiji: Both. You are doing the mantra consciously and that purification goes on unconsciously.

Disciple: Is it just like it brings up samskaras and you understand it and put it back?

Swamiji: Some samskaras may come up but it is not in that way. When you go on repeating the mantra, every moment, it goes on sending impression after impression, the might and glory of God. Mantra and other things fill the whole chitta and even if you get some sort of thoughts, there will be good vibrations, good thoughts. All other thoughts are purified or washed away. The entire chitta is changed by mantra.

Disciple: That means you do not have to go to this process we discussed of the psychiatrist who makes a man remember some suppressed things?

Swamiji: They have got a small process, that is all. Just to bring out some hidden things which are in the chitta. They are giving a sort of relief to the patient. They find out that he or she was in in love with a certain person and that love was frustrated, so they bring it up and give some kind of explanation. That is all they can do. What else can they do?

Disciple: Are there things like hindrances or worse?

Swamiji: By doing your mantra-jap, all those things get destroyed. All those things, hindrances and everything, get destroyed. Mantra has power. It can purify. The psychiatrists are doing only a little of this, tidbits. They are giving a good consolation. They ask them to do good things. In this way, they give a sort of relief momentarily. Thereby, they don't become wise people, do they, after going to the psychiatrist?

Disciple: No.

Swamiji: They feel a little momentary relief because some sort of difficulty is overcome. It is not a difficulty at all in a deeper sense but, for them, because they are trained in the worldly sense, they find a sort of relief, somebody to give them a sort of consolation. That is nothing at all. In a deeper sense, it is nothing. There is no help.

But, unlike that, mantra helps a person so deeply. It goes deeper and deeper and helps the same people, if they also take mantra. We find many people come in a horrible state, not just one screw loose, and after a few days when they have taken mantra and done meditation, there will be good results for them. They find there is peace and they have brightness in the face and eyes. They regain it in that way, so it is doing miraculous work.

Disciple: Swamiji, if you break a stone will there then be two Atmans?

Swamiji: Many Atmans. Every particle has an Atman, not one, not two, millions and billions in this much of a stone. There will be millions according to your atom theory. How can you deny it? So, what is your difficulty there?

Disciple: How can the stone come to a higher incarnation?

Swamiji: When that stone is ground and made into ashes, then it takes birth in some other life. In that way, it comes lastly to man. It takes some millions and billions of years. So, how to know when it began, this creation? There is no end to it. How it began, nobody can tell you. If you can tell that thing, when, where and how, then you can know when God was created. Then who created that God? And that God must have some others. There also you come to Infinity. You are nowhere. So, that will be an illogical question. You have to stop somewhere. Say there is God, or we have called it "The Ocean of Consciousness by Itself." It is eternal, infinite without beginning, without middle and without end. There only you have to stop or else there will be confusion.

Disciple: Swamiji, are there other solar systems similar to this?

Swamiji: Why do you worry? Take care of your solar system here. Why all these questions? They must have the same system. Every star you see is a sun. There are some stars where the light has not yet reached. They are so far away. The Milky Way in the sky, there are so many. There is no end to it. Your astronomers get stunned when they go there. They feel confused.

Disciple: But it seems that the scientists only think that there is this solar system.

Swamiji: Yes, they can say only that much when they don't understand and get confused thinking and thinking.

Disciple: Some of them believe in God.

Swamiji: Oh, as if God is waiting for their information or their Godhood disappears if the scientists do not say God is existing, as if He is waiting for the recognition of the scientist, oh horrible thing. Your understanding is limited. Whatever you conceive is all limitations of the mind. It can never know Infinity. The mind is finite. It can only know finite things. In a relative way, you can speak of all those cock-and-bull stories.

Disciple: Yes, but Swamiji, if you go on analysing this finite thing...

Swamiji: How long will you go on analyzing, analyzing, analyzing. You must come to a point. You must end somewhere and there you can keep silent. Live in silence now. If you live in silence, you go to Samadhi. That is the secret. When there are no thoughts, no analysing, no projections, then you go back to your Source. That is Samadhi. Is it clear or anything else?

Disciple: Yes, but I have to think it over.

Disciple: How to explain the different Samadhi states?

Swamiji: First you have dwaita, two things and then you go to visishta adwaita. I have been telling you last year also the story.

A salt doll, it wants to know the ocean, the depth of the ocean. Now, it starts from a long distance and it sees the ocean and it is rather afraid. It says,"What a vast expanse of water, water everywhere." That is dwaita. Your God is something else. He is the creator. You are the created being, so you are at His mercy, at His grace. You think you are helpless without His grace. You can't do anything. Then this doll goes and goes, comes near the sea and takes a little water, sips it, and then it says, "This is also water, salt water. I am also salt in solid form and this is in liquid form. This is the difference. I am a portion of that also. I am a part and particle of that thing." That is the second stage. You come to that pitch. You understand God is all-pervading. He is infinite, eternal, everything, so many things and, at the same time, you think you are also part of that thing. Then this doll enters the ocean. No sooner than it enters the ocean, it melts and becomes One with it. So, that is adwaita. These are the three stages, how it can be explained.

So, religion begins with the idea of duality. You have got the idea of hell and heaven. And when you make progress, you come to the second stage and then when fear gets extinguished, no demarcation, that disappears slowly and then you come closer and closer and lastly you come to the last point, Nirvikalpa Samadhi state, and you become one with it. That is why you say, "I am Brahman. I am Brahman. There is no Brahman separate from you. He is your innermost being. I am that." That is the last point.

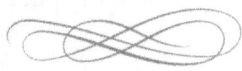

June 29, 1973

Reading: *(Disturbances to meditation: First, from the gross body, secondly from the subtle body and from external agencies like a loud noise) Thirdly, disturbances may arise from the causal body and from divinity, such as heavy storm, lightning, thunder, etc. The uttering of "Om Shanti" for the third time implies prayer to God to save us from all kinds of disturbances that arise from the causal body and from cosmic agencies.*

Disciple: You say divinity such as thunder and a storm?

Swamiji: A storm is caused by divinity. That is all. Who has caused it? It comes from God, as it were, so it is put in a general way. If you want to discuss logically, there is only One, we say. It is all illusion then. Who will ask when they come to this point? So too, the illusion is gone. You have to play with the illusion. All these prayers have no meaning when you go to higher pitches. When you go to higher pitches, there are no prayers also. You can't pray, to whom to pray? Until you come to that high pitch, there are temples, there are churches and paGodas. Everything is real. The world is real. The body is real. You can't deny it. All of a sudden you can't make a step and say, "Everything is an illusion, God alone is real." Ordinarily, when everything is going well, you think, "Why should I pray to others? Who can help me? I will stand by myself." That "I" is strong there. Suddenly you get downright kicks. Then you feel, "Why does this failure come? What is the cause? How did I fail?" Then you want someone to help you. The ego gets a good snubbing and kicking. In this way, it learns slowly and steadily. Then one concludes: "Who cares for anyone? Nobody will care for anyone in the world." So, when pain comes, everyone wants help from whatever side it may come. Are you ready to accept it then?

Disciple: Is that to say that the illusion will become subtler and subtler?

Swamiji: The illusion will be the same but the binding force, the effect on the mind, will become subtler and subtler as you go on discriminating and discarding. When the mind becomes finer and subtler, the binding force of the mind becomes less and less. Do you understand the difference between the two?

Disciple: Swamiji, I don't quite understand it, but I think it is like if you are bound by ordinary objects like money and house and all that.

Swamiji: The money is there, the problem is there, but the bondage you felt in the beginning is not so great if you go on discriminating and discarding. The binding force will not be so strong when you go on making progress. The desire is there, the necessity is there, but you do not feel the misery. That is what I mean.

Disciple: Swamiji, is it not so that a subtle attachment can be more dangerous for a sadhaka than a gross attachment?

Swamiji: Both are dangerous, but subtle attachment you can control easily. Gross attachment should be avoided first. It is like this. Say you have a small dog. You have taken it, always carrying it in this way (on the shoulder), petting it, kissing it. You have done all those things. The dog has taken you as its own in such a way, sleeping, even they may eat together. Some are of that nature. After some time, the spirit of renunciation comes there and now the person concerned pushes the dog away saying, "Oh rascal, why should I get attached to you?" But the dog doesn't understand when the person is acting in that way. It comes and jumps when he is careless and licks the face and mouth and everything. So, the habit is there. Now, what is to be done? Every time it comes, he takes a stick and beats it. The dog will learn and then the tendency of the dog will stop.

Likewise, you have so many desires which you have cherished like taking the dog on your shoulder — so it is coming on you. Now, kick it, give nice beatings. Every time it comes, give a beating. After some time, it will learn and it will not disturb you.

Disciple: Swamiji, is it the same process with mother and child?

Swamiji: Why do you go to such a distance?

Disciple: Is it the same process when a mother takes sannyas? The spirit of renunciation is there but you can't kick your child.

Swamiji: Don't kick the child like a dog. How can you? There is nothing like that. Not in that way. There is much difference. There is a way to make children understand also, slowly and steadily. Here it is not in that way. After all, a dog is a dog and a child is a child. You can't make a comparison there. It is a wrong thing. They must be given love but don't get attached.

Suppose you are in the kindergarten class and many children are coming. What is your duty there? You love every child and treat them kindly, understand that much. If you see some of the children weeping, you will take them on your lap and give a kiss and take them to your bosom saying: "My John," "My Sita" or some other name. You say "My baby, my child" but yet, you know in your heart of hearts, "It is not my baby." If you can keep that attitude, then there is nothing binding. Don't treat them like dogs. Think that the children belong to God, put that idea. It is the easiest way to live in the world without attachment.

Disciple: Can you describe any way to keep a corpse?
Swamiji: You burn it immediately. Only the Tibetans keep a corpse.
Disciple: Swamiji, can the soul take birth immediately or is there a fixed time for the soul to reincarnate?
Swamiji: Even if you take a soul which has immediately gone and entered the womb of a woman, then there will still be time. One year is there. In that way there is time, immediately you cannot take birth. If one takes birth in a lower life, the time is decreased, but generally there will be a little time. There is a gap. Some immediately take birth which means they migrate to another body, enter the womb of some other person, and some may wait. Some sinful people remain as ghosts. Then you have some big gaps. Are there ghosts or not? Have you seen any?
Disciple: I haven't seen any.
Swamiji: You don't believe?
Disciple: Yes, I do.
Swamiji: Our neighbour keeps one or two. He has got a house and the ghosts appear there. If you want to see them, you can go at night. But don't play with them. There are many people who say they have seen them. I have not seen them but I have felt it on one or two occasions.
Disciple: How have you?
Swamiji: How? It is a long story. I think it was in 1932. Once I went to a certain place the source of the Kaveri River in South India. In that place, people have received many blows. Nobody will remain there at night. Even the temple priests go away from the place, nobody lives there. I wanted to go to that place before going to the Himalayas. I was young then. Two elderly people were with me. We were staying about

seven miles away. The whole day we were busy worshipping and other things. It was the rainy season also. In the evening about five or five thirty on that day was a lunar eclipse, and on those days especially, there is all this danger and the ghosts are very ferocious.

Anyway, we heard so many cock-and-bull stories but actually, people have been injured there also. Many have gone mad. Many have been terribly injured. So, towards evening I had a desire that I must go to that particular place and meditate the whole night. That was my desire. In those days, I was very stubborn. Whatever thought came, I would act. I would never care for anybody. No one could stop me, so I said, "I am going." Then I told these elderly people, "I am going tonight. You wait here and come tomorrow, not today," I said. They tried to persuade me not to go. I said, "No." So, they were disappointed, poor people, and they were also terribly afraid. "I am going alone," and then they said, "We are also coming." "I don't want anyone. I want to go alone," I said.

That was a jungle, full of forest and the rainy season also. And there is no real road. It was muddy and slippery. The mud was so fine, just like butter. If you put your hand in it, it slipped away like anything. Then also there you can't wear any shoes. It is forbidden to wear shoes in that area. You have to walk barefoot.

So, I started and these people were looking for a lantern and other things for the night. I said, "You go back. I don't want you to come. I want to go alone," and started. The priest of the temple was also there. He had come to town. He was following and after going about two or three hundred meters, he went away by a short cut to his home and I was going on alone. I went and went and there was sunset. It became dark and it was cloudy also. I couldn't see the moon. So, I was walking. There was drizzle also, not heavy rain, but drizzle and, somehow, I was walking and in one place I actually fell down. I rolled and got up.

Then I went slowly and when I reached the place, it was pitch dark there. There was a temple but you can't remain there. There was a guesthouse but it was all locked up. There was no place to sit. So, I went and found the lower piece of wood that supports a door. There was only a little portion, this much, and I had only one blanket. That is all. I sat for meditation.

I was meditating and after one or two hours those two old men with the lamp and other things came searching and they were terribly afraid.

They went to the temple. There were no traces of me. They had heard so many things but then lastly, they came down to see whether I was in that house and they found me there sitting and they were happy.

Anyway, I got up, now we were three. Where to spend the whole night? So, we pushed doors here and there and it was full of rain. There was heavy rain there, more than two hundred inches of rainfall per year. Too heavy rainfall there, so the walls and other things were all wet, also on a hilltop. Then we pushed and one door gave way. We entered it and searched for firewood. In one corner, there was firewood but it was wet. We brought it in. There was a small veranda so we got two planks of wood which were meant for making big doors. We leanead on one. One we kept on this side and another that side. We put all the rubbish wood together and we poured kerosene on it and made a bonfire.

So, we were talking. Those two people were talking and sitting on that side and I was sitting on the other side and there was a big fire. One man was a bit egoistic. He began talking, "Oh, people talk all sorts of cock-and-bull stories. What is there? That is nothing." When he was talking, immediately, in the adjoining room, which was closed and nobody was there, a cat began mewing. From where did it come? How it could come? How it could come inside? There were no traces. But the other man was wise, he scolded the man and he prayed to God to be excused. Immediately the cat stopped mewing and disappeared. It was in that way we have felt it. I have seen it actually.

In this way, there are some places where we can actually see the things. Because I was not egoistic, I had nothing to fear. I was just going in a devotional mood. I had no challenge to the Gods or Goddesses, nothing to quarrel with anyone. I was going with a true spirit, with a devotional attitude. I never challenged them or anything. So, I was free but I also saw and actually heard the noise close by in a closed place. It disappeared and there was no trace of that cat or any other things. So, there may be so many causes.

Disciple: Are people who stick to their sadhana troubled by that?
Swamiji: No, it has not got power. Your mantra and Ishta-Devata will protect you. That is the secret. Thereby, don't challenge and or quarrel with any ghost, avoid such things. Don't be egoistic but at the same time go on with your mantra and meditation and the whole atmosphere will change. Such things will have no power also. That is the secret.

Disciple: Swamiji, can one give relief to a ghost by sending good thoughts?

Swamiji: You can help the ghost also. That is why they help. In India, they have got the system of doing Sandhya ceremony morning and evening. They send good thoughts to the departed spirits, ancestors, in that way they can also help. When a man dies in India, the general custom is they go on singing God's name or reading the Gita. They do it even now. The custom is there.

Disciple: What happens to the Self when a man dies?

Swamiji: The whole thing gets concentrated in the spiritual heart center. It is the seat of the Self and it migrates from body to body along with the Self, the subtle body, mind, the subtle senses, kundalini shakti. They remain in the causal state. Causal state you understand?

Disciple: I think.

Swamiji: In seed form, if you take the small seed of a tree and open the seed, you can't see the tree, but still the future tree is in that seed, that is called causal state. They go back to the seed form, all the things, all your chitta, mind-stuff. Everything is there back in the causal state. In the next birth, they come there, the mind and other things. The projection comes there.

There was one man, Tulsidas, he was always meditating but he had not come in contact with reality, God-Realization. He used to go to the forest and wash his feet and other things under a particular tree where a ghost was living. By pouring water every day that tree was always kept green. So, that ghost was pleased with this man. One day the ghost said, "You go to a certain place, the monkey God Mahavir, will come there. He will come in the form of an old man and pretend to be very aged and sick but he is Hanuman. He wants to hear the Ramayana recitation. You go and catch him and he will tell you what to do."

The next day, the man went early. There was a big hall where they used to have Ramayana readings. First, as the ghost said, an old man came with a big stick as if he was going to fall down, in this way shaking. He went to a particular corner and sat there and when all had left, he used to leave last. He was the first to come and the last to go.

So, accordingly, when all went away Tulsidas went and caught his legs, "You can't deceive me. You must tell me what I have to do, how I can attain God-realization?" That man pretended as if he knew nothing.

He said, "Oh, I don't know anything. I am an old man. Leave me. Don't catch me." But Tulsidas did not leave him. He caught him firmly, "I will not leave you. Don't deceive me." When he was so firm in his determination, the old man said, "All right, go to such and such a place and you will have the darshan of God." Accordingly, he goes and meditates and gets it in that way. So, good and bad things are also there among the ghosts. There are some good ones and there are some evil ones.

Now it is time. Open the window.

June 30, 1973

Disciple: Where does a Living Free man go after death?

Swamiji: He does not go anywhere. The mind and everything merges completely in infinity. It is just like putting a drop of water on a red, hot iron. It makes a hissing sound and then it merges there. Likewise, the Jivan-Mukta does not go anywhere. Going and coming is for ordinary people. Is it clear?

Disciple: Is there any connection, any more connection, between, for instance, the Guru and his disciple?

Swamiji: Ah, what a horrible thing. Why do you bring that connection there? You are talking of a Jivan-Mukta, then Guru and disciple. Why do you bring it in that way? What do you want there? There are two points in that thing, don't make a confusion. You want the Guru to remain with you, to help you, all right. So long as you remember the Guru, the Guru is with you. That is the answer for one question. For your other question, what becomes of a Jivan-Mukta, you have got the answer already.

Disciple: The first question was my real question.

Swamiji: I have solved it. What more do you want? Why do you confuse then? Why do you bring me there? Let me have leave. In a general way, you bring the topic. Don't bring any personal things. Now, what do you want? Come. What is your question? Come forward.

Disciple: I am afraid if my Guru disappears.

Swamiji: He will not disappear; so long as a single disciple remains, the Guru will be there.
Disciple: That is good.
Swamiji: Why should he disappear? He will be with you. He will be with the disciples. Then, what do you want more?
Disciple: So, he is not a Jivan-Mukta. He is not free?
Swamiji: Then again you put a confusion. You want both things. Either you take one side or the other side. I gave the answer about Jivan-Mukta earlier. If a Jivan-Mukta wants to leave the body, the question comes there. Here, Jivan-Mukta may not leave the body also. After leaving the body, he may remain in the subtle body just to help the disciples if he wants. That is another thing. Satisfied?
Disciple: As long as the Guru has a disciple who has not realized, can he merge?
Swamiji: Not in that way. It is left to the choice of the Guru. If he wants, he can merge leaving all the disciples. If he wants to remain to help them, he can remain. Both are possible, in that way.
Disciple: But isn't there some cosmic law that he has to obey?
Swamiji: The Jivan-Mukta is beyond all these cosmic laws. He, Himself, is the lawmaker. So, nothing can bind Him. It is for ordinary people. If the Jivan-Muktas want, they can leave the body dead, at will. If they want to prolong, they can also do it. So, both are possible there. They are beyond the laws.
Disciple: Swamiji, is there no time limit for the body to exist?
Swamiji: I am telling. They can change the body also if they like. By supernatural powers, they can do all those things. Then?
Disciple: What is meant by chitta akasa?
Swamiji: Akasa has been divided into several groups. One is the all-pervading akasa, maha-akasa. Akasa you understand? "Ether", you call it. Then there is jala akasa, akasa seen in the water pond. And the akasa reflected inside a pot is called ghata akasa. And then you have got chitta akasa, akasa inside the chitta. Whatever projection you make in the mind, you project the whole scene. You close your eyes, akasa is inside your brain. It is just like a mirror projecting the akasa. In a different way, the akasa is in different groups.

So, similarly, the Jiva or the Self is just like being confined inside the body and now this ghata, ghata means pot, this pot contains five things.

That is the Jiva, individual Self. Then there is the mind, intellect, ego and chitta. This pot consists of these now. Death means only the gross body dies. There are so many other things of which this pot consists. It is not destroyed. This destruction takes place only in the state of Nirvikalpa Samadhi. The so-called pot goes to pieces, so it is one with the akasa. You understand?
Disciple: Yes.

Disciple: The vision of the Ishta-Devata, is it perceived actually in the heart or in the chitta-akasa?
Swamiji: That may be both places. Sometimes you may see it in the heart center as well as in the brain center.

July 1, 1973

Disciple: What produces the sounds heard from a man during meditation?
Swamiji: Especially when the kundalini shakti goes to the heart center, then you hear the natural sound. That sound belongs to the pranava. From there you can hear OM. Not only OM, there are a variety of sounds. That is a cosmic sound, not a constructed sound. It is just like the distant roar of the sea or a waterfall or like the humming of bees. There are about ten sounds in that way; the last sound one hears is pranava, OM. Side by side, one has the vision of the Ishta-Devata or Guru and sometimes light in the form of the moon or a ball of fire or a rising sun. It can be taken as a universal symbol. There is a mantra also, but it is not for all. The mantra OM is taken only for jnana-yoga. It is dangerous to use. It may strike the kundalini shakti and untimely wake it up. It is just like doing pranayama. So, never do it without knowing the thing properly through a teacher or a Guru. So many people I have seen in India after living thirty or forty years take OM and go on meditating on OM. They don't know how to meditate. Always they say, "I am Brahman, I am Brahman," but they don't become Brahman at all. That "I" grows and they become so stupid and vulgar. Many Brahma-Jnanis come in that way to me and I give them kicks there, or I say,

"What have you learned?" There are so many hidden things also behind all these words. In writing the books, they can't give all these secrets. It is not possible. It must be given and understood by a Guru only.

Disciple: Swamiji, what is the difference between subjective and objective visions?

Swamiji: Subjective, you may see inside while meditating but if you have objective visions, you can see a person face to face just as you can see human beings, just as you are talking with your friends.

Disciple: Can such a vision be witnessed by another person?

Swamiji: No, it is not possible. Only those who have similar classification or purification of the mind can see it. All cannot. That is why it is said, a vision may be subjective or objective and at the same time, it is beyond both. You understand it?

Suppose you are thinking of a particular object constantly and then the mind suddenly projects the scene. That is subjective vision. That is one way. The objective vision, there you are not thinking of anything and suddenly it appears before you. The man who has not purified his mind cannot see the vision, so in a way, it cannot be strictly objective, but still, it is an objective vision for you.

Disciple: Swamiji, is it actually a mental vision?

Swamiji: Which one?

Disciple: Both the subjective and the objective vision.

Swamiji: Both are mental, all right. The whole universe is mental in a way.

Disciple: What I mean is, can it ever be a social reality because the other one cannot see it?

Swamiji: It is not possible there. Some ghosts may be both. You can see it, he can also see, both of you can see a ghost. But in purification, there may be a difference. That God or Goddess may want to show favour to one man but not to the other. He may not be fit for that favour.

Disciple: The vision Ramakrishna had, was that an objective vision?

Swamiji: First he had subjective. Then he had to work twelve years, again and again, and lastly, he could see it and speak with Kali whenever he wanted. Nobody was seeing it. Others could not see, but he could see.

Disciple: Is it a higher development?

Swamiji: That requires further development there.

Disciple: Because of his intense devotion?

Swamiji: That is all right. Everything is devotional. It began with subjective and then it became objective, in that way. After all, it is not a permanent thing. One has to go further, higher up. Many people make a hubbub. They want to become popular and they say they have God vision. That is not a real thing.

Disciple: Swamiji, as an object of meditation, I have used different kinds of photos, is that all right?

Swamiji: If you want to concentrate, take one photo, one particular photo. If one day you concentrate on one and the second day another, that means you are giving wrong impressions to the mind.

Disciple: Even if it is the same Guru?

Swamiji: All right, it doesn't matter, but only one photo for concentration. That will speed your growth. If you go on changing, there is no strength of work. In that way, don't do it. Take one particular photo which appeals to you the most and proceed with it. When the mind gets concentrated on the photo, it also will drop down. The mantra will stop also. Proceed further. Don't drag it to the photo or anything. Many people make that mistake. Don't do it.

Disciple: But, should one not repeat the mantra again and again, I mean go back to the sound of the mantra?

Swamiji: You have started with the mantra. Now the mantra has stopped and you have come to concentration. Then why should you repeat it there in that state? Why do you force the mind back? Do you want to go up or do you want to go down? When the mind goes deeper and deeper, you can't utter the mantra. The form will also disappear. What is the confusion there?

Disciple: Then it goes up to light?

Swamiji: Yes, if you can see light, forget all these things.

Disciple: The mind merges in the Ishta-Devata, yes?

Swamiji: You are making a big confusion there. You are passing the Ishta-Devata also. You are going to light. Work it out, when you come to that state.

Disciple: What is forcing the mind back?

Swamiji: Your ego and stupidity.

July 2, 1973

Reading: *When the three gunas make a stir, they create a sound. This sound is not gross as heard by ordinary men. It is the most subtle aspect of a sound or the very starting point of a sound as experienced by a yogic-mind.*

Swamiji: It is not only there. Even in your body, you have got so many things. Suppose you want to produce some kind of sound. First, it must come from the mind-stuff, chitta. There everything remains in a causal state. In that state, what you are going to say, you have no idea. Anyway, the idea you have given, you are making a stir, the force produces the sound actually and that sound makes a stir and moves to here, manipura. That is called para and pashyanti. Still, you don't know. When it comes to the heart center, you are aware of the sound. It becomes a desire. Immediately it goes to the brain center and there it becomes a thought. Then you know what you are going to say. This process is constantly taking place with every one, and, in the same way, in the state of, so-called, creation.

Disciple: Swamiji, in the chitta, all the knowledge remains in its causal form. Are there different levels because the mind can only get a part of it?

Swamiji: It is only a little, very little. It is just like an iceberg, only a small portion is above sea level. The subconscious plane is bigger and the unconscious plane is very big.

Disciple: But one can get a part of it from the unconscious state?

Swamiji: You can take the whole thing if you want it. If you want to know your past births, you can get it but it is a mere waste of time, a mere curiosity only. It will not help you in any way.

Disciple: Swamiji, the kundalini shakti has all powers and all possibilities and the past, present and future are in it but how can it be purified?

Swamiji: You are making a confusion between kundalini shakti and chitta. There are so many impressions in the chitta, good and bad. By mantra, you can purify it. Purification means you want only good things. Is it clear or not?

Disciple: Is it the same thing with karma and effort? When everything is there, how to change it? How to purify it?

Swamiji: Then how can it bind you also?

Disciple: It cannot bind. You are not bound.

Swamiji: Then go beyond it. If you can, keep the mind in balance in all things. If something good comes, don't be happy. If something bad comes, don't be sorrowful. Keep the balance. Then it is all right. You have solved the problem. But why do you feel, "I am happy. I am sorrowful?"

Disciple: I feel that.

Swamiji: Then automatically, there is ignorance. Get rid of all those things. Then when you consider all those things, there is purity and impurity. All those things come there. But when you go to higher pitches, there is nothing. In the lower stages, you feel all these difficulties. In this way, purification of the chitta is necessary and it is done by mantra. You will get good thoughts then.

Disciple: How to discriminate between pure love and sensual love?

Swamiji: In sensual love, you feel attracted through the senses. In pure love, there are no sense irritations.

Disciple: But will the senses not always be involved?

Swamiji: A little, but in pure love, there will not be any sense-attraction. In pure love, you are not bound in any way. You are prepared even to give your life. In all other selfish love, there is some motive behind. If that is not fulfilled, you will revolt immediately. If your desire is not fulfilled, you get annoyed. In pure love, there is no expectation. There you always want to give and give. Generally, it is said that if there is no barter, no hatred, no fear and there is no selfish motive, then it is called pure love.

Disciple: Are pure love and selfish love, by nature, the same?

Swamiji: By nature, they are the same, but the effect on you is quite different. Some people misunderstand it. They think they have pure love but lust is hidden behind. Take as an example, the love between a boy and a girl. In the beginning, they say, "Oh, we are just as brother and sister." But lust is hidden behind, veiled as a beautiful coat, just like lipstick. Later on, it will develop into lust. Lust was there all the time.

But, when the love is very pure, it is another kind. There is no attraction of lust at all. There is no sex-attraction but this state of love is not easy. Then there are other kinds of love, for instance, among friends. There, pure love is also very difficult. The two friends expect something from each other and find some value in it. Thereby, the love arises. But when something happens which is against your hidden desire, then hatred will develop. Then the very sight of your friend makes you feel bad. You cannot tolerate him.

When there is pure love, you will always be generous. You will not expect anything. You will only give. There is no fear of anything there. Ordinarily, if a young woman is alone on the street and a mad bull comes running towards her, she will run away just to save her life. But if her only baby is playing in the street and a mad bull comes running, then she will not think of her own life. She will run out and face the bull in order to save the baby. There will be no fear. This is pure love. The mother will always give love to her baby without expecting anything in return. There is no barter. She will serve the baby wholeheartedly. Likewise, she will have no fear and no hatred. These are the symptoms of pure love.

Disciple: Then all women get a chance to develop unselfish love when they have a baby?

Swamiji: Not all! Some are very horrible. They rather eat away the baby! But the chance is there. Not only for mothers, for all. In the ashram, pure love can also be developed when you are living together side by side. There is cooperation and a good chance to become unselfish.

Disciple: Can lower kinds of love develop into pure love?

Swamiji: Yes, why not? Both ways are possible. Sometimes it begins with so-called pure love and it may develop in a wrong direction. Some people begin with ordinary love and it develops into pure love, both are possible. If one is careless, pure love can develop into lust. But if one is careful, lust can develop into pure love. It depends on how you handle it.

Disciple: Can real, pure love only be had in Samadhi?

Swamiji: In love, there are so many grades. The highest kind is Samadhi, but still there are different grades of love.

Disciple: But the ego will always be there to want something.

Swamiji: Without ego, there is no love. You have to keep the ego in order to love. Even in loving God, the ego is there. It must be there.

Disciple: But the ego always desires something or expects something.

Swamiji: Yes, that is why love has been divided into so many attitudes or grades. Some people take God as their child or baby. Others take God as their friend or as their Master and feel themselves as the servant of God. There are different attitudes in love. Bhakti-Yoga suits the taste and tendency of different people. But in all these attitudes, the ego is there. It does not want to merge. It wants love from God. But you should not expect that love. You only give. You do not pray for anything either, but you want the company of God. That is also a desire, but it is a high desire.

Disciple: Can there be pain in pure love?

Swamiji: Yes, when the beloved is far away, then the pain is there. Why not? That is why adwaita says, "Oh, kick out all this love. You are That yourself. Why then be worried about all this? Don't be at the mercy of anybody's grace." But one must be very strong to keep this view.

July 3, 1973

Reading: *When the three Gunas make a stir, they create a sound. This sound is not gross as heard by ordinary men. It is the most subtle aspect of a sound or the very starting point of a sound as experienced by a Yogic-mind.*

Swamiji: So, until and unless you get the knowledge from chitta, you can never produce anything. It is a mysterious thing, a most wonderful thing how the chitta can keep all your past knowledge. You might have read so many books. You might have seen so many people. You might have visited so many places. Everything is kept in the chitta. Only you have to say one word, take for example, you say "Copenhagen." You get the whole thing concerning that particular town. You only press the button and you go on speaking for hours together. How it is kept, it is so wonderful. If you think deeply on the subject, it is most wonderful.

Reading: *Shabda-Brahman is the causal state of all manifested sounds, and It is the All-pervading, undifferentiated Power while a mantra is Its particular manifestation. From Shabda-Brahman originate the whole universe and its beings.*

Swamiji: "OM" is known as the Maha Bija Mantra. All sounds, all mantras and other words start from OM and they end with OM. So, Brahma, Vishnu and Shiva, all the three are in that OM. They stand for creation, preservation and destruction. It is not merely a constructed word. It has got tremendous power with it and it will also wake up the kundalini shakti easily. So, it is better not to meditate on OM before the time is ripe. Many people take it up in a hasty way, "Why should there be any danger? It is the greatest mantra," this and that thing. Then they make use of it and wake up the shakti. There will be a partial rising. It will bring difficulties; so, it is better to have patience.

Disciple: Swamiji, is it given as a universal mantra which can be used?

Swamiji: It is universal in that it is in each and every man. It does not belong to India or to England or Denmark or any other country. Each and every man is the owner of that. Just to avoid this friction, it was put there in that way, not to make any quarrel, just to give room to all sorts of people. In the book, "The Basis of Universal Religion", it is given in a logical way so people, who do not believe in God, when they read the book, they may understand.

Disciple: Is it possible to live as a sadhaka without having doubt?

Swamiji: So many do not have any doubts when they have full faith in their Guru and other things. They follow the thing, whatever he says. They obey and follow it and they have speedy results.

Disciple: Can we follow you blindly?

Swamiji: Don't follow blindly. I am not teaching you or any one blind faith. Every step you take, I tell you, reason it. That is why we use so much time discussing this and that. It may be a good question. It may be a wrong one. We answer it, we satisfy them. You may have some doubts in the beginning but there should not be any major doubt regarding your sadhana. There are so many other doubts. They get cleared up when you go on meditating and making progress. Automatically, all these things drop away.

Disciple: I am still, in the third year, talking about creation but I cannot understand it.

Swamiji: You see, in a deeper sense, when you go to the last point, there is no creation. When you say God is all-pervading, infinite and eternal, then there can be only One Infinity.

Disciple: Yes.

Swamiji: All right, when you say there is only One Infinity, how do you define Infinity? Infinity is a thing without beginning, without middle and without end. You understand?

Disciple: Yes.

Swamiji: Then, with such a thing, there can be only One. Who is there to create and from where? In infinity, you cannot increase or decrease even an atom. You agree with it?

Disciple: Yes.

Swamiji: Then there is no creation.

Disciple: But you can change the atoms.

Swamiji: When you go to the last point there is only One. There is only force.

Disciple: Does that mean I do not exist?

Swamiji: Actually, you do not. Your existence is only by ignorance. All are in a particular dream which is a big dream. When you go deeper and deeper, all these things disappear. When you go to Nirvikalpa Samadhi, there are not two things. There is no bondage and no Freedom.

Science has been analyzing matter and they have come to the atom and there are negative and positive forces which they call electrons and protons. Now, after splitting that, they have come to the point that there is only energy. But I tell them further, there can never be energy without Consciousness, that is the last point. That is called God or Brahman or your Self. So, you are That. You are One with It. So, don't be afraid of going back to that state.

July 4, 1973
Swamiji: If you have any questions, come forward.
Disciple: What is the distinction between blind faith and full faith?
Swamiji: Blind faith is without reasoning, but it is not possible to have blind faith in that way. Faith is always with reasoning. For the time being, you can say that, "I am having blind faith," but afterwards, that blind faith will not work. After some time, it will break, so it is always with reason. To start with, you may say that you have blind faith. Many people are deceived by propaganda, but after some time, they find out their mistake. So, where is that blind faith then? It is gone. So, there cannot be anything called blind faith. It is momentary in that way. It must have reasoning behind. You must have satisfaction. Is it clear?
Disciple: Partly.
Swamiji: And what is the other thing?
Disciple: Full faith we talked about yesterday.
Swamiji: When you have full faith, you will work it out and there is no shaking. Whatever comes from full faith, it is reasonable and you will not give it up. You will have no doubts on that. You understand?
Disciple: Yes.

Disciple: Yesterday we talked about pure love and you said that in the last state, there is no love. How to understand it?
Swamiji: The last point before Samadhi is called prem. When you hear the name of God, there will be a kind of goose bumps. That is all higher developments. In the last point, the lover and the Beloved become one. In Samadhi, there are two ways. In Savikalpa, you want the vision of God, God and nothing else in that state. But you don't want to merge. You want to keep the thing and you separate. Then only, there is that love. In Nirvikalpa, that love has become One. The lower thing has gone. There is only One Thing. Everything merges completely. The "I" is no more. You are one with it. You are That Thing.
Disciple: I think it is impossible to want Nirvikalpa before you have attained Savikalpa.
Swamiji: Then have it. You see, a Jnani will not worry about Savikalpa. If a God appears, he will say, "I don't want it. Get out." He will not believe in any names and forms. Even in Savikalpa, he does not care for Savikalpa.

Disciple: Will one automatically get Nirvikalpa after concentrating for half an hour in all cases?

Swamiji: As if it is so easy to make the mind merge in one point completely. Even if you have only a few seconds of concentration in the morning, you will have peace for the whole day. If you can succeed in that way, that is a great attainment. That must be a man of great will power. From one place, you have to bring the mind to one point and keep it there for twelve seconds. It is a high attainment.

Disciple: Before that, there will be Savikalpa also?

Swamiji: Savikalpa has not come at all there. That is another state. That is raja-yoga. You have not come to any kind of Samadhi.

Disciple: But it is described that he will be struggling with different kinds of Savikalpa Samadhi.

Swamiji: That is another thing. Savikalpa is already a high attainment.

Disciple: But there is described some degree.

Swamiji: Even then, that is in a different way. Here it is dealing with raja-yoga. Even taking raja-yoga, some may go with form. You go higher and higher, then you come to the point where the mind constantly lives in the object of your Ishta-Devata. It may all go to subtler and subtler things. But still, to keep to that object of your meditation is not easy. It takes a lot of training. So, to come to Savikalpa Samadhi is a high attainment.

July 5, 1973

Disciple: Swamiji, why do some come back to this world from Nirvikalpa and some not? What is the difference there?

Swamiji: You see, if you give one teaspoonful of brandy or whisky to a child as a medicine, it gets intoxicated. A drunkard may drink half a bottle and there may be some other experts in drinking even one bottle. Why do some get intoxicated so soon and some not? What explanation can you give for that?

Disciple: They are used to it.

Swamiji: Some may be great people in that way. They are used to it. They can tolerate that thing and they can come down. If you are strong enough, you come down. If you are weak, you merge completely.

Disciple: All are perfect there?

Swamiji: Perfection may be, that is all right. Even by smelling the brandy also you taste the brandy, then what is the difference there? All must get intoxicated. Some are intoxicated by merely smelling, some by drinking a little and some by drinking one bottle. Then how do you explain it? It is similar with the man of Nirvikalpa.

Disciple: Is it not weakness to come down from that state?

Swamiji: Is it weakness to drink one bottle? Still, if he is strong enough, he can walk. Why weakness or strength? He is not weak. He is not strong. He can digest that much. He has power.

July 6, 1973

Reading: *The word "Om" with Its three letters (AUM) represents Trinity. Thus, "Om" stands for Brahma, the Creator and His Creative Power; Vishnu, the Preserver and His Protecting Power, and Shiva, the Destroyer and His Destroying Power.*

Disciple: Can it be used by every one?

Swamiji: All the week, I have been telling, don't take "OM". It is for those who follow the jnana path. It is given in a general way to satisfy the curiosity of different people and sects so they cannot quarrel or make a claim, in that way it is put. In every mantra, "OM" comes, but don't take it separately. It is only for sannyasis and those who follow jnana-yoga.

Disciple: Would you like to explain what is meant by the astral plane?

Swamiji: Astral plane. There may be so many subtle things. "Subtle body," I have called it. There may be so many innumerable planes. Man has gone to the moon and found no life there. It does not mean that there is no life. Life existing there may not be seen by you, so you are in a different vibration. In this way, the entire space is covered by Consciousness. There is not a place without Consciousness.

Disciple: Swamiji, self-confidence and faith, is that the same thing?
Swamiji: No, they are two different things. If you have no self-confidence, that is due to weakness. You don't want to take the responsibility. To have faith in God, what He will do, you are depending on God fully, so you have faith in Him. You have got full belief in the existence of God and His might and glory. That is called shraddha. Then what is your difficulty there?
Disciple: I thought there was a connection.
Swamiji: There may be partly, you can say. Those who have full faith in God have confidence in that way. But generally, you will say you have full faith in God or in your Guru or in the scriptures. Here, self-confidence is a lower thing. It is connected with your small "I".

Reading: *We call this plane as the unconscious plane, because an ordinary man is quite unconscious of this vast storage of knowledge.*
Swamiji: If necessary, you can also recall it but it is a mere waste of time. There is a thing called samyama. Suppose you take a particular idea and you want to know more. Taking that idea, you think over the matter and then go into a sort of trance. When you come back from the trance, you have all the knowledge. You can know anything and everything. Many people, those who don't come to the highest pitch, make use of this knowledge. That is called samyama.

In recognizing warships during the last war, they used a pendulum and went into a sort of trance and they could tell exactly where the warships were. They got some supernatural powers by concentrating and they made use of it for worldly purposes. That is why they keep everything a secret in yoga. It is very dangerous to make use of it in that way.

Disciple: Swamiji, is it possible to raise the kundalini shakti without a moral code?
Swamiji: It is impossible. There may be partial rising.
Disciple: Is that what they use when they use siddhis?
Swamiji: Yes.

Disciple: But they must use very much concentration to reach that state?

Swamiji: That concentration may come in deep sorrow also. Many intellectuals have partial rising. With some people, after they have been drinking, it also wakes up. In some cases, with strong medicine and with LSD and hash, in so many ways, people may get partial rising. The after-effect is very terrible and many suffer.

Disciple: So, before you observe the rules of yama and niyama completely, it cannot rise up fully?

Swamiji: Not only that. Not before you attain three-fold purity. That means purity of the body, purity of the nadis and purity of the mind. When you go on with life, your body will gain purity. The sweat of the body will indicate how far a man or woman has progressed spiritually. When a man is becoming purified, even the sweat that comes, that is also not so bad. Those who have been meditating, there it will change completely. When you go to higher pitches, it is a very sweet smell, an agreeable smell that changes completely.

When the shakti is forced, there will be partial rising. Many people, before attaining this three-fold purity, do intense pranayama. Especially number four and five and thereby there will be partial rising. The effect is very bad. Especially you will have sexual falls. It is the first and foremost fall for a sadhaka.

Disciple: With mantra-jap, will there also be partial rising?

Swamiji: You will have to be careful there. Generally, it will not come in that way. Don't tackle it; don't try to raise it up. Many people want to get a response quickly. Don't do all those things. Go on with mantra-jap and meditation and you will gain three-fold purity automatically, but you must be careful always. Even after doing mantra-jap and meditation, never get up suddenly and do any kind of work. Sit for five or ten minutes at least and then go out. Until and unless the currents go up to the brain center, you cannot have good concentration. It is working there. So, it should not come down suddenly. For that thing, sit quiet. If the current is too strong, do pranayama number three and it will come down slowly. Many people get abnormal sexual craving if the shakti comes down too quickly.

Disciple: You say don't tackle the shakti but haven't you written somewhere how to wake it up?

Swamiji: That is why the Guru gives you personal instruction. He does not ask you to do that. The book only gives a certain formula. It does not give the secrets. Many people make the mistake of taking the book and following the book without the help of a Guru. "The book has all the instructions, why should I not follow it? Why should I have a Guru?" Ego comes there. Then they get blows and kicks. That is dangerous. That is why; always learn it from a person who knows the thing. That is safe. He will tell you, in a way, how to do it and if you are egoistic and too proud of yourself, he will also kick you. There are so many stupid people. They are so proud. "Why should I bend my knees?" I say, "Don't bend, stand erect." I tell them in that way and then again, they come. I kick them there, go and stand on your feet. For such people, they have to study again and again. I will make them work.

Last year, one man came when I was in Rungsted, a suburb of Copenhagen. He asked, "Is it necessary to have a Guru?" "Not necessary," I said. Then, "I have been studying books and other things." "Yes, it is better not to have a Guru." Then on the next day he said, "Oh, I have a strong desire to have a Guru. I want a mantra." I kept quiet and he came the next day and I said, "You are not fit now. Wait. I am going to Gylling. You can go there." I wanted to see him. "I will see you there." "No, no. I will come tomorrow," he said. "That is all right. You come tomorrow." And the next day, he did not turn up. Then he came to Gylling last year. I turned him out. "You are not fit to take it. I will not give you mantra." I had a great desire not to give; so, I turned him out. So, he had to wait for one more year and this year he was polite. He came with his wife. He was begging. "Last year I came." "Yes, you were not fit for it then." "I want to take it now. I have come with my wife." "All right, now you can take it." When they are egoistic, it is so terrible. I poke them and leave them there.

Disciple: So, there is a big chance to end up in the madhouse?

Swamiji: Oh, I don't agree with you in that way. We are keeping people from the madhouse. That is a contradictory thing. We have helped keep them from the madhouse and you say to the madhouse. It is impossible. Many poor people, they would have lost their life completely, many of the youngsters. So, it is a great help.

Disciple: Swamiji, I was thinking that if you read the book about the kundalini shakti...

Swamiji: Don't read it. It is not for practising. That book is written only to save people from danger. That is the aim, not for making people suffer or other things. I was seeing so many people suffering without knowing anything. Many people make so-called kundalini-yoga, that is a stupid idea. It has no meaning. I have brought the idea, in any yoga and whatever work you do, you are tackling the shakti. It may be knowingly or unknowingly. Every deep thinking means you are unconsciously attacking the shakti. That is how in deep sorrow, a person by constantly thinking of the object of sorrow, they go mad in that way. There will be abnormal heat and when the heat currents go to the brain center, the discriminating faculty of the mind is destroyed. In many of the cases with LSD, it is too strong. It goes up and destroys the brain. Some have a sort of experience but the after-effect is very bad. The vast majority of people sink low to animal life.

Disciple: Is that faculty a gross faculty or is it a subtle faculty, that which has been destroyed?

Swamiji: It is a part of your brain, a functioning of the brain. It is not a faculty.

Disciple: So, it can be mended also?

Swamiji: That is why your doctors are mending you by shock treatment. The excess currents are taken away from the body. That is a very dangerous process also.

Disciple: I have read that a yogi doesn't feel the electric shock.

Swamiji: Don't go for all those experiments. By supernatural powers, you can do it. That is not a great thing. Don't touch it. They may die and they may catch me. They will say, "Swamiji told us."

July 7, 1973

Swamiji: Yesterday, we were discussing mantra-jap and waking up the kundalini shakti. By mantra-jap there will be partial rising but the current will not be so strong so you can easily control it. That is the difference. With all that, the full rising must come. With purity of the

body, nadis and mind, it rises up fully. Until then, there must be a little hard struggle. Ups and downs there will be. So, is it clear that point?
Disciple: Yes.

Disciple: In your new edition of "Brahmacharya for Boys and Girls", you write, "If you can control one of the yama and niyama rules, you can control them all?"
Swamiji: A perfect brahmachari must be perfect in thought, word and deed. That means he must have perfect control over his mind. When he is a perfect master over the mind in any one subject, all the other subjects also must be there. To control the mind means yama and niyama automatically follow. Is it clear?
Disciple: Yes, it is clear but it must be fantastically difficult to give up desires of all kinds.
Swamiji: We say, keep up the higher desires, give up the lower desires and then slowly and steadily come up to the higher and higher points. You cannot eradicate all desires. Keep up good desires and give up the bad ones.

Disciple: Swamiji, if you are going to play a big piano concert, which is very concentrated work, isn't it a kind of high pitch?
Swamiji: I have divided concentration into more than a hundred ways. So, what our aim here is, concentration of mind at will, on one point, on One Thing. There, with your piano, songs and other things, there are a variety of things coming; so, it is another way of concentration and that kind of concentration is highly developed even in lower animals and insects. It is also highly developed, higher than in you people in many respects, but they can't control the mind.

In mind-control, you must come to one point, one thing. It is taking mantra-jap on one subject, on one point slowly, slowly. There also, you have to take a gross thing first and then go to subtler and subtler and then the subtlest point. That requires a lot of training. That is the difference.

An ordinary man going to the cinema, he also gets concentrated, but there are a variety of objects. A man reading a novel, he is also concentrated there. Many people without reading a newspaper, they can't eat or drink or anything. As soon as they get up, they read the newspaper. They are so concentrated.

Disciple: But Swamiji, isn't there a difference between this kind of passive concentration and active concentration?
Swamiji: There, also, imagination is on a variety of subjects. It is not on one subject.
Disciple: Yes, but still, it is on the way to one subject, in the process.
Swamiji: It is the process, if you want it. Many end there alone. They don't want to proceed. A man wants to become a good writer of novels. He stops there only. He wants money and a little comfort. It is all right. That is what he wants.
Disciple: But isn't he inspired when he makes his music?
Swamiji: He is getting some thoughts. There are a variety of thoughts. That is not one thought as in meditation.
Disciple: But still, it is more difficult than to read the newspaper, I think?
Swamiji: Who says it is easy? I did not say that. There are different ways, but the highest way is at will on one subject and then coming to one point. Even the scientists do not come to that point. If you can develop that, then only you can go to Samadhi.
Disciple: Yes, but I do not exactly understand what one point means?
Swamiji: You are taking God's name, your mantra, and then you are thinking of the mantra and then the image of God. On that only, you have to concentrate, not here and there. The mind will wander; so many thoughts will come, here and there. It is lack of concentration. When you get concentrated, then the thoughts cannot come. But in creating a novel or poetry, there you have to imagine so many things and you are giving a link, a connection. That is all.
Disciple: Swamiji, is it like coming in contact in a deeper kind of concentration?
Swamiji: I have written somewhere, I think in the book, "Revelation", "Poetry scents of Divinity, ecstasy tastes It a little, but Samadhi tastes, re-tastes, and merges in It. Again, poetry merges in ecstasy and ecstasy in Samadhi." There is a sort of concentration. That is all right. He is above the ordinary man but with that, you cannot go any further. That must stop there. In ecstasy, there is a deeper state of bhava. That means a sort of trance and you enter the circle. Even then you have not gone to the point. It is in Samadhi only you go to the point.

Disciple: Does that mean that concentration in art and concentration in composing are only child's play compared to the real concentration?
Swamiji: In a way, you can say that it is a lower state. If you want to go to higher pitches, automatically you will feel disgusted with all these things. The time will come when you find no value for it. You will say, "I want to retire now." Until one gets a severe kick, then everything will come. You will say, "It is all unreal. I don't want all those silly things. Let me retire now."
Disciple: In the west, Swamiji, I think devotional people will sing and play for God.
Swamiji: You see, it is some sort of sentimental feeling. Sometimes they weep also and they stop there. It does not mean they have attained anything. When there is nothing else, something is better than nothing. It will make a man very great. So, they will make him a saint immediately.
Disciple: Is it not to be great, just to have the ability to give expression for feelings?
Swamiji: That is a lower way. But you can take up some songs, side by side and then devote your time for meditation.

Reading: *The easiest and, at the same time, most efficacious method adopted to make the mind pure, serene and one-pointed is mantra-jap.*
Swamiji: In this way, mantra helps you. You have got so many desires and thoughts. In order to get rid of them, make one thing strong. That is mantra. When the mind gets concentrated on that one point, you can go beyond that one point. That is the secret there.

Reading: *It is the mantra that should fill the mind all the twenty-four hours.*
Swamiji: When you go on deeply, always repeating the mantra, even in sleep, a sort of vibration goes on. That is what is meant by going without sleep. Don't go mad. When you go on with deep interest, even in breathing, there will be mantra. The vibration is there. It becomes an automatic process but it will take time. Many people say, "I have been uttering so much mantra-jap, still there are so many thoughts." It will take time. Don't get disheartened. Go on with the mantra and after

some time all these wandering thoughts will become less and less. That is the secret. But have patience in the beginning. Continue the mantra and the whole Chitta will get changed and you will attain purification. Whatever thoughts come, they will be good, not bad. So, pay much attention to mantra in the beginning.

Disciple: In many kinds of work, it is impossible to concentrate on the mantra because you have to concentrate on the work.

Swamiji: That is the exception. Before going to work, take the mantra and then merge in the work and in the breaks, if there is a chance, remember it. It must become a habit, in that way. Even teaching or writing, whatever you do must become a sort of worship, that is the way you have to proceed. Afterwards when you finish the work, offer the fruits. Don't hanker for it.

Disciple: The mantra can be pronounced in different ways. Is it very important that it is done correctly?

Swamiji: It does not matter. If a child says "father", sometimes it may be an abusive term but the father or mother does not get annoyed. They only embrace the child. So, if God knows that you are doing it with a good motive, God will embrace you for the fault. He will not be annoyed. Suppose a young baby is just learning to speak and says, "Father is a fool." Then you will say, he has uttered the word, "Fool", and he will kiss and embrace the child. If another man tells you that you are a fool, he will be bombarded.

July 8, 1973

Disciple: How can one misuse the mantra?

Swamiji: When you are using it, suppose you are annoyed with some person and you are using the mantra and you are attacking that person again and again. That is misuse. That will injure the person and it will injure you also. Both are not safe.

Disciple: Will the mantra have less effect if it is not kept secret?

Swamiji: You will have a fall. If you go on telling your mantra to other people, some may discourage you. People will say so many things. Some people, out of pride, go and tell to their friend, "Oh, I had this kind of experience and that kind of experience." The friend might have been doing long practice but he has had no response, but you had speedy result, so he will be against you. Afterwards, you have to weep and weep to come to that point again. You lose that point and you have to work twice as hard to come to that pitch again. So, everything must be kept secret. If at all you have anything, any direction to be taken, you share your concerns with your Guru. That is all. There you have to be very strict or else you have to suffer. There is no fun in this thing. Be sincere and be strong also. It is a temptation when you get some sort of response to go and tell it to other people. "I had this thing. Did you have anything?" They want to compare but there is not a common mind.

Disciple: Swamiji, can one use the mantra to avoid getting annoyed?

Swamiji: You go on with it. To control the mind, you have to use the mantra constantly. When anything comes, your anger or other things, overcome it. Repeat the mantra constantly. Engage the mind in thinking of the mantra. Is it clear?

Disciple: Not quite. Before you said not to use the mantra when one is annoyed with a person.

Swamiji: You are not using the mantra on the annoying person. If you do that thing, it is wrong. But you are trying to repeat the mantra and forget the other thing. There is a difference in that thing or no?

Disciple: Yes.

Reading: *All and sundry should not presume to be Gurus and select the mantra for their disciples. Only a man of God-Realization, i.e. one who has attained Samadhi, can know what the Ishta-Mantra of a disciple should be and it is only he who can give him initiation.*

Swamiji: There will be two ways. There is Savikalpa and Nirvikalpa. A man who has attained Savikalpa is also a man of high attainment; so, he can also take the position there.

Disciple: Are Savikalpa and Maha-Samadhi the same thing?

Swamiji: When a monk dies, he has gone to Maha-Samadhi.

Disciple: Can a man who has attained Savikalpa show the way to Nirvikalpa?

Swamiji: He cannot show it, but he will show the path that he has taken. That is why all this trouble in religion comes. So many sects make a confusion and quarrel. It is due to this. Many people take it to be the last point and they say there is nothing beyond it. "We don't want it." That is the quarrel going on between sdwaita, visishta-adwaita and dwaita. Many people want only this much. If there is some sort of disease, they will pray to God and make some offerings. The priest will pray to God on behalf of your son so he will be cured. Sometimes, he may get a cure due to some other cause, but the credit will go to the priest and to his God. In this way, they go on. People want only this much. Who cares for Moksha?

July 9, 1973
Reading: *When once the Guru and the mantra have been chosen all doubts must be brushed aside. It would be infinitely better to let a bullet pierce one's heart than to entertain any doubt.*
Swamiji: Don't use any bullet. Your police will come running to me. You must understand the meaning. Don't make any mistake in that way. You have to take the spirit, but don't have any doubt.

Reading: *In the beginning, therefore, the mantra should be repeated very often. One should not worry about the wandering mind but work regularly and systematically.*
Swamiji: Here many people make a mistake. Many people complain, "I am taking the mantra, but the mind wanders here and there" and some abruptly come to the conclusion that it has no meaning. They think that when once they take the mantra, the whole mind must concentrate. That is what they understand. It is a wrong idea. Every one has to struggle in the beginning and when you go on systematically repeating the mantra, then slowly and steadily the mind calms down and you will enjoy the mantra and concentration will go deeper and deeper. So, don't be discouraged by it. Every one has the same difficulty. You have to work it out faithfully. Many have committed so many sins then suddenly they want to have everything. That is not possible; so, you must have patience.

After some time, you will understand yourself. There is peace now. You love the work more and more and you will want to devote more and more time. Many people also find it difficult. The work is there and they don't want to get up. There also, the mind plays a trick. If one is allowed to sit, then the mind does not want to sit longer. When there is work and you have to get up, it wants to escape work and be easy-going. There also you have to control it. So, both work and meditation must go side by side.

If you take it in that way, life will be healthy and happy or else it will be one-sided. Often it goes like that when you go on working, you will feel disgusted with the work, "Oh, work is too heavy." Only the mind is playing. If the same man goes on meditating without any work, then meditation also becomes too heavy. The stupid mind deceives a person so you have to sit tight upon it, control it and divide the time also. During the time of work, the mind must work and during the time of meditation, the mind must meditate. In that way, regulate the time. Then it will come under your control or else it will control you and you will become a slave.

Reading: *One should have infinite patience and perseverance and should never get dejected if no definite change in the mind is affected.*
Swamiji: Change will be there always but how to measure it? How to know it? Some may attain easily because they have worked in past lives. So many lives they have spent. The vast majority of people have to work hard. That is what is meant. Never get dejected by all these things. One has to face it.

Reading: *When performing mantra-jap one should keep the meaning of the mantra in the mind and think firmly that God is actually sitting in the heart center.*
Swamiji: So, mantra is there. Meaning is there. When you go on uttering the mantra, if you always repeat the meaning, that will be distracting or it will confuse your concentration. Take the mantra and think it means this and then go on repeating the mantra only. That will bring one-pointedness easily. Then think of your Ishta-Devata that has been directed to you and concentrate on that thing. When concentration deepens, the mantra becomes slow and it may also stop.

The form may also disappear. It will take you to the last point slowly. Many people make a mistake here and they search for supernatural powers or they want to see how far the kundalini shakti has come. Many get afraid of death when the breathing becomes slow. When the mind goes deeper and deeper, the mantra also will stop. Many drag it down to mantra again. That is a wrong idea. Allow it to work. Follow it and there you have to focus, as it were. Focusing as a flash light, the whole light will come to one point. Without a point, the mind cannot merge in Infinity. When you work it out, you will understand it. When you are coming to this point, never be afraid of death. Why should you be afraid of stopping breathing? It is all a misfortune to think in that way. Be bold. Thinking of God, even if you die, you will have Moksha. That is all right. It is not easy to die. So be brave there. Forget everything. Dive deep, come what may. Then such people go to the point.

Disciple: Is it good to concentrate on different chakras?

Swamiji: There are different methods. There are different alphabets and different lotuses in the chakras. Don't go for that. It will wake up the kundalini shakti. If you want Samadhi, take one point and merge it there.

Disciple: What is the other kind of mantra-jap? You mentioned two kinds.

Swamiji: With dhyana and without. Dhyana means with the meaning. It is too tedious. First, take the mantra, remember the meaning and then go on with the mantra. The meaning will go automatically. That is the easiest way. Or else you will be dividing the mind into two portions. It is too tedious. There, many people make a mistake when they start with the lotus with eight petals and then they bring the Ishta-Devata and then the mantra. Now there are three things so they want to put all three at one time. That is also a mistake. So, imagine that the lotus is there. In the middle of the lotus, think of your Ishta-Devata and now forget the lotus and think of the form itself and the repetition of the mantra will go on mentally. The mind must be put on one point. Then the result is speedy.

Disciple: Guru and Ishta-Devata is that the same?

Swamiji: You are a newcomer?

Disciple: No.

Swamiji: How long have you been here? How many years? Such a strange question to ask. That is a private question you must not ask in such a public way.

Disciple: Swamiji, how to avoid being afraid when the heart is going to stop?

Swamiji: You see, that is a misfortune, I am telling. You should never get frightened there. When the shakti rises up along the sushumna nadi to the last point, it is the symptom of Samadhi. There the breathing stops completely. But if you are afraid in the middle, it will not go there. The shakti will fall down. You will lose the concentration and to come to that point again. It takes a lot of time. You have to weep for it, several years. It is not so easy. Sometimes you get a fortune, just like a hidden treasure, but if you lose it then you have to wait. So, one must be careful there. Fear comes with the ego. That dirty ego is hiding, so it is deceiving you. That is a critical point there. You must be very careful. Think, "I have taken God's name," and leave it unto God completely.

Disciple: What is the best to think when a person is dying?

Swamiji: To take God's name, repeat your mantra. That is the best thing. You must be joyful in seeing a man who has died. An old man has died and it is just like you have a new coat. An old coat is worn out. You are throwing it away. He has taken a new coat. You must be happy there.

I remember an incident in my own life. I was young, I had just renounced the world. Suddenly some people brought me the news that one of the younger brothers had died. It was so terrible. Suddenly it caught me. I was struggling to get rid of all this so-called attachment. For three days, I had to struggle. After some time, three or four years, I was in Rishikesh and was at a high pitch. Then the postman brought me the news. Mother had died. Then I laughed at it only. Then I said, "What is that? It has no meaning. What is life and what is death?" But there are stages. That is the natural state when nothing upsets you. Generally, we say, when a man dies, if you cry, it disturbs the person who has died. That is the secret there.

Disciple: It holds him back?

Swamiji: It holds. Many people they don't weep. They suppress it. It is a very dangerous thing. It can develop into a mental disorder. Some go mad also. In India, they have a sect who are trained. When a man or

woman dies, they come and weep. They go on in such a way to make them weep. All the forces go away by weeping. It is an art there.
Disciple: What happens if a man dies by accident?
Swamiji: That is not good. He has to remain as a ghost. He does not get a new coat there.
Disciple: Even if you have learned to say your mantra all the time?
Swamiji: Then you will not die also. Then you will not have a car accident. You will not have such a bad death. The mantra will not allow you to die in that way. Generally, when a man dies after a long disease or old age, all the forces of the body and mind concentrate in the spiritual heart center. Then, such a person knows where to take the next birth. But in an accidental death or suicide, it has not come to that point; so, one does not know where to go to the next birth. Immediately, he has to remain as a ghost in the subtle body. Nobody can avoid it. Then there is death for that body also. According to karma, he may have a good birth or a bad birth. Generally, committing suicide is not good karma. It is a very bad thing; thereby, you increase your sins. It is not a solution to get rid of the troubles and tribulations of this life to commit suicide. You make your life worse. One should never try that.

During the time of death, whatever preoccupation you have during the whole lifetime that predominates. Even by doing a little mantra-jap, one cannot expect that during the time of death, he will have the mantra. If you have been practising it, it is all right. It will come to your help. That is samskara. That impression works easily. Many people are in a dilemma there. They see some people coming, some soldiers catching them and dragging them. They talk so much nonsense. They have hallucinations. It is all due to their bad deeds. It is coming there.
Disciple: You can see it on their face.
Swamiji: So horrible they look. Some have a very peaceful death. Those who have been meditating, they have a peaceful death. Even after death, there is some satisfaction. There is some brightness. That you can see.

Reading: *Mantra-Jap should never be done in a hurry. The mantra should always be pronounced very distinctly. It should neither be repeated too quickly nor too slowly.*

Swamiji: But when you are doing it in your daily work, that rule may not apply there. It is an exception that you have to keep in mind. Some people may think, "I cannot do it with shraddha (faith) while doing work. So, it is better to stop it." That is bad. Do it there also. But the same attention as during the time of meditation cannot be there. Work is there. Mantra is there. So many things, there you have to divide. The same sort of concentration will not continue there. You have to make a distinction but it must go on. It will help.

Reading: *The number of jap to be done should be fixed according to one's capacity and convenience.*
Swamiji: Generally, when you go on doing a fixed amount of malas, you cannot escape. When you are in a period of action, you feel that mantra-jap is more attractive. You want to do more and more. But when reaction time comes, you don't want to sit for five minutes even. Then you have got the mala. A certain amount of japa should be done. You have to do it. You have a hold over it also if you have the tendency to fall asleep. These are some of the methods to make the mind active. That is all. When you go to deeper states, then there is no need for a mala. Automatically you continue without the mala. Until you come to that point, the mala will help you in so many ways.

July 11, 1973
Disciple: Swamiji, is Ramakrishna not a great man?
Swamiji: Why do you worry about Ramakrishna? It is not our function. If you have any other things, come forward. I have not come here to preach about Ramakrishna, Jesus or any other Krishna. I have come to teach you Truth. Those who want it, come forward. If you want this man or that man, it is not my problem. It is not my business also. Whether the Vedas have the prominent things or the Bible is a good thing or the Koran is the best, it is not my purpose there. I have nothing to say against anything. Our duty is to deal with Truth. That I have been telling. So, if you have any problems, come forward.

Disciple: Is it the effort that causes the evolution of a man?
Swamiji: Everything is there. Without effort, nobody can come up.
Disciple: Without effort, there is no evolution?
Swamiji: No evolution. How can there be? Then you must put someone else, you must bring a God. It is absolutely an unnecessary thing and absurd also. Effort is on behalf of you. That means your past effort giving fruit, that is called karma-phala. Without effort, there is no evolution or involution. Both are there. Wrong effort means going down. With right effort you go up. Both are with you. Nobody can help in that way. Every individual has to work. With right effort, you can rise up. With wrong effort, you sink down. Both are possible.
Disciple: It is said that no one can escape prarabdha-karma.
Swamiji: It can be overcome also by intensifying the effort. Suppose a cobra has given you a bite. There is poison in the body but if there is taken proper care with proper medicine. In due time, you can be saved. If it is neglected, it will kill you. So, the poison is just like prarabdha. It has come to you, now, by right effort, you can overcome it.
Disciple: It is said in the book that prarabdha cannot be resolved.
Swamiji: Not in that way. There are so many things which can be avoided. If the karma is too strong, it will defeat you. The force of the karma differs. It may be too strong. It may be middle or it may be mild. There are so many milder and middle things which can be controlled by right effort. If it is too strong, one has to pay terribly. They want to make progress but they are pulled down. That is owing to wrong things they have done in the past.
Disciple: Is the best way to overcome bad karma just to keep calm?
Swamiji: You have to work. When it comes, face it boldly. Think, "I have done something wrong. I have to face it. Who else will face it?" Put that question. Don't commit suicide. That is too bad. Then you are increasing your karma to lower life, very bad karma. So, you can never escape it. Escaping can be done by taking the right path. Mantra-Jap and meditation will help you.
Disciple: Can you never put a why? Why you have to suffer? Why is it so bad?
Swamiji: There is no why. You are all suffering. If you ask a young man who has got so-called young blood, "Please don't do it." Then he will say, "Who are you to tell me? Why should I not do it?" He puts that

question to you. The same man when the thing comes, he has to weep and weep. Then how can it come, why and how? If you have one birth theory, then you have to criticize your God who created you. It is absurd. It has no meaning there. You are responsible for everything. If you do something good, you will enjoy life. If you do something bad, you have to pay for it. That is all your own making.

Disciple: Swamiji, you write in one of your books that if there is a conflict between the heart and the head, follow the heart. What does that mean?

Swamiji: Suppose you are going to do something wrong, then there is a conflict between your head and heart. The impure mind, that is the head, it says do it; but, the inner voice, your inner conscience, says don't do it. That is the heart. You understand?

Disciple: Yes.

July 12, 1973
Reading: *Writing of mantra-jap.*
Swamiji: Writing mantra will help you more during the time of reaction. It is more concentrating. It will be a help to every one in the long winter nights when the devils are coming. All will come during those winter months. Many succumb to all temptations in the long winter nights. So, it will help many. That is profitable. First, do it with mala. When you feel tired, writing can be taken side by side. It will help very much because, when writing, you have to put much concentration on the mantra. Mentally you have to repeat the mantra. The mind cannot go here and there when you are writing. That can be done in small books made from waste paper in your press. Write with small, small letters. That will make you more concentrated. If you scribble, that will be easy-going. Use small script, in this way, so many lines. That will be another training for the mind.

Reading: *Besides this, a sadhaka (spiritual aspirant) must do the mantra-jap mentally wherever he goes and in whatever he does.*

Swamiji: That, every one is doing. Every one has to practise that also. Instead of allowing the mind to think of a variety of things with many thoughts, you have to make one thought strong – that is mantra. Then, one has to go beyond that also, when the whole chitta is filled with mantra. When the chitta is purified, then automatically wherever you go, whatever work you do, the mantra will vibrate. That is the secret. So, mantra does not go on in vain. It has a great force behind it. The more you can do mantra-jap, automatically you control the mind and senses also. You will benefit very much. Sadhana means this. You have to be alert. There will be difficulties, but overcome them. You have to make a hard struggle and after some time, you will have the benefit. One can enjoy the effects or the results of the work. Then you will understand it.

Reading: *There is yet another method of doing mantra-jap. It is to read the mantra-jap. Get the Ishta-Mantra printed or written in bold letters — one hundred and eight mantras to a page or get a small pocket book of one hundred and eight pages with only one mantra printed or written on a page.*
Swamiji: If you have written already, that small book can be used for reading. After writing, that can serve both purposes. That book is not to be thrown away; so, the value must increase ten times. It is an important book then.
Disciple: It is difficult to sit straight when you write.
Swamiji: Try to sit straight. Write when sitting straight at a table. That is better. Don't bend. When I was a young boy, a brahmachari, I was meditating. Out of devotion, I used to bend. When you come to concentration sometimes you bend automatically. One monk, he saw me and scolded me like anything. He said, "Why are you bending like an old man?" It pained me rather. Then from that very moment, I took it up. When I was sitting, I would be straight, walking straight. It was too painful for him. Then he began to say, "Why are you walking straight, sitting straight." I said, "I will do it." I did not say anything more to him and I kept up that thing forever from that very moment. You have to pick up. A sadhaka's attitude must be like a bee, it goes to a variety of flowers but it only takes the honey. Even the wicked sort of

man or sinful man, he has something very good which you are lacking. Learn that thing from him.

Reading: *In chitta, all the past knowledge of different objects, events, incidents, etc., is kept arranged in different pigeon-holes as it were.*
Swamiji: Many people make a confusion there. They will say, "How can there be pigeon-holes?" It is just to give a rough idea about it. How wonderfully it works by giving one an idea. There are so many things concerning that subject, whatever it may be. They are all kept in different places, as it were, not exactly in that way. Everything remains in the causal state. That is why there is so much confusion in western psychology. They can't make out anything. They can never understand it, until and unless they take the help of their own mind and dive deeply into the subject, that means mind-control. When the mind is controlled, then you can understand mind-functions. Then you can understand what is meant by chitta and where it is stored. Now, as it is, it is an automatic process. They don't know from where it comes. Western psychology means only the brain center. They have done much work in that research. That is all right, as long as they are concerned with the physical things. But the subtle part is beyond their understanding. That is why they say, "Every thought creates a furrow in the brain center." It is impossible. If you have to collect furrows and then repeat it, it is terrible. You can't bring any knowledge. It is not only furrows. The shakti, by its infinite powers, keeps all memory in the causal state and whenever it is necessary, it supplies the knowledge.

For example, if you take the word, "father", it has two sets of meanings there. One is particular and another is general. When you say "father", in a general way, what is meant by "father"? All the knowledge you have gathered up to now is there in the chitta. You can go on speaking about the word "father": what is the attitude, how he has behaved to his children, all the things come there. If we say, "Your father", there you have got some other meaning. You think of a particular man as a father, the whole thing comes there. How beautifully it is kept there, a most wonderful thing it is. You cannot imagine. Only one button pressed and the word, "father" or "your father" and the whole thing comes. You do not think about the matter. The supply goes on and you go on speaking, how wonderful.

Suppose if it was to be in furrows, how to apply to the furrows? So many words you have heard about the father. How can it come through a furrow? It is quite impossible. Think over it. In the course of a day, so many words, so many things. You keep everything. It is so nicely kept, so wonderful. Even after ten years, you can recall an incident. It is there already. That is nothing short of a wonder. It is a great wonder. How it tackles the subject without any effort on your side. Everything is arranged so perfectly and it is not forgotten also. From your childhood, if you want it, everything is there. Likewise, the past birth memory is also there if you want to recall it. It is a miraculous thing.

Reading: *As soon as the thought occurs, the subtle form of the thought-object occupies the mind. This shows that every desire and every thought has a subtle form behind it.*
Swamiji: So, in a nutshell, name and form always go side by side. In that last point, God is formless. It has no name and no form, but to go to that state every one of you, every one in this universe you can say, has to start with name and form. Without a form you cannot conceive anything. That is why symbols came into prominence in every religion. To concentrate, there must be an object. You cannot conceive of Nirakara. That is the formless aspect. Even if you say, "God is all-pervading," then you have to think of this akasa everywhere or you have to think of the big ocean, that is also a form. So, to begin with, it is just like a child learning the alphabet. Without the alphabet, you cannot read or write. Likewise, the symbols are necessary and there are a variety of symbols. Taking one, the mind gets concentrated easily. After that, you go to higher and higher pitches. That is the secret.

Reading: *There can be neither any desire nor any thought without first mentally seeing an object or without projecting a subtle mental image of a thing or object.*
Swamiji: So, name, form and meaning, these three things always go together. This is the function of the mind even in imagination as I told you some days back. You are the biggest creator. Whatever you imagine, you have created something there. If you are fanciful, you can create so many things. You can invent so many things.

Reading: *Without the mental projection of the image of the thought-object there cannot come any knowledge of it. That is to say, name and subtle form always go together, and the two are quite inseparable.*
Swamiji: So many religious sects, without knowing this, they make a big hubbub and quarrel for nothing. That only shows their ignorance on an important thing like that. If they actually know this, then there is no quarrel between a church and a temple, a paGoda or a mosque. It is all from stupid ideas that they quarrel. So, if you really know the meaning, then there is compromise. Let them do. Let them worship. Why should we be enemies?

Reading: *Even a man who has attained Nirvikalpa Samadhi, has to think with the help of a subtle form when he comes down to the plane of relative Consciousness.*
Swamiji: The mind can work under these conditions only. Subject, object and knowledge, these three things will always be there. When you go to Nirvikalpa Samadhi, there is no more mind, subject, object and knowledge. They become one. Then what remains is the Ocean of Consciousness by Itself or in Itself.

Reading: *God is only One without a second. He is Eternal, Infinite, Unchangeable, Immovable, Birthless, Growthless, Decayless, Deathless, Sexless and Formless.*
Swamiji: In the long run, in the last point, there is nothing. There is nothing material, nothing efficient, nothing whatsoever — only One Thing. When you say God is Infinite, there can be only One Infinity. So, the word creation has no meaning. It is absurd to say something is created. Out of what, from where, that means you are limiting the unlimited. God creates from where? At the same time, every religion says that God is All-Pervading, Eternal and Infinite. That is only One Thing then. How can you create from where? If there is something remaining side by side with God that means you are limiting the unlimited. So that God has become a limited being like you. Thereby, that God loses the Godhead. He is also a created being like you. When you say God is Infinite, Omnipotent, Omnipresent, Omniscient, there can only be One such thing. There is not a thing without it. How can a

second thing be there to create, comes the question? You catch the point? Yes or no?
Disciple: Yes.
Swamiji: There comes the question from where it can create? How it can create? How can it increase or decrease? So, there is a big problem there. All these things you have to wipe off. For ordinary people, for ignorant people, those who are young babies like you, we have to give some sort of "milk", just to attract them and make them understand but you don't tell them the last point. You say it is confusing there. Then they will say, "It is impossible. How could it be? We see creation. We see so many things. How to deny it?" Then the last word they can say is, "Oh, that man is mad. He talks so much nonsense."

In order to avoid all this confusion, they have brought the Maya Theory - maya working on God. Then again comes the question. So, however you put it, it is a dilemma and that dilemma will remain forever. It can never be answered. It is impossible. Only when you go to Nirvikalpa will it be solved. Then there is no dilemma. You have no questions.

Disciple: Will it help to say the mantra without understanding the meaning?
Swamiji: Even without understanding the meaning, it has value. But it is more beneficial if you know it. It is just like someone is standing on the seashore and another man pushes him and he falls into the water. If you understand the meaning, you knowingly go for a swim. But both ways, you have the benefit of a bath.

Disciple: I would ask, if one is meditating, is it always necessary to use the mantra or can one listen to one's heartbeat or the wind blowing or something?
Swamiji: If you join the mantra with the wind blowing or the heart beating, it is far better. Mantra will help you more. Mantra with the heart beat or the sound from the wind will help you more.

July 13, 1973

Reading: *Thus, in expressions of all kinds, however fine the wordings thereof may be, man as man with a finite mind, can never conceive of Infinity or the Formless Aspect of Brahman without the aid of a symbol or an image which may be either gross or subtle.*

Swamiji: That is why all symbols come in every religion. You cannot make progress without it. All cannot take up jnana-yoga. They must come to a high pitch of evolution. They must have an intense desire to be free, have control over the mind and senses and constant discrimination between the real and the unreal. These are some of the qualifications for taking up jnana-yoga. Many, without having the attainment, make a big show. Some hear or read some books about jnana-yoga and they become "jnanis" and they want to discard all these names and forms. They cannot grasp anything. They can't make any progress also. The growth gets stranded, as it were. Only the ego grows automatically. That is a dangerous thing.

Disciple: If one begins to concentrate on an image and then continues with a point of the image, next time you sit for meditation, can you begin with the point?

Swamiji: If you can do it, it is good but you cannot always come to the point in that way. Start with the gross form and then go to the point and if you proceed further that point will also disappear.

Reading: *The founders of different religions have prescribed different methods and different symbols for the use of their followers for the worship of God, to suit their tastes and in conformity with their spiritual growth.*

Swamiji: That you have to understand. Don't make any unnecessary quarrel. Who is right, who is wrong? It is none of your business. Follow your own method and give choice to others also. That is a happy growth. If you think it is the right path and he is wrong, that is wrong. Let him also have a chance. When he goes on doing his work, he, himself, will

understand what is good and what is wrong and how to proceed. The best method is not to interfere with the affairs of others. Is it clear?
Disciple: Yes.
Swamiji: When devotion is there, when love is there, the mind easily gets concentrated on anything. That is another secret. The Tibetans have a story. A disciple went to a Guru and wanted to take mantra. The Guru gave him mantra but he did not succeed in concentration. The disciple went to the Guru and said, "I didn't succeed in concentrating. I find it difficult." Then the Guru asked, "Whom do you like most?" And he said, "I have a big buffalo. I like it very much." The Guru said, "Concentrate on the buffalo." He was living inside a cave. The door was very small. He had to crawl in. After a few days, he attained concentration. He thought he had big horns because he, himself, had become a big buffalo. For many days, he did not go out. He thought, "That door is too small. I am a big buffalo." So, he was sitting quietly. The Guru thought, "Why is he not coming?" so he went in search of the disciple and he found the cave and called, "How are you?" "I am quite all right. My mind is so concentrated." "Come out," the Guru called. "Gurudev, how can I come out? I have got big horns and such a big body. The door is very small. How can I come out?"

So, he identified himself with the buffalo, his God was buffalo. In this way, it is all mind's play. Mind easily gets concentrated on a thing which you love and like the most. That is the secret. That is why they give a variety of symbols of Gods and Goddesses. That is another secret.

Reading: As the vast majority of men and women do not regulate their sexual-life, they generally possess weak will power.
Swamiji: That can be seen even among the youth, it may be boys or it may be girls. Where there is no sexual control, their will power also becomes very weak. Is there any objection to this point by anyone? Those who meditate, they can clearly find it out. Generally, those who do not live a life of brahmacharya, their will power remains very weak – so, also intellect. You have seen such people among your students?
Disciple: Yes, a lot.
Swamiji: You can see easily how it is. How it makes them helpless. The mind also becomes fickle-minded and weak.
Disciple: When they reach the age of fourteen or fifteen.

Swamiji: Many people begin their sex life much earlier. They are so stupid because they have no guidance. They become a prey to it. By the time they reach the age of eighteen or twenty, everything is exhausted. The creative power is gone and they are good for nothing. In a way, they may look very healthy, in appearance only, but actually it is not so. They have a variety of diseases. They cannot withstand a hard life. You don't ask them to observe absolute brahmacharya, but at least to regulate their sexual life. It is the greatest loss that a person can have in this world. Especially people who observe celibacy at a young age, they shine well. But when they begin sexual life, they fall down. There is no energy to study further. They don't want to study. That is why young children have so much energy to play and play because celibacy is there. The energy is there. That is the secret.

You cannot minimize such an important subject. That is why they say in spiritual life also, when one is established in perfect brahmacharya, that means in thought, word and deed, three fourths of the sadhana is over. For such a man, only one fourth remains. He can attain Samadhi easily.

July 14, 1973
Reading: *A ruffled state of mind, ficklemindedness, unsteadiness, loss of cheerfulness, loss of self-confidence, doubt, procrastination, unsteady gaze, haggard looks, peevishness, loss of memory, clouded intellect, lustful desires and thoughts, fear, etc., are all the symptoms of weak will power.*
Swamiji: If you have any doubts, come forward. That we can easily see, when new people come after smoking hash and other things. When you ask them, "When did you smoke hash last?" They pretend as though they have forgotten everything long ago and it is only one week back. The face will indicate so. One case came today and said, "I only stopped yesterday." If you are prepared to give it up, at least you must struggle and use your will power. So, where is the will power? It is all gone. It is a miserable state, especially for girls. Boys also suffer terribly but, to a

certain extent, they can withstand it. The girls will immediately have all sorts of maladies and it will tell very badly on their whole life. It is a terrible thing. Such people we are helping. That is why they call me "the King of the hippies." After taking LSD and hash, they come to a certain understanding that the whole world is unreal but that there is something real. But your church cannot guide them, your doctors cannot help them and your government cannot control them. Such people come to me.

So many people have come up. Every one is a hero now. Every one of you must come forward now and boldly tell about the necessity of brahmacharya. I remember some five or six years back, one boy came back from India after taking sannyas. He began talking of brahmacharya in Copenhagen. They said, "He is a mad man." They wanted to throw stones at him. What a horrible state it was. So, now, at least, we have come to a point where we can emphasize, put much force and say it is necessary. Nobody can come forward to face it or challenge it. Besides, we have given a challenge to the whole world, not only to Denmark, a small speck. To the whole world, I have given a challenge. Come forward, we say. Whoever has a doubt, we will prove the necessity for brahmacharya without any fear. Many of the pseudo-yogis who have come up to now, they are not talking about that subject at all. It is too terrible for them. They wouldn't have gotten a single penny if they had talked about brahmacharya; so, they are taking an easy way. Yoga means only hatha yoga. We have to walk with the head, not with the feet.

Up to now, I have not made any sort of propaganda, not even for the books. People who read one book, they go for all the other books automatically. It is spreading from mouth to mouth, not by any paper advertisement. We have made a very sound basis, a strong foundation. So, it is for you people to make use of it and work it out. Never lose it. Be strong, all of you.

Reading: *Never lose hope. Be full of high hopes and keep high ideals before you. Have infinite faith – faith in yourself, faith in God, faith in the words of your Guru and faith in the Scriptures. Never look down upon yourself. Never brood over your weaknesses, drawbacks, sins and falls. If you are a sinner today, you can be a Saint tomorrow, only* *if you will. Self-confidence will fill you with infinite strength and power. Good thoughts and noble deeds will make you great; improper desires, thoughts and acts will make you sink lower.*

Disciple: How to discard stupid, vulgar as well as good desires? I know that both have to be discarded.

Swamiji: First, stick to the good and then go above both.

Disciple: How to discard the low and stupid things?

Swamiji: Suppose you know that if you put a finger in a burning fire it will burn. If the desire comes to put the finger in the fire, will you then put it?

Disciple: No, then I would burn my finger.

Swamiji: So, you know what is good and what is bad. In the same way, when an evil desire comes, say you feel hungry and somebody's apple orchard is there. The desire comes to your mind, "Let me take some fruit." That is an evil desire, so your inner voice says, "No. Don't take another man's property." Control it. What is the difficulty there? You know yourself, what is good and what is bad.

Similarly, get rid of all bad things. Whenever a bad desire comes up, bring the other side. Tell yourself that stealing is very bad. You must be honest, truthful, chaste and good, bring that forward. In that way, overcome the bad things.

Suppose the desire comes to eat more and more. Then tell the mind, "If I eat more, I will fall sick." So, put the discrimination there. "Would you like to eat one morsel more and be sick? What do you want?" Put the question to the mind. Then come to this conclusion, "If I eat more, I will fall sick tomorrow. So, it is better not to eat." Bring the good qualities. Discard the bad. Understand this.

Disciple: I think people love each other very little.

Swamiji: Very little?

Disciple: Because when a weak person, for instance, takes hash and other bad things, such a person needs our help and I think we have to give it.

Swamiji: First help yourself before helping another person. Suppose a man is going to drown and you don't know how to swim. If you jump into the water to save him, what will happen to you? If you are an expert in swimming, then only you can save the person. But if you do not know how to swim and you jump in the water, both will die. In that way, it will happen.

Disciple: But it is good to help others.

Swamiji: It is a fashion to speak in that way. A beggar thinks that he will give a charity a million dollars but he has not even one kroner for his meals. His charity is just like your so-called help. It has no meaning. First, be strong yourself, then only can you help others. Live the life. Build up your character. If you are strong, then only you can help others or else you will be destroyed. At that point, many people make a mistake about so-called charity.

So, even when some have learned a few yoga asanas, they say, "I have benefited so much. I must help the world now." What a horrible thing, when they themselves do not know how to do it perfectly and they want to help the world immediately. What kind of help can you do then? The ego is playing false with you. One becomes egoistic and thinks, "I have got success. I must help," that is ego. That help will go to pieces. Both will suffer. It is not help there. You can't help in that way.

Disciple: Swamiji, if a man feels vairagya (renunciation) because of some disappointments and he wants to renounce and take the vow of celibacy, will this state be permanent or momentary?

Swamiji: In that case, one must be careful. When vairagya comes, you must have patience or you must take precautions at least. Say a person is in love with a person who dies suddenly. Or a man has a great loss in business, money or prestige, then comes a sort of vairagya. Then he says, "Why, this worldly life is wretched. It is better to renounce and go away." That is called Markata Vairagya. Markata means monkey. Every night a monkey and his wife climb up a tree. It is very cold. Clasping their baby by its legs, they hold it between each other, thereby keeping themselves warm. Then the monkey says to its wife: "Tomorrow I will make a warm house" and when the morning comes and the sun sends its warming rays, it forgets the house. Then again at night, it gets cold and it will remember. So, the whole winter passes away. The whole life passes away. The house will never come.

Likewise, when there is some difficulty, Markata Vairagya comes. One has received a kick and he wants to renounce the world. That vairagya is called Markata Vairagya. That is only vairagya for the time being.

After some time, they go back to the world they left. All the things come one by one.

Real vairagya is when you have got everything, all comforts and there is no difficulty, no misfortune. In spite of that thing, you hear the inner voice. You have the great desire to renounce the world. Such a man renounces and goes. He never turns back. That is real vairagya.

Then your question, if a man gets momentary vairagya, what he has to do? Then he must take precautions. You should not be loose there. You must have satsanga. That is the company of the good, reading good books and above all, your daily meditation. That is the best remedy. Your daily meditations must be kept regular and systematic. And keep up some work also side by side to engage the mind fully. When you have heavy work, in spite of that, keep up morning and evening meditation, at least. When you are doing any kind of work, repeat the mantra. It must be your constant friend. The mantra must vibrate constantly, whatever work you do, wherever you go, mentally it must go on as a sort of vibration. And think, whatever work you do, it belongs to God, "I am doing His work. The body is meant for God. It is only an instrument. It belongs to Him entirely." Keep that idea. Work it out and all the defects can be controlled.

One has to continue in this way. The mind will not always be in the same strength. Especially during the time of reaction, one wants to run away. One wants to be easy-going and even your mantra and meditation become monotonous. You don't have any taste for it and think, "What is there, the mantra has no power. Why should I worry and waste my life?" In this way, many people go back to what they have given up. That is a misfortune rather. That is, during the time of reaction especially, every one must be very careful. Regulate your life. Whatever work you do, keep at least morning and evening meditation. There must be no compromise with it. When the meditation time comes, whatever work you do, throw it aside. There must be no compromise. In that way, stick to your time regularly and will power also grows side by side. Even if you forget to remember God, when the particular hour comes you have to remember. You need not see the clock. Automatically, the mind will be thinking of God and your mantra. In that way, it becomes a habit with the mind. So, one must be strict and follow the routine at any cost and afterwards it becomes very easy.

Disciple: It is said that one should have balance of mind in joy and sorrow. Is sorrow itself not loss of balance of mind? How can one have balance of mind there?

Swamiji: When you don't feel happy, then why should you feel sorrow?

Disciple: There can be so many reasons.

Swamiji: Why so many reasons. There is no reason. The "I" is the devil hiding there. That is the cause of all those things. When you think, "I have given up the 'I' to God. The body is His. Everything is given to God." Then when sorrow comes, it is all His will. You take it easily. And when joy comes, you will also say, "It is His will." In that way, you don't say, "I am happy." And at the same time, you don't say, "I am miserable." That "I" is no more. The cause of all this misery is the devil "I" that is playing mischief.

You have to give up both. When joyful, "I am joyful" should not come there. And when sorrow and misery come, you don't say, "I am miserable." Both are God's will. Take it in an easy way. Both good and bad, pleasure and pain, in all the pairs of opposites, you must think, "Oh Lord, it is Your will." That is an easy way. You don't get upset by tidbits.

Generally, if you have got one kroner more, you will be very happy. You will dance like anything and if you have lost two kroners, you will be weeping. Then that "I" is there. So, you have to kill the "I" by keeping God in front constantly. That is the devotional side, to keep one's Lord in front everywhere, in every work. In this way, when success and failure and all those things come, think "It is your will" and you take it easily. If the "I" is there, then you are miserable with sorrow.

Disciple: When nature has given us the senses to feel sorrow and joy, why is it better then not to feel anything?

Swamiji: Has God made it or have you? You feel it. You have made everything. When you go in a deeper sense, there is no sorrow and no happiness also. Your mind has made everything. Mind is the cause of everything. You can't blame God for anything. He has given everything. He has given you the intellect also. By the aid of the intellect, you can control your emotions, if you make proper use of it. If you misuse the intellect, you degenerate. You will be a miserable slave of your emotions and you will suffer hellfire. In order to gain control, you are doing sadhana. That is the only process.

There is not a single thing which is absolutely good or absolutely bad. A thing which you call very good has a portion of bad too. And a thing which you call very bad has a portion good too. It is a mixture in that way. When you come to higher pitches, you understand that these things have no value. They are all mind's play. You come to that point. Make it clear.

Disciple: But to practise sadhana as devotion, will one not have to make use of mind's creation in a way?

Swamiji: It is all right. Have devotion in order to control the mind but don't stand there alone. Rise up. When you go to higher pitches, when you come to Jnana or Wisdom or Samadhi State, all these things disappear. You don't take anything as good or bad. Both lose their power. Then you discard both. As long as you have the idea of happiness, sorrow must be there side by side. You have to go above both.

Guru Purnima

Today is the Full Moon day. In India, they call it Guru Purnima. On this day, monks and devotees worship their Gurus. There are some Sanskrit Pathshalas (Sanskrit schools) where some rich people give free education with free lodging and boarding to some Brahmin students. There the students call their teachers as Gurus and worship their teachers today.

This Purnima is also called by the name Vyasa-Purnima as Vyasa was born on this day. Up to the advent of Vyasa, the four vedas — Rig Veda, Yajur Veda, Sama Veda and Atharva Veda – were with certain Brahmin families only as their hereditary properties. There were no books and the people had to keep the whole Vedas in memory and this sacred knowledge was passed from father to son as a hereditary property. This great Rishi, Vyasa, with the help of his disciples, brought the Vedas into book form and also the eighteen Puranas. Thus, the Rishi Vyasa became very famous and he was called a great Guru. So, the Guru Purnima and worshipping the Guru on this day starts with the great Rishi Vyasa.

July 16, 1973

Reading: *The Symptoms of Growing Will Power: Purity, serenity and steadiness of the mind, good concentration, peace, calmness, self-control, lack of evil desires, steady gaze, strong memory, good character, self-confidence, lack of procrastination, clear intellect, quick and apt decisions are some of the sure symptoms of growing will power.*

Swamiji: Any doubts on these points? These are all the symptoms of growing will power. It comes with purity of the mind. All sorts of weaknesses are there but when you grow in purity, all this wickedness, the evils, they also go down or you control them easily. Any doubt on this point? Come forward.

Disciple: Swamiji, will all these weaknesses and drawbacks be there but not be able to bind you? Is it in that way?

Swamiji: What do you mean by it?

Disciple: The chitta will be full of these things.

Swamiji: How can it be when you go on purifying? What do you mean by purification then?

Disciple: Does that mean that the good side becomes strong?

Swamiji: The bad things are suppressed. They have no room to play.

Disciple: But they are there still?

Swamiji: A little. That will not disturb you at all.

Disciple: So, if they come, you can kick them out?

Swamiji: Suppose one drop of poison is in a tub of water. It is strong now. Then you go on pouring water into some more buckets. What becomes of the poison? It is there but it has no power. Even if you drink it, it will not kill you. Likewise, all these evil things get destroyed in that way. The more you think of better things, the more you do mantra-jap, that is what is meant by purification. When evil thoughts come, bring forth good thoughts constantly and the evil thoughts become weaker and weaker. The same thought may appear after some time, after some months or even years, but it has no binding force.

Disciple: But how can memory then get stronge if one has not bad thoughts anymore?
Swamiji: What is your question?
Disciple: If one does not have the bad thoughts anymore?
Swamiji: That is what we were telling just now. They are weak. What do you mean by memory? Strong memory means he may remember the thing but the binding force is no more. Then what is your difficulty there?
Disciple: One should forget the bad things.
Swamiji: Even if the bad things come, they have no binding force. So long as you have the idea of good thoughts, bad thoughts will be there also. But they have no binding force. You know what they are. They cannot overpower you; whereas, in an ordinary person, the bad thoughts overpower him. They make him act in a wrong way. Here it is not possible for them to act. As I told you just now, one drop of poison put in a big tank, poison is there, but how can it take over the tank. In that way, your major portion is all good things and the small things are not binding you. It will not injure you in any way. So, the memory of bad things may remain but it does not mean it will overpower you. Is it clear or no?
Disciple: It is clear.

Reading: *For, purity and steadiness of the mind, strong memory, automatic control over all the senses and the gaining of gigantic will power always go together.*
Swamiji: When the mind is fickle, when the impurity of so many thoughts come, such a man cannot have a steady look. He will be turning this side and that side. Even when speaking he will be so fickle-minded. When he speaks about a certain thing, he will not come to an end. He will take up some other subject and will never come to any conclusion. But yet he goes on speaking and speaking without knowing. It has no meaning also. From one point to another, from one subject to another, he doesn't finish anything. That also shows the weakness of the person. A man who has got peace of mind, he will be steady. His gaze and other things will be always steady. He will not be shaking this side and that side, so restless. That only shows the impurity of the mind. Any questions?

Disciple: There is no reason for speaking then.
Swamiji: In reality, there is no purpose. But you want someone to hear you, so you will catch hold of someone who knows nothing. You will want to speak about yoga. "That is a new philosophy, come forward. I will speak to you." You don't know what it is but you want some stupid fools to hear you. They will think, "He is a great scholar. He speaks so much about yoga, eastern and western psychology and philosophy. He knows so many things." Whether you know it or not, the people who hear you will also appreciate you. Then you think, "I have gained something. I am a big man now." So, your ego also grows there. Then you want to help the world. You understand. That is how the idea of help comes. One, two, three, four people listen to you very patiently and you go on speaking. That speaking you cannot control when automatic currents come up. People hear you, they say, "He is a great scholar." That puffs you up and now you want to serve the world. You must avoid all such things if you want to make progress.

Reading: *A pure mind is always steady and a steady mind is always calm, serene and peaceful.*
Swamiji: There the intellect also works in a clear way. The judgment you come to after discriminating and deciding a thing means you have a clear-cut vision there. You always make the right decisions. If your decision is in a wrong way or your argument is in a wrong way then you come to a wrong conclusion and you suffer very much. Whatever you do, you do it in a wrong way. So, everything depends upon your intellect, how you discriminate and decide.
Disciple: Swamiji, now we have been talking about will power, habits, effort, everything. I would like to ask, who is the judge and who is judging?
Swamiji: You, yourself, are judging. The chitta is recording everything.
Disciple: I understand that but the answer does not satisfy me.
Swamiji: Then you must bring a God there who judges. There must be a thing which judges everything. If you don't want to admit your own inner voice, inner Consciousness, then you must bring a God. The chitta is recording everything and according to the samskaras, the fruit will be there also. It is just like you are putting a particular seed that will

sprout, you cannot avoid it. That is why it is said, "What you sow, that you reap." And that sowing takes place in the form of desires, thoughts and acts. If it is a good one, automatically you have a good result. If it is a bad one, you will get a bad result. So, you cannot make any other man responsible for it. Automatically you get the result. You cannot change it because the shakti is there, recording the whole thing.

Accordingly, it shapes your fortune or misfortune. All these things are kept arranged side by side. It has all powers and all possibilities. Nobody can do a thing in a secret way and escape punishment because your inner voice is there. You cannot avoid it. If you do charity, the benefit will also come there but don't become egoistic. If you are actually doing good work, making progress, you won't be proud of it. On the other hand, an ordinary man, with a little tidbits of success, he makes a big show of everything. He has no control over the mind. When a tree is full of fruits and flowers, it bends low and a tree which has no fruit and flowers, it stands straight.

July 17, 1973
Reading: *It will thus be seen that desires are of two kinds, viz., desire to possess things agreeable and desire to avoid things disagreeable.*
Swamiji: It is also a desire to like or to hate. In one sense, desires are the cause of this samsara: the wheel of birth, growth, decay and death. All desires come because you want them. You live in the world and behind all those things comes the ego idea. That is the impulse. Keeping the ego, you want so many things. If the ego is absent, there is no need for anything.
Disciple: Does that mean that a serious sadhaka must have absolutely no interest in anything else but Samadhi?
Swamiji: The aim is there but is it possible to have it? Is it possible in the initial stages? You have to have so many things, so many objects. Slowly and steadily, you have to give it all up. For that we say, keep good desires and good thoughts in the beginning, then go on. Mantra will help you in that respect. When you proceed to higher and higher

pitches, then you come to a point where you have to discard that also. All desires automatically fall away before you enter the state of Samadhi.

Disciple: When a man is born with a talent, is it then a desire to fulfil that samskara, for example, music?

Swamiji: All right. Even music can be converted to a sort of sadhana. Did I ever deny it?

Disciple: No.

Swamiji: Then you have to give a new direction to your desire. Make the music beautiful and appealing to your sadhana. It can also be converted to a sort of sadhana. But don't get attached to it. Make music for the sake of music, like a master, not like a slave. If you take precaution with art and turn the mind and think it is meant for God, in that way, art also can be made into a sort of karma-yoga. Then, when you come to a high pitch, everything dies. Music and art have no meaning there. You find so much peace and bliss in mind-control. You have no time to think of your art. It is so painful. You cannot think of lower things. Automatically you change. To start with, take the impressions you have gained in the past birth and work it out. That is also one of the ways.

Reading: *Most of the evils of the world, such as lying, swindling, debauchery, theft, murder, etc., owe their very existence to the fact that unsuccessful, desire-stricken men generally resort to foul means to achieve the objects of their unfulfilled desires.*

Swamiji: Many people go and do in that way. They have some strong desires and when they are not fulfilled, then they begin smoking, drinking and doing all other things. There they fall. The wife is unhappy with the husband and he goes on drinking just to forget the thing. Some have got some terrible sorrow and just to get rid of it, they begin drinking and afterwards it becomes a terrible thing for them. The whole life is spoiled. Many people do the same mistake in taking hash. They want to rise up suddenly. They can't do it. The mind wanders in a circle and in order to forget it, they want to smoke hash. They always die in that circle. They can never rise up. In this way, habit comes.

Reading: *Had it not been for his desires, man would have easily known his own True Nature and enjoyed perfect Peace, and Bliss in life.*

Swamiji: It is their multifarious desires in a variety of ways that drag the mind out constantly and make you helpless. The mind becomes weak and stupid. That is the cause of all the miseries in this world. So, you have to eradicate and kill all the desires. The easiest method is to keep up one desire and that is the desire for God-Realization. Mantra-Jap will help you enormously in that direction — in killing and rooting out all kinds of desires. After that, it will be easy to control that desire also and go into Samadhi State without desires. That is the secret there. Yesterday, you were asking about strong memory. Was the answer satisfactory?

Disciple: Yes.

Swamiji: Strong memory means, whatever is once read, they remember it. They need not repeat it again and they don't forget it easily. There are some people, they have to read a passage twice, three or four times, and then they commit it into memory. There are some other people who have got a very bad memory. Even a hundred times they read it. After one hour you ask them and they have forgotten it. Strong memory means that all the old Samskaras can be brought up, if necessary, but they are not disturbing you. You are a master of them.

Disciple: Did you say yesterday that the yogi knows where he goes after leaving the body?

Swamiji: Not only yogis, you also know.

Disciple: But can you tell me where you are going?

Swamiji: Where? I have not yet decided. Why should you worry about me? I will decide it when the time comes, not now. What a stupid question you are putting. It has no meaning. You want to kill me? We are talking about a dying man, not a yogi.

Disciple: I have read that a man from India can do astral travels. Is it possible?

Swamiji: Not only in India, in Europe they can also do it.

Disciple: Are they free souls?

Swamiji: They are not free. The body remains dead as long as they are gone and if he does not come back, he is a dead man.

Disciple: When we die, only the gross body dies. Where does the subtle body go?
Swamiji: It may be travelling or it may take birth somewhere immediately or it may wait for some time.
Disciple: Can they live on other planets?
Swamiji: It is possible. They can live on the same earth or some other planet if they want.

July 18, 1973
Disciple: Modern science thinks that they have proven that memory is in the brain center.
Swamiji: How?
Disciple: They have developed habits in rats and then they go to the center of the memory in the brain center and transfer it to another rat and then it will act as per the training of the first rat.
Swamiji: That is a one-sided view. You cannot prove it in that way. If memories were to act in that way, it is terrible.
Disciple: They have done this.
Swamiji: Some vibration is there. Some of the daily vibrations are there in the brain center. Some of them in the heart center but the knowledge is not there.
Disciple: It is some physical thing.
Swamiji: It is a physical transformation which is natural because you are daily doing some acts. Whether the same thing acts as memory after some time, that you have to see. They have made some experiments, I think, in Russia. They hang a bell and when the particular time comes, they will ring the bell and feed the dog. After doing it daily, it becomes a habit. After some time, they ring the bell but they don't give any food and there is saliva coming from its tongue. That is how a habit works. Memory is somewhere else. To get the meaning or memory of a thing, it comes to the brain center in a particular way. Similarly, by repeating a thing often, it will remain as a vibration there, maybe as a sort of

memory. But the stuff for that memory is somewhere else. They can't detect it in this way.

Disciple: Yes.

Swamiji: How to recall the memory of past births? Some people have got that capacity. I remember an incident in Delhi four or five years back. A young boy of four used to say recalling his past birth, "I have a wife and I have a daughter." It became fun for many. They began to laugh at him. He was sent to school and there, also, he began to say, "I have a wife and I have a daughter." The boys began to tease him like anything and lastly the teacher went to the grandfather, he had no father, and said, "Please take care of him." The grandfather was going to beat him but the boy started crying, "I have a wife and a daughter." "Where," the grandfather said. "There is a house in that village and there is a widow and she has a daughter. Four or five years ago that man died and he has taken birth in an adjoining village"; so, the grandfather could not beat him. "I am going there today. I will make inquiries and then come back," he said. So, he went. It was exactly five years back that there was a man and he died and he had a daughter too. The wife was still alive. Then there was much hubbub. The wife wanted to see her husband and the elder sister was there also. So, without telling anyone, they came to the house and the boy went inside. "It is my wife and it is my sister-in-law, that other one." So, they began weeping, wife and husband. Then they got consoled.

Afterwards, there was a big hubbub. The parapsychologists went and made inquiries and then they concluded — "It is a fact. The boy can recall his past life and memory lives in the form of furrows in the brain. So, with death, the furrows in the brain center are destroyed so we don't know how he can remember." That was their stupid conclusion.

It is all one-sided. Your psychology is only making research on the gross plane. Memory can never live in the gross form, in the form of furrows. It is impossible. Perhaps they may be thinking of the tape recorder or gramophone record. The immediate things which are an everyday occurrence. Such vibrations may remain in the brain center but knowledge comes from the chitta where it is kept in causal form.

Disciple: But they take it as proof for the theory.

Swamiji: For a few days, the memory may remain in that way. Suppose you want to recall your childhood memory, where is it? It is still there. If you cultivate mind-control, you can recall the whole thing, not only of this birth, also from past births. How can it remain there in the form of furrows? It is impossible. Then how can they explain dream-state? They can't explain it. The mind is not functioning in the brain center when you dream. How can you explain the dream? They only say, "We don't know." How can they explain the difference between the waking-state and the dream-state? What makes the difference? They don't know. They know something in the brain center has some effect. I don't criticize them, the doctors and modern science. But the subtle things do not come under investigation. That is what I mean to say. Don't conclude that I have been criticizing anything. It is not in that way. They have done much work, no doubt. That is a creditable thing.

But still, to come to the right conclusion, you have to go further. You have to come back to mind-control. You have to take the help of your own mind if you want to go to deeper things. That is the best instrument. There they are lacking. In order to know the mystery of your own mind and mind function, the chitta, or what you call mind-stuff, there you have to dive deeper. It is not easy. It is a life long struggle. There they fail. Science has come to the splitting of the atom and they have come to the understanding that there is only force and it is travelling with enormous speed.

Disciple: Will it lead them to God?

Swamiji: How can it? If you understand that Brahman is the cause, then there is no more Brahman.

Disciple: But this theory of one constant energy, isn't it near to Adwaita Theory?

Swamiji: If it can be proved, it becomes a limited thing and that thing is unlimited, beyond the scope of the mind, beyond understanding of the mind, the subtlest of the subtle. So, that can never come under investigation. It is impossible. To go to that region, the mind must merge in the experience. That is a mysterious thing. Because it is the cause of all causes, or in other words, the subject of all subjects, it can never be objectified. You understand objectified?

Disciple: Yes.

Swamiji: That is the knower of everything. How to know the knower? That is illogical. It is impossible. That is why it is said that God can never be known in one sense. How to jump on your own shoulder? It is impossible. And, in another sense, God is more than known to you because it is your innermost being – your own Consciousness. What proof do you want to say you are existing? On the other side, it is unknown. It is two contradictory terms. When you enter that region, mind, ego and everything are no more there. Even the kundalini shakti merges. They go back to the Source. Knowingly, you enter there. You become one with your True Nature, your Consciousness. That can never be known by an external instrument. It is quite impossible.

Disciple: Is it Consciousness only?

Swamiji: I have called it "The Ocean of Consciousness By Itself". There is nothing else. There is no scientist, no scientific instrument, no one else to make experiments with it.

Disciple: I sometimes think that the way we are working is very exclusive because there are so many millions of people in the world.

Swamiji: But to know the Truth, to work for it, it is not exclusive. It is worth having. You have to struggle. It is only a question of time. Every one has to go back to the Source. So, we are trying to curtail the same and reach it as soon as possible. Effort must be there. When you know the path, it is better. Let us work slowly at first. At least there is hope in the future. Let us not give up. There is no guarantee that all can reach in the same life. That is not the question here. But we must know the path, how to work, where to end — the aim.

Disciple: Yes.

Swamiji: We don't ask you to give up your music and other things and come to this line absolutely. Have more money also we say, have all comforts.

Disciple: At the same time, you have said that it is only child's play and it is nothing compared with mind-control.

Swamiji: But, with all that, you have to be in the play. You cannot avoid the play. You cannot give up the world suddenly and go away. Only you must know that it is a play. Don't be serious. You have to take part in a drama. You know it is a drama, not a real thing. But still, you must be a good actor.

Disciple: It is very hard, Swamiji.

Swamiji: Why? It is easy. That is nothing. So, every one must have the game, finish it now. It is all right or no? One has to play the game and then finish it.

July 19, 1973
Disciple: Democracy is based on the thought that every one is born equal.
Swamiji: Oh horrible. As living beings, they are equal; but in growth they differ. In birth, as Jivas, that is all right. We may say all are of one kind, the whole universe, but in growth, there is much difference. Then why should there be a prime minister? He has power, then the ministers and then there are some officers.
Disciple: They say it is because they have had different circumstances. They have not all had the same experiences.
Swamiji: Not the same. Select five people from different categories, give them equal status and circumstances and see how they develop.
Disciple: They don't believe in it.
Swamiji: Why should they not make experiments? In America, they have made experiments and there are intellectual groups now among the children. They test and see to which group the children belong. All are not equal. It is all one-sided views. To say all are equal, it can never be in that way. We have got our camp. Say there are some people who have been working very hard and they have got good results. There are also some drones who eat and sleep. Now, you want to equalize a man who has worked very hard, who has better results, and a man who has not worked and has no result. Then he will be the enemy of the man. "Why should he make progress? Why not I? I also lived in the camp." Yes, they must be equal. That is democracy?
Disciple: It is because of their parents, they will say.
Swamiji: Now everything is equalized. They have got Freedom. You have got four fixed meditation times, food and everything. They have all kinds of facilities, then why is it that some make more progress than others? Even by birth, some have good parents and some have bad parents. Why? Who made it?
Disciple: They say it is society.
Swamiji: Society. It has no meaning.

Disciple: No, they think that these differences are due to genetics, heredity from the parents. They think that the child is having defects from the parents, for instance.

Swamiji: And then the parents may go to their parents. Their parents to their parents and lastly, they must go to Adam and Eve. The sin of Eve is destroying the whole of genetics. So, it must go back. So, it comes again, your original sin.

Disciple: They have a theory back to the monkeys.

Swamiji: Oh, it is a horrible theory. That is Darwin. It has no meaning.

Disciple: They teach the children in the school about Darwin's Theory.

Swamiji: They teach everything. What else to teach?

Disciple: But they have studied this genetic influence of the children to find out heredity is the cause of the difference.

Swamiji: You must go to the pregnant woman. That is to be counted there. If the mother is in a sorrowful mood or in a good mood, it has an effect on the child. During that season, they should never have sex. It has a very bad effect on the child. Then again comes the cinema and all sorts of vulgar things. Even the hearing and reading must be all good things if you want to improve. The mother must be kept in a healthy condition. If that is not kept, you can never expect anything from the child. You have to take proper care of the coming child. Even then, there will be differences between parents and parents, children and children. All can never be equal. You can try to give the same facilities to ten children, same education, same teacher, same everything. Still, they will develop in ten different directions.

Disciple: This they have seen. But they explain it out of the genetic composition.

Swamiji: If you go to a tree or a plant and study it, you can see how much difference there is in the leaves. Not even two are equal or two apples from the same tree. See how much they differ both in colour and size. How will you explain it? You have to accept the Reincarnation Theory some day.

Disciple: But Swamiji, doesn't democracy mean that all get a chance to develop?

Swamiji: I am telling, here, we are giving democracy in this way. Now develop. We have given all the facilities. Some do not want to work and, at the same time, if they are enemies of other people that is very wrong.

That is what I mean. Such people only talk of democracy. Those who work hard have no time to think of all these things. Here your government is doing so much work. If a person is sick and unable to work, you have got a pension. But, in India, it is terrible. You will go to the dogs immediately with nobody to help you.

Here you don't understand the difficulty that is felt in other countries. You have so many other facilities, especially in a country like this. You have no other resources except your farming. With this simple farming, they have made such wonderful progress. They have given all sorts of comforts. There is plenty to eat for the young people coming now. You people have forgotten it completely. There are so many other countries, in spite of having plenty of other resources, they have not progressed so much.

All youngsters, you must be careful there. Don't lose what you have gained. What your ancestors have given you. Add to it. Make it rich. If the coming generations are too careless and lazy, then the prosperity will go away.

Reading: *As a matter of fact, each is a strange mixture of good and evil. A close analysis reveals that even an act which is called very good has something bad in it and an act that is termed very bad is not without a tinge of goodness in it.*

Swamiji: Never take up this thing. In the beginning, it is very dangerous. Everything is good and bad. What is the use of making good? So, it is an easy excuse to do bad things. Every one will say, "Where is the necessity of making good if everything is a mixture of good and bad?" It is not in that way. Don't make a confusion. In the beginning, take what you generally understand is good and leave the bad things. When you evolve and come to a high pitch, when you have gained mind-control, then you will understand there is nothing which is absolutely bad and nothing absolutely good. Everything is a mixture. Then go beyond both. Here comes the aim of yama and niyama.

July 21, 1973

Reading: *Sometimes a man may, however, build castles in the air; that is to say, he may desire for things imaginary. But very often such desires are only fanciful and not strong. Ordinarily, a man desires for objects that he has seen and enjoyed and such desires being very strong and powerful, he is led into action almost immediately.*

Swamiji: Take that desire of constantly thinking of an invention. They make a design, they plan it, how to do it, what to do. It may also be strong. In making a radio or television, it is all wonderful things. They have done great work, so much energy, time and concentration of mind on these points. It is not easy. They have made so many experiments. We have to give credit to them. They have done a lot of work. How they could find out the sound vibration and how they have made the apparatus to receive it? And an ordinary tape, how they can record it? It is all miracles. It is also yoga in a way though externalizing. If they had spent as much energy to realize their True Nature, they could have done some more miraculous thing. They could have attained easily also because there is a high concentration of mind.

Reading: *The force of a desire or a thought differs and it is of three main kinds, i.e., mild, middling and intense.*

Swamiji: That can further be divided into so many groups. The same desire may differ in strength according to so many things, if you feel tired or fresh, if you take interest or not. Then again comes circumstances – place and time. In so many ways, it can be divided.

Disciple: Some desires are not caused in this way, but by some outside agents, special sexual desires by Jivas who want to take birth.

Swamiji: That doesn't matter. That you have to kick out and say "No".

Disciple: How can that manifest as a desire in a person?

Swamiji: It enters the body so that desire may come. It enters the body of some wrong person. It is wrong for them to enter the body of a brahmachari or brahmacharini. That is a wrong selection, that stupid Jiva. So, it must be kicked out. Say "No". Kick it so it should not come there.

Disciple: How does it manifest? Just as an ordinary desire?

Swamiji: The Jiva enters the body in so many different ways, in the form of eating, through food and drinking. Some powerful ones, they can enter directly without the aid of anything. When you have got mantra, you are strong. Everything can be kicked out. Don't be loose. Don't give place and think, "Some Jivas want to take birth, let me have it." Don't go in that way. Kick it out. "It is not the right place for you, get out, rascal," you say in that way. "Some Jivas want to come. I have given birth to a child." That is a stupid idea. Don't be so generous and weak in that way.

Disciple: Swamiji, how can it be that one can desire a thing without knowing it?

Swamiji: That we have been explaining. How a desire comes up in the body in so many ways. You have read the book, "The End of Philosophy"? There are fifteen ways how a desire arises in the mind. When the kundalini shakti gets heated, it carries automatic thought currents and they are the cause of a dream. By automatic thought currents, your desire suddenly appears in the mind.

Disciple: Of these fifteen causes, which is the strongest cause for a thought to arise?

Swamiji: Daily you will have so many things. The willing process is the strongest.

Disciple: Is it not the senses coming in contact, for instance, with the eyes?

Swamiji: That is also by the willing process.

Disciple: In creating desires?

Swamiji: In a general way, the eyes are powerful but some are attached to smell, some to sight, some to sound, some to taste and some to touch. All are very powerful with man. All the five senses are equally developed in man only. In lower life, they have got one of the senses predominating over the other four. But the devil man, he has got all the five senses equally developed. So, many temptations will be there.

July 22, 1973

Reading: *A subtle desire is the cause of a gross desire and a gross desire, in turn, is the cause of a thought. When a desire develops it becomes a thought.*

Swamiji: There are different ways how a thought arises in the mind. This has not been touched by western or eastern psychology and philosophy. They have only given the senses coming in touch with the sense organs. They produce desires and thoughts. For them, desires and thoughts are the same thing.

Disciple: What is the difference?

Swamiji: One is subtle and the other is gross.

Disciple: That is just words.

Swamiji: Because you can't understand, you say it is words. It is a subtle stage, I am telling, before a desire becomes a thought. A desire is the cause of a thought. When it comes to the heart center, you understand it. There it becomes gross.

Disciple: Where does the desire come from?

Swamiji: It comes from muladhara chakra. That is the starting point.

Disciple: Who is the knower? Is the ego the knower here?

Swamiji: Ego is not. The knowing function is the mind. The Self is only a witness. The mind gets its life and light from the Self. Without Self, the mind cannot exist. So, the mind is only an instrument of the Self to know the world. And further, the mind knows the world through the five senses. This is the connection. In the waking-state, the mind is working in the brain center. Then in dream-state it works in the lower brain. And in deep-sleep-state, the mind merges, goes back to the Self and remains in the causal state so you are not aware of the world.

Disciple: Where am "I" then?

Swamiji: You are there. The real "I" is there, your True Nature.

Disciple: And why don't I know it then?

Swamiji: Because the mind is no more. It has merged in the Self.

Disciple: I am going there every day and still I don't know?

Swamiji: This is your ignorance. That is the most mysterious thing and your misfortune also. Every one is going there, right to the Source, but due to ignorance, one forgets it. It is all in the mind only. The world is nothing but a projection of your own mind. Daily you are going to your True Nature and, in that state, nothing is there. It proves though, you are the Self that remains in the body as a witness only. Secondarily, it proves, everything is in the mind. Now, in Samadhi, you knowingly go to that state. But in sleep, somebody pushes you there to that state and you come back, as it were, without any change.

Disciple: What is this, then, that is here now?

Swamiji: That is your ego that is deceiving you. Mind, ego, senses, all the things they are working now. They are fooling you; so, you have to control them just to go back to your Source. So, the effort made to know your True Nature is religion or philosophy in a nutshell.

Disciple: Mind is not controlling automatically?

Swamiji: One side is controlling and one side is discriminating all the things. It is all different functions of the mind.

Disciple: Like heartbeats or digestion, mind is not controlling?

Swamiji: Mind is not controlling that thing. It is not the mind. There, the kundalini shakti is taking part. The mind is also under the control of the shakti.

Disciple: Well, I understand it but why am I still identifying myself with the body then?

Swamiji: That is bondage. Get rid of it now.

Disciple: It must be lack of understanding.

Swamiji: That is what we are teaching. Get rid of that blunder, that ignorance. You are identifying in a wrong way. Even generally, when you say, "my body", do you say, "I am the body," and then "my brain, my senses, my ego". Now find out what is that "you". You say, "my body". That means you are not the body. Automatically you deny it. Even the most ignorant man does it.

Disciple: Yes.

Swamiji: Then you say, "my mind". In all these things, you say "mine, mine". You don't say, "I am the mind, the brain, the ego." Now, who are you? Every one is practising sadhana. It is just to find out your True Nature, that real "I", not this ego.

Disciple: But how to remember the mantra always?

Swamiji: All right. You have to make it a habit. The mind will divide into two parts. Then, one part is only speaking and another part will be thinking of your mantra It will develop in that way. It can divide in that way so you will not forget. The senses drag the mind out constantly so you become weak. When the habit becomes stronger to the other side, it will go on automatically when you are eating, drinking, sleeping, whatever you are doing.

Disciple: Swamiji, could you please explain the meaning of the food mantra?

Swamiji: The meaning:
"The offering is Brahman. The food is Brahman.
The fire in which the offering is done is also Brahman.
He who does the offering is Brahman.
By seeing Brahman in everything, one goes to Brahman."

And in Sanskrit:
brahmarpranam, brahma havir
brahmagnau brahmana hutam
brahmaivatena gantavyam
brahma karma samadhina

July 23, 1973

Disciple: How to control desires?
Swamiji: That we have been explaining every day last week. You have not yet understood? You have to control the mind. The easiest method is mantra-jap. Go on with the mantra. It will serve every purpose. Mantra purifies the body, nadis, mind, chitta and everything. There will be only mantra and mantra alone. Go on with it. Be strong with that one thing. You will be all right. That is the easiest method.
Disciple: What is the function of Lakshmi Nadi?
Swamiji: It is just taking the currents.
Disciple: Which kind of currents?
Swamiji: Kundalini currents. Nerve currents.
Disciple: Is Saraswati taking the thought currents?
Swamiji: No, it is not working in that way. The function is connected with the flow of the nostril. You breathe only through one nostril for two and a half hours to three hours at a time and then it changes to the other nostril.

Disciple: So, when the left nostril is in flow, there will be more automatic thought currents then?

Swamiji: It is not in that way. When the left is in flow, there will be mildness. You will be cool and composed. The mind is not so fickle-minded. You have control and sometimes good meditations too. If you want to make a compromise of peace, the left should be in flow. When the right is in flow, they go for talking or lecturing or, if there is warfare, to defeat the enemy. This is rajasic. Some people observe only to eat when the right nostril is in flow then there will be good digestion. There will be a lot of energy and heat in the system. So, the right nostril produces heat and the left is cooling. That is how they function.

Disciple: Can you get reaction due to too much meditation?

Swamiji: In the early stages there will be reaction but it can be controlled also. Some may get reaction often and some only now and then. With some, it lasts for one or two days. Others may have severe reaction for one or two months even. It is all due to your past karma. People who do not meditate may also get reaction, but they don't know what it is. They may call it depression or they will say, "I feel so miserable." Many take up drinking and go to pieces. When you have reaction, you feel an unknown sorrow. You have no cause for it. You don't know why, how, where, when, but you feel so miserable. If you search for it, there is no cause but, at the same time, you have no peace of mind and that is a very, very miserable state. You can't eat, you can't drink, you can't speak with others, and you can't sleep. Then, what else can you do? Only to commit suicide, that is the easiest method. I have seen many people. That is a very dangerous game. When you come to a certain pitch, you know how to tackle the kundalini shakti. You can take it to another center so there is no more reaction. Those who regularly meditate can easily control any sort of reaction also. So, systematic work is necessary. By pranayama, you can change it.

In sadhana, there will be ups and downs. Sometimes you have a fall. That does not matter. Rise up. I have been telling that the road is so slippery. I tell you, roll with the fall, fall and roll and then get up. In that way, go on. Don't get discouraged. If you remain in the same mud, you will die. You have to roll and get up.

July 24, 1973

Reading: *The mind works automatically in a particular way as a result of the early training it has received.*

Swamiji: So, everything depends upon how you train the mind. A number of habits make the character of a man. When a thing is repeated often, it becomes a habit. This is the secret. According to your one birth theory, a thing which is inherited cannot be changed. That is how they give Freedom to the children from the very childhood. It has no meaning. It is completely ruining the children. The word control is unknown. Whatever desire comes, one accepts it and acts accordingly. Now, if you want good results, you have to train them in the right way. Discard the bad things and always try to follow the good things. It is the only way. You have to give Freedom to the children. That is all right but there is a limit for it. You have to keep a close watch and whenever they go to the wrong side, take them and mend them. Then they can take up good things. Children can take bad things easily, not only children, every one takes bad things easier than good things. So, it is very difficult. It is better not to give such Freedom. When they grow up, even two people cannot mix together. Every one wants to have their own views and they go on quarrelling for nothing. There is no agreement. That is terrible. The reasoning power is no more there and now they are engaging psychiatrists just to console them. They are grown up and about to die so they go to a psychiatrist to learn what they should have learned from childhood. It is easy to bend a young plant in whatever direction you want but when it is grown to a tree, it will break if you try to bend it.

Reading: *How to control Desires. There may be some people of virtuous samskaras (good past merits) who may accomplish this uphill task within a short time, but they constitute the exceptions rather than the rule.*

Swamiji: So, such people have come with great merits. They are born perfect. From childhood they are Jnanis. In India, they have some mythological stories. I have told the story about Jadabharata who was an emperor to start with. He had great merits but by misfortune, he came in touch with a deer and he became a mother to that deer. While dying, he was so attached to his deer that he became a deer in the next birth. So, those who are attached to cats, rats, dogs and other things, they will take birth as an animal.

The same kind of story: Recently, there was a goat in Rishikesh. It's actions and everything were just like a human being. It was called Matru. That goat was not mixing with others. It was living aloof. Daily it used to go into a temple and meditate three hours at a stretch. In the morning, it used to go for a walk. It was acting just like human beings and people used to respect it. At fixed hours, it would go for bhiksha. It would eat and go away, nothing more. Then it went on pilgrimage and came back. On one occasion, they said, "You better come to us." It was about a hundred miles. It was travelling alone on the road and there a Muslim butcher saw the big goat, so big and fat, he said, "It is a good one. I will earn hundreds of rupees by cutting it up." He tied it and it followed him. He did not say anything. Next day it was to be taken to the butcher's house to be cut but immediately that fellow got cholera and died. People made inquiries and found out he had tied Matru. They said, "Horrible creature. What have you done? Your whole family will go to pieces. Let him go at once." And they let him go. In the last days of its life that goat had some wound on the leg and it went to the doctor who gave it a bandage. But Matru got a fever and died. Then there was a claim that some monks wanted it to be cremated like a monk and others that it should be as a householder. There was a quarrel. Lastly, it was said that it was a monk. So, it was given all credits and a glorious burial like a monk.

So, how to account for all those things? The scientists will say it is all bogus stories but so many things are actual facts. There may be some past connection. Man does not know anything. They say it is all by chance. What is that chance? Nobody knows. How to get all these merits from the very childhood? From birth they make it all by chance. That is all mere escaping the real facts. It is not a story. Every one has seen it. It is a fact. Every one knows it there in Rishikesh.

Disciple: But Swamiji, how can one become an animal because one likes an animal?

Swamiji: Suppose if one is too much attached. While leaving the body, the thought might have been there; so, he has to take birth in that way. That is why it is said in the Bhagavad Gita, whatever thought you have when you leave the body, that will be predominating in your next birth.

Disciple: But when a dog dies and the thoughts are with the owner?

Swamiji: If it concentrates on a man, it will have a higher birth. If you are too close to a particular person, you will become a child and will get birth in the same family.

Disciple: When one dies with the mantra, what will happen then?

Swamiji: You go to Mantra Devata. That is a good birth. You will have a lift.

Disciple: Already while living, you can see some people coming to look more and more like their dog.

Swamiji: Yes, there is a close similarity between a dog and the man, man and the dog. By looking at the dog, you can understand the man also. It is difficult to explain but you can make it out. Even the formation, their face, there is some similarity. If you carefully watch them, you can immediately say that person is the master of that dog. In that way, don't get attached to anything.

Disciple: What do you mean by "attached to"?

Swamiji: Attachment you don't understand? Too much love. Give little love. Give your full love to God, instead of loving all these animals and worldly things. It is a mere waste of time. So, if you want to do anything, practise mind-control. When the thought of the dog comes there, in this way, it is dangerous. Many people have no attachment. They create attachment to a dog or a cat. Wherever they want to go, they will carry that dog. They can't love human beings. They want animals. They are very kind to animals but very cruel to human beings, horrible creatures. Their philosophy and theory is so horrible. Some of your dogs are more comfortable than your king. They have no worries. They have good food and everything. They will have a bed and be washed and some servants to robe him, a good life then.

Disciple: So, is that good karma?

Swamiji: Yes, it is good karma. It might have been their ancestors, some grandfather or grandmother, who was fond of the children, has taken life as a dog to watch a family.

Once a monk went to a house of a sweetmeat seller. That man was not very rich. Whatever he got of extra money, he used to put it in a big pot and keep it in a hole in the wall. There were no banks in olden times. One day a monk went there and he had torn cloth. He was a great man and unmindful of it. They gave him food and fresh cloth and cleaned everything. The monk took pity on the man and said, "Now come with me. I will show you the path to Godealization." Then the man said, "Oh, you see, I have a young wife. I have children. How can I go at this age? Let the children grow and the wife also becomes aged. Then I will come. Give me five years."

So, five years passed, the monk kept his oath. The monk came there. "Will you come now?" Then the man said, "You see the children are all grown up. Now they must be married. So, let me have another five years." So, five years went on and again the monk came. By that time everything was collapsing. The house was nothing. The man had become almost old and had an aged wife. Then he said, "All right, give me five years more to mend the house and other things." After a few days, the man died. After the given time, the monk came there and he asked. There was nobody. The children were ploughing the fields and a very old bullock was there. It had no food, nothing whatsoever and the boys were beating him like anything with a big stick. It's whole back was full of wounds. Still, it was going on working and working.

Now the monk understood what had happened. The man had died and had become the bullock. It was still serving the children. Now, the monk gave Jnana, that means wisdom to remember the past birth. "Now you can see the condition of the fields. I am working day and night so that they may have something to eat. So, at least give me five more years." All right, the monk said. Five years were gone and the monk came back. After a few days, the bullock had died. The house was half broken and everything fallen also. The boys were all here and there, scoundrels.

Now there was a dog. When the monk arrived, it was growling. It had not even the strength to bark but still it was guarding the house. Then the monk saw that the bullock had become the dog, "Will you come at last now?" Then, the man said, "See the state of the house." Because the money was there, it was guarding the money so the robbers could not take away the money. So, he said, "Let me have three years more." "All right," the monk said. He went away. After a few months, everything fell down and the money was covered. After the agreed time, the monk came back. He called the boys. They were here and there like coolies and he told them, "Come here, I will show you the money." They were very happy because they had nothing to eat. They went on digging. After digging so much, they said, "Oh, you are a rascal. You are telling lies. Where is the money? We will crush you down," they said. "No, no, have patience," he said, "Dig further." They went on digging and digging, then a cobra came hissing. It jumped like anything. "Kill it," he said, "Give it a beating." They took the pot with the money and bolted away. The cobra was the man who became the cobra. He was guarding the money. At last he said, "Now, I will come." In that way, your attachment deceives you in so many ways.

July 25, 1973
Disciple: Swamiji, is an hallucination a waking dream?
Swamiji: In a way, you can say in that way. With hallucinations, you are seeing something or you are creating something. Your screw is somehow loose so you see so many things. Many people say they see demons.
Disciple: What is the difference between a vision and an hallucination?
Swamiji: In a vision, the screw is not loose. The screw is tied. That is a vision. But in a hallucination, there is something loose. That is the difference.
Disciple: If you think long enough on a certain thing, doesn't it become an hallucination?
Swamiji: It is not hallucination in that way. It disappears if you concentrate on a light for long. For example, you see the one light and then in the place of one light, when the eyes are concentrated, you see two lights. Further, if you go, you come back to one light. When you are concentrated, the eyes are cut off from the light. Then, if you go further, it disappears. So, it is not called hallucination there. Hallucination is

when suddenly you project something you see mentally. There may be some defect in the brain.
Disciple: Do alcohol, hash and LSD produce hallucinations?
Swamiji: They all produce hallucinations.
Disciple: Yes, but does it spoil anything?
Swamiji: Yes, in the brain center, the discriminating faculty of a man is gone. That means it produces abnormal heat and it goes to the brain and produces hallucinations.
Disciple: Is sadhana the only way to repair the brain?
Swamiji: Yes. And medicine if it helps is well and good but we don't find any medicine so far helping. The easiest method is there must be celibacy and side by side mantra-jap and meditation. That will help. We have seen marvellous improvement with many, so we have got confidence to say this. They have now a charming appearance. That is the best.

July 26, 1973
Reading: *Apart from these great men, ordinary people have to work hard day and night for months and years together to banish all desires of the mind. In fact, complete eradication of all desires takes place only after the attainment of Nirvikalpa Samadhi.*
Swamiji: Yesterday, we were discussing that there may be people who are born with great merits. They are the exceptions rather, but for other people, they have to work hard. So, never get discouraged. It takes a long time. It does not matter. You have chosen the path, the right path. Now work it out. That is the right way. Don't weep, don't cry, and don't remain without sleep. Those are all bad things you have to control. Have patience and work it out. It must come. Every one must get it. It is only a question of time.

Reading: *It is in this state that the mind along with chitta merges in the Supreme Spirit or Brahman and all desires in their gross, subtle and causal states are destroyed.*

Swamiji: Destroyed, then there must be another thing. Some may ask what about memory? The mind is a purified mind and ego is also called purified. The mind works from the Superconscious plane. That is called Turiya State.

Disciple: Swamiji, does that mean that you rediscover the world when you come down?

Swamiji: It is not rediscovering. Everything is already there. After all, what is the world? It is a false thing so you will have to make patchwork. This morning I was seeing, it is just like so many divisions, so many branches of learning. It is just like different rivers coming and coming and the last point is the ocean. Whatever river, whatever side you follow, the last point is the ocean. That ocean will eat away everything. That is God. In whatever direction you go, it may be science, it may be good things or bad. In whatever direction you come, all must end in that. Some rivers may be with pure water, some with muddy water, some with poison. All must come to the ocean and end there. The ocean will eat away everything. There is nothing else.

Reading: *When such a man's (he is known as Jivan-Mukta i.e., Living Free) mind comes down from that Transcendental State to the plane of relative-Consciousness, he is no more bound by desires of any kind whatsoever, because he sees Brahman and Brahman alone behind all names and forms of this universe.*

Swamiji: The senses come in touch with sense objects and produce thoughts but there is no reaction to them. For an ordinary man, there is reaction. You understand what is meant by reaction? Suppose you see a beautiful flower, the eyes perceive it, then there is the desire and thought also. The desire for the flower comes there. But here, it is not in that way. Everything gets burned. There is no more desire for anything. An ordinary man is the desirer of desires. He always has the desire. He has to struggle but here it is an automatic process. It has no more value. That is the difference there.

Reading: *After the attainment of Nirvikalpa Samadhi when the mind of the Jivan-Mukta comes down to the plane of relative-Consciousness and begins to work the body and the senses, he retains the purified ego.*

Swamiji: So, there you see, to retain the body there must be duality. He has to come down. There must be the ego. Without the ego, even the breathing cannot take place. But the ego of a Jivan-Mukta, he has not an ordinary ego. That is a purified ego. In that way, he retains the body, thereby he is not bound by anything.

Disciple: I have asked Swamiji before, I thought that this development was very exclusive when you compare it with the many people living on earth. Now, we have Swamiji's unique authorship. I want to ask Swamiji, if Swamiji has a big plan?

Swamiji: I have no plan at all. You see, more than twenty years back, they wanted me in America. They sent an invitation and they were prepared to meet all my expenses but I said, "No." I did not want to go. Slowly my books came to Denmark and some of you wanted to translate them, I never asked anyone. Even then, they were terribly afraid of two books especially the one on psychology and the one on brahmacharya. They never touched them at all. They thought some stones might fall on their heads if they translated those books. So, it is only recently, last year, they were translated by some of you people.

I was avoiding making ashrams, also even in India. By chance, it also came. They wanted that I must have some place to remain in old age. A small plot about 150 square yards was purchased in Rishikesh and a kutir was built. I had no money also to publish the books but by chance it also came. I never expected it. I never planned it. I never wanted to go anywhere. Then the Delhi Ashram came and that also by mysterious ways. I never wanted it and it came in search of me and then it was built without money. Afterwards, money also came.

Some of the youngsters coming here wanted this plot of land. Gopal, a Danish disciple, thought ashram people must have their own place and that they must maintain themselves by having a plot of land; so, he purchased the land. He had no money and some of you people came forward, a heavy debt was there. After that, the youngsters went to Delhi for training and then I told them: you can go back to Denmark. There is a plot of land. We wanted food without poison. Go and live there. So, they went there and they began working and by fun I also said one day: I will go there. I never liked it. It is too terrible for me to travel because I can never go out even for a walk there.

After the first visit, I never thought of coming again. Then, everything was in chaos. I got an urgent letter that everything was going to pieces. "You are the only man to save it." I had to decide in five minutes about last year's trip (in 1972) and I said, "Yes, I am coming." I had some money, so by chance the Guru plot came there just to make the camp area. It was to be sold because we had a lot of debt. All this was planned by you people but I have corrected it. Last year, they had the cowshed here but I gave the suggestion that it would be a very good meditation hall and so it has come now.

Disciple: Does that mean that Swamiji is indifferent if it becomes a worldwide organization?

Swamiji: If it comes, I am not weeping. If it does not come, I am not sorry. If it comes, I am not happy, so it is both. Even now when I have so many disciples, I don't think of myself that I am a Guru in that way. You see, I have not come to preach any religion. I have come to teach only Truth.

Disciple: Certainly, it is a plan of the universe.

Swamiji: Oh, let Him plan Himself. Let Him have his plan. He may have some plan. Let Him have it. I don't worry. Let Him have it. It is His will. But I am free. I am no more. I have no plans. He may have some plan. That is all right. Let Him have it.

July 27, 1973

Reading: When a desire arises in the mind, try to remain indifferent to it. Do not mind it; do not care for it; do not pay any attention to it. Let it come and go unceremoniously. At the same time do not tax the mind and do not get worried and irritated.

Swamiji: Here you have to learn these important things. Many people make a hubbub over it. Why should this desire come? It is in the chitta. It must come. But don't pay any attention to it. Drive it off. Remain indifferent. If you are worried, it means you give importance to that thing and that desire becomes stronger and stronger. That is the secret. So, discard it. That is the easy method.

Reading: *If you would become a desirer of desires, they would catch hold of you and make you dance like a puppet.*

Swamiji: If you are worried, it means you are giving prominence to it. That desire becomes deeper and deeper. You are giving wrong impressions there, in that way. It is better to kill it and kick it out. That is the best way. Don't invite it for dinner. Kick it without mercy. Then it will go away. So, be strong there. It is all mind's play. Everything is mind. Your whole mind is playing mischief so you must be strict there. A portion of the mind is acting on another. Both are the mind's play. Even discrimination, one side and the other side, you divide the mind into two parts as it were. So, you must be strong there. Any doubts on these points?

Disciple: Yes Swamiji. When one begins to practise meditation, is it only the bad things in chitta that are killed or also the good things?

Swamiji: Yes, in a way, good and bad, both. It is not the question of destroying. You get purified. When you have no bad thoughts, there is no value for good thoughts also, both get purified. Purified means you can keep the mind calm, it is just like a big tank without any waves. Good desires are also disturbing you. That is also a sort of wave. So, both must go. In order to do that, you take the good ones just to kill the bad ones and then you come to a state where desires are unnecessary. You go beyond it. The best thing is to make mantra the predominating desire. Let it vibrate day and night then you will get purification. In a deeper sense, it means calmness. Even good desires are also a disturbance to the mind but still the flow of prana is smooth there. It is not disturbing so much but that also must stop when you go to higher pitches. Somebody was asking if everything gets destroyed when you go to Samadhi. Destruction is not in that sense. Purification does not mean that. Memory may remain there but it is not disturbing you. The highest kind of purity is to keep the mind blank from all desires. It may be good. It may be bad.

Disciple: It sounds very beautiful but is it at all possible to live along those lines? When you meditate, it is okay. You can try to keep your mind calm. But, as soon as you leave it, your mind is going out.

Swamiji: In the beginning, it may run. Afterwards, when it gets accustomed, it may not run in that way. It won't be wild. Some thoughts may come.

Disciple: When will you start to improve?

Swamiji: The improvement starts with the beginning of the meditation itself. It has already started. Now you have to improve it.

Disciple: Yes.

Swamiji: Even in fifteen days, if you work honestly, you can understand there is a great change in the mind. I have been watching some of the people in the camp. When they came first, they were so stupid, just like mad men. After doing sadhana for some time, there is some charm in their faces. There is so much change. Already you have started the play. Now you have to have patience and continue. That is all. It is a miraculous thing. So many have been improving, both boys and girls. You can see that.

Disciple: But Swamiji, for most of the people, it will be impossible in daily life to keep the program of the camp. It is only for when you have holidays.

Swamiji: Camp is all right. We are giving allowance to such people. Those who cannot follow four meditations, keep at least morning and evening. Every one can do it. The camp is only a trial for those who can devote full time to sadhana. For those who have work, they have to adjust. You have to learn to adjust. If you are sick today, tomorrow the other man may be sick. If he does not help you, you will not go to help the other man. So, there must be mutual understanding. Cooperation must be there. We want that love. Many people who come here to the camp, they feel that love is here which is rather missing among the so-called householders nowadays. We are creating that love here and we have to develop it further.

Disciple: The other day you said we have to meditate half an hour in the morning and in the evening.

Swamiji: For ordinary people, it is at least half an hour to start with. Not less than half an hour morning and evening. Then, in daytime, when you are doing physical work, engage the mind in thinking of the mantra. If you are too busy, then begin the work with mantra and offer the work unto God. Make every work as a worship. Every man can do it. There is no difficulty. If you have patience and continue, after some time it becomes a habit. Whatever work you do, there is no complaint over it. It may be good. It may be bad. It is nothing. Say it is God's will. There you have the right to say it is all God's will. So, you have no choice,

whatever comes, you take it. Then you have peace of mind not disturbed by anything, or else if you keep the ego, it wants selection. The work becomes too heavy. Every one must learn how to adjust to circumstances and take the work as God-sent. It is His work. That is the easiest way to make every work as worship. You understand?
Disciple: Yes.
Swamiji: In the beginning, it will be difficult. You find it difficult. Stick to it. After some days or months, you will be able to do it easily. Automatically, the work will go on and you will feel pleasure. You have no pain when you take the work in such a way. Then, you don't feel the work as heavy. You take it as light as anything. You forget everything. That becomes an easy process there. Even amidst the heaviest work, you are at ease. Is it clear? You see, I have to work at least twelve to fourteen hours daily. Every day I have this much work for nothing.
Disciple: For nothing?
Swamiji: Work is there but nobody compels me and I am not tied also. So, I take it easy, no responsibility also. So tackle the thing rightfully. Don't run away. Then everything will become easy.
Disciple: Swamiji, is it cowardice to leave a work you don't like. Is it really cowardice making a choice?
Swamiji: Why should you go in that way? When you have taken a work, face it and work it out. Nothing is easy. Such people, they want to do something here, something there and accomplish nothing. Stick to one thing and then you will do better. The same work will become easy. Many people make a mistake. "Oh, it is too heavy work." What will they get without heavy work? Everything is heavy. To leave the work is heavier. They want to run away. That is escaping rather. That is wrong. Such people cannot make any progress either in meditation. Give them time to meditate. "You meditate the whole day and night," tell them. Now see how long they will meditate. Then they want to sleep. Mind deceives man in so many ways. Don't believe the devil mind. You must sit tight upon it.
Disciple: I think our problem is more that we have so many kinds of work we can choose from. We can choose our work so much here in Denmark. You know I want to move to another place?
Swamiji: That is weakness. They don't stick to one place. They want to do this side, that side. It is just like people they go on rolling and

rolling one place to another. That is a disgusting thing. That is failure. It is better to stick to one place and make yourself comfortable. If you remain in one job, one place, you have all the comforts. They will come. Then you can do your sadhana. With a wandering life, you can't do your sadhana. It is a mere waste of time. If you cultivate that habit at a young age, you can't sit quietly in one place in old age. You will go from one ashram to another. That we have seen. Many people lose their whole life for nothing. They will quote in that way, "A monk should not sit in one place." They want to make a wandering life. That is terrible.

Disciple: But if you stay so long in one place, you will get very much attached. If you move, you may be non-attached.

Swamiji: Attachment is not easy in that way. Even if your mind is not attached in keeping plenty of things, then you are attached already. Everything is in the mind.

Disciple: How can you develop non-attachment?

Swamiji: You have to do it little-by-little. If you have two coats, give one to some poor people. If you have four pairs of socks, give two. What is necessary, keep. Don't go for unnecessary things. You have to go into detail in food, eating, drinking. You have to control yourself, but don't deny the body. Give what is necessary. Don't get attached to anything but externally keep what is necessary. It does not mean that if you are suffering and the doctor gives you medicine that you throw away the medicine. That is not proper. You have to give something for restoring the health, so never neglect it.

July 28, 1973

Disciple: Swamiji, why is it necessary to sleep with the head in a special direction?

Swamiji: There is a close similarity between your nerve currents and electricity. If you keep two magnets with similar poles touching one another, they lose their magnetic power after some time. But, if you keep them with opposite poles, they don't lose their power. The head indicates the North Pole and feet the South Pole. That is why you should keep your head to the south and feet to the north.

Reading: *Have a definite aim in life and stick to it at all costs. Always keep in mind the sanctity of human life and its four-fold aim, viz., Dharma, Artha, Kama and Moksha (virtuous life of righteousness, accumulation of wealth through fair means, lawful enjoyments according to the injunctions of the Scriptures and, lastly, attainment of Freedom or Moksha).*

Swamiji: It is a big subject. I think we have discussed it in one of the books. First, you have to live a righteous life. First comes the student life. He has to observe brahmacharya, live a hard life of discipline and build up good health also. According to their system (Hindu scriptures), they have to live in celibacy up to the age of twenty-five and after that, those who want it, can take up the householder life. After begetting one or two children, they used to observe celibacy. Just to keep up the line of heritage, they live a sexual life.

Second stage is Artha. They have to earn money in a lawful way to maintain a family and educate the children. A portion of the money must go to charitable purposes to help the nation, the sick and the needy. It is not for his own stomach and family. Both wife and husband have to carry on the local customs with fasting, prayers and feasts.

When the children are grown up and well educated, they take over the responsibility for the family. And husband and wife used to retire to the third, Vanaprastha, and lastly sannyas. There they have to cultivate further mantra-jap and meditation, sandhya and so many other things. There they used to live a simple forest life but it is all gone now, so we have to adjust.

Lastly comes Moksha. The aim of life is Moksha. So, we are not against any kind of life. There are two ways from the life of brahmacharya. If they want it, they can go directly to sannyas life. We don't compel anyone. It is left to their choice. The end and aim of life is Moksha.

Disciple: Will you tell us the meaning of mouna?
Swamiji: The aim of mouna is to repeat the mantra as much as possible and meditate, not to make a show of anything. That is one way. The second way is to keep a notebook and pencil and ask for whatever they need but it is troubling other people. It is better to speak. The best

thing will be, if possible, not to speak much. Every day observe mouna, speak little and sweet words, if at all there is a need and then stop. It is the best way, if you can do it. Control it every day, every moment. What is necessary, speak. It is similar with food also. You must regulate it. Don't be driven by your tongue or palate. You have to control both, speech and tongue. That will be a wise thing.

Disciple: Can you explain the difference between subjective and objective visions?

Swamiji: Suppose you are seeing a thing with closed eyes. You are seeing a thing mentally, that is subjective vision. You have been thinking of a particular object continuously that projects the scene. That is called subjective. With an objective vision, you see a thing or object with open eyes suddenly without thinking of the object at all. Is it clear to you?

Disciple: Yes.

Swamiji: But still, you cannot call that vision as strictly objective because a man who may be sitting by your side, he will not see it. Because his mind is impure, he can't see it. Only a man or woman who has purified the mind will see it. So, you cannot call it strictly an objective vision. That point, you catch me?

Disciple: Yes.

July 29, 1973

Reading: *In enjoying one desired object, you give rise to hundreds of new desires connected with that one act which gives you only momentary pleasure. The after-effect is everlasting pain and misery. It is by curbing and controlling all desires that you can gain Peace and Bliss. Repress, restrain and check them before they become too strong or else you will be thrown into eternal perdition.*

Swamiji: Eternal perdition, don't take the words exactly. You take only the meaning. Long suffering is called eternal perdition. That is all. Eternal heaven and hell, as we have been discussing, are only childish games. To make a man righteous, work hard and take the right line, that is the meaning behind all these things.

Disciple: Swamiji, how can it be that people we call "genius" often end in the madhouse? We say, "From being a genius to a mad-cap, there is not far between."

Swamiji: All inspired people, the so-called "geniuses", they have partial rising of the shakti. There will be heat going to the brain center, constantly strong currents. First, they can't sleep. If you ask those geniuses, they can't sleep, I think?

Disciple: When they are working on a subject, they can't sleep.

Swamiji: That is what I am saying. Genius comes in that way. First, they can't sleep, then the sleeplessness continues and they go to the madhouse.

Disciple: Yes, but they can be a genius for many years before they go to the madhouse.

Swamiji: That is all right. It is possible.

Disciple: Isn't it a question of the creative power, if they can go on creating?

Swamiji: All creative power comes with the partial rising of the shakti. The shakti must rise up you see.

Disciple: Yes, as long as you can check this partial rising.

Swamiji: He might have worked on the subject in a past life so knowledge was there. Now, with the partial rising of the shakti, it comes up and you call him a genius. When it is beyond his control, then he goes mad.

Disciple: Many great artists say this, "If I do not work, I will go mad."

Swamiji: That is a fact.

Disciple: They have to work all the time.

Swamiji: They have cultivated that habit. Then there is a limit for that also. When they go beyond the limit, they go to the madhouse. That is all.

Disciple: Those people who are just mad and those who are possessed, they are, here in the west, called mad - all of them.

Swamiji: That is some evil spirits taking possession of a person. They don't live always in that way. Sometimes it comes. It may remain in the person for one or two hours. Then it goes away.

Disciple: These people they call momentarily mad.

Swamiji: That is not madness in that way. They are possessed. That is not madness.
Disciple: No.
Swamiji: They have given a wrong word. They don't admit devils. Sometimes they will speak some strange language also.
Disciple: Yes. How is it possible that there can be two Jivas in one body?
Swamiji: When the devil enters, you are no more. You are suppressed. You can't speak. You have no will power of your own. You are kept down as a slave. It acts and speaks through your body. Sometimes they want to eat and drink. They ask for it. If you are a man of strong will power, you will never allow it. If you are weak and timid, then only they can come.
Disciple: Where do they enter through?
Swamiji: In so many ways, during sleep or through food and drink.
Disciple: How to get free of them?
Swamiji: Some tantrics, they can control it. If you are strong enough in your mantra, they cannot come also. The main thing is to make your mantra strong. That will save you from all these troubles. Be strong.

July 30, 1973
Reading: *Ordinary meditation means deep thought and serious contemplation and revolving things in the mind. But in the spiritual realm meditation connotes serious thinking about and constant living in one's Ishta-Devata and Ishta-Mantra (God and Its Name) and diving deep into the Ishta-Devata's Divine qualities.*
Swamiji: The easiest method here is to go on with your mantra-jap. But, in the first stage, you cannot meditate properly. It is not easy. When you take precautions and go on with the mantra, it will take you to meditation. That is the secret. It is a point one has to keep in mind. Go on. Devote your time with mantra-jap. Go on repeating the mantra. Many other thoughts will come in the beginning. Therefore, many people make a complaint saying, "I get so many thoughts. I cannot

meditate. I can't sit. I can't repeat the mantra also." Sometimes people feel like that. But have patience and continue the process. Slowly and steadily, it will become easier for you. Go on with the mantra. By constantly repeating the mantra, the mind will settle down and you will get deep concentration later on. So, go on with the mantra. That is the way.

Reading: *As has been said, the mind is a subtle thing without any form and colour of its own. But it takes the form and colour of the thought-object. The mind of an average man cannot conceive of God without the aid of a name and form. And the form may be gross or subtle. When one constantly takes the Divine Name (mantra) and lives in the Divine Form, one's mind takes after that Form of God and casts away all past impure and sinful desires and thoughts. Meditation is the key to the purity of the mind and the heart.*

Swamiji: Here, "mind and heart" mean the same. It is an English term. Sometimes people speak of an "inner voice" and they make a confusion there because they don't know what that thought is or from where it comes. They feel it in the heart region so they take "mind and heart" as one thing. This is actually a wrong idea though we are using the English phrase here. In a deeper sense, there is no heart function. How could there be? Knowledge comes from chitta. But they don't know chitta. Therefore, they have put it as "mind and heart" but "heart" has no meaning here. Only the feeling is at the heart center. Every one feels desire, hatred, anger, sorrow or joy in the heart. When there is sorrow, you feel the heart squeezed, as it were, and then comes weeping. Something gushes up from the region of the spleen which you cannot control. The feeling overpowers you and you begin to weep or laugh. Every one can watch it. So, all the emotions creep up from chitta but you feel them at the heart center.

To return to our subject: The easiest method to control the mind is to not worry about meditation. Go on with the mantra. When other thoughts come, go on! Repeat the mantra quickly, as quickly as possible. Then the disturbing thoughts will disappear. Go on with your mantra and you gain concentration after some time. Don't get confused there. In this way, you have to proceed. So, you cannot meditate in the beginning. That is why I tell every one to go on with the mantra. That will develop into meditation.

Then again, when you go on with regular and systematic work, after some time, the mantra also will stop and you go to higher pitches. When the mantra stops, don't drag the mind down to mantra again! The mantra stops but the mind will be going with the meaning in the subtle region. Your mind gets concentrated in a subtle way. Go on with it. Pursue the concentration! Don't drag the mind to mantra. That means you are disturbing your own concentration and growth. Don't do it. There you must be careful.

Another trouble is: Some people start with meditation in the heart center and they say, "The mind easily gets concentrated on another place." It doesn't matter. Then, forget the body, wherever it goes. Allow the concentration to grow. Then you can develop it.

Then some others have difficulties with heat coming up. Their kundalini is rising up and they want to see that kundalini. If they watch it, everything is gone! The mind must get rid of everything or else the concentration is gone. But some have a tendency to watch the kundalini: "My kundalini has woken up. My kundalini has come to this center." Some will say: "The current was coming. How did it come up? Through which nadis?" These are horrible questions for nothing. Thereby, the ego grows unconsciously.

Then, some people have the tendency to tackle the kundalini shakti, "Let me wake it up soon." Then they go on with too much pranayama or other exercises. Though they are not told to do pranayama, they do it. And then they hide it also. When there are some bad results, they hide them and say, "I have got some pain here." They hide it because they are ashamed. They know they will be caught and asked, "Why have you taken up that thing without telling?" So, they make some lame excuses and say they have got some severe pain in the lungs or they say, "I can't breathe." These are all dangerous things. So, one must be careful there.

Never tackle the shakti! It is a very, very bad thing. Don't meddle with it. It is a dangerous game. Thereby, you are playing with your own life. Allow the shakti as it is. In due time, it will rise up when you gain threefold purity: of the body, the nadis and the mind. When you go on with mantra-jap, it brings purity of the body, nadis and mind. All the three kinds of purity take place with mantra-jap. That is the easiest process. And when you go on with mantra-jap, the shakti automatically works by Itself. The shakti will take care of Itself. Don't worry about it. Don't tackle it untimely. Don't raise it up by force. That's a dangerous game. Take precautions there and keep this in mind always, every one of you.

Reading: *Without meditation no Knowledge and no Wisdom is possible. When we seriously think and meditate upon God, His might and glories, the mind begins constantly to live in those high, noble and sublime ideas and gets metamorphosed slowly but surely till in the long run those very noble and sublime ideas manifest themselves in it. Contrarily, an ordinary mind living constantly in low, mundane things of the senses becomes impure, weak and sinful.*

Swamiji: It was only in this respect that I sometimes criticized the Christian idea of the so-called "original sin". The original sin committed by Eve. That is still going on even now, for every one. Then again, they have the repentance, "O God, I am a sinner. I have committed this thing. Forgive me!" Thereby, you are giving wrong impressions to the mind and chitta. That means, by constantly thinking wrong thoughts, you become a sinner ere long. Really, it is so. As you think, that you become. What you have sown in the past in the form of desires, thoughts and acts you are reaping now, in this birth. And now you have to rise up! If you have done some wrong things, sinful things and slips, all right. Get it out now! Make a firm resolve and say, "I will not do it hereafter. I must be strong." Then you will be strong. On the other hand, again and again thinking of the past sins, you are giving wrong impressions to the mind and chitta. Actually, you become a sinner ere long. Never do that thing. Say, "I have done sins. All right. That is gone. Hereafter, I will not do it. I must not do it." Be strong in that way. Rise up! And then really you will rise up.

The mind is a subtle force having Consciousness at its back. Whatever thought you have, the mind projects the thought form accordingly. So, when you constantly think about your past sins, you are giving wrong impressions to the chitta. And they accumulate there. On the other hand, if you give strong and good impressions, the mind constantly lives in them and you become good ere long. So, never make such mistakes in life. That is a great misfortune to think in that way.

Reading: *In short, rise and fall of a man depends entirely upon his own desires and thoughts.*

Swamiji: So, no one else is responsible for your rise or fall. There is no God to put you to hell or to raise you to heaven. Both are in you. It is with your mind. The way of your thinking, how you live, is decisive. If you take the right line, right thinking, you rise up. By wrong thinking, you go down. All these things, this play is made by you only. Nobody else has made it. Every one of you is responsible for it. Nobody else. You can't blame anyone. Don't be weak in that way.

Reading: *Meditation is of two kinds, vis., Saguna (with form) and Nirguna (without form). Saguna meditation means contemplation in one's own heart center on the Form of one's Ishta-Devata (the Deity that one likes and loves the most) and Its Divine qualities. Nirguna meditation is contemplation on the Formless Aspect of Brahman. It is easier and safer for an ordinary man to meditate upon the Saguna Aspect of God, because he cannot contemplate without the aid of a name and a form. The Formless Aspect of God is very difficult to comprehend and much more difficult to contemplate upon. It can be conceived, understood and realized in Nirvikalpa Samadhi only. In this state alone does pure adwaita (absolute monism) prevail. Apart from this state, life means perception of dwaita (duality). An impure mind can think of the Supreme Reality only with the aid of a name and a form.*

Swamiji: Are there any difficulties with this? Many people want to take that Nirguna aspect. They think, "Why all these forms? They are all false. I must go to the formless aspect." There are also some sects in India who make a big quarrel. They think, "All forms are false. Why should we worship them?" And some of the priests going to preach Christianity from the west call the whole of Hinduism idolatrous. They say, "They are worshipping images." And the Christians do the same. It may be that the Hindus are using black stones and the Christians have white marble stones because they are rich. But the marble stones and the beautiful churches are also images. Then, why should the Christians hate the Hindus? That is mere ignorance. If you have tolerance, if you have patience and go deep into the subject, you will understand the necessity of form in meditation. To meditate, you require some sort of gross form. Whatever form you take, your progress depends upon your faith and sincerity and work.

When you go deeper in meditation, you will not stand in the same place. That's why they say in an English proverb, "It is good to be born in church but very bad to die in church." The meaning is that it is good to be born with all good environments, going to church, having devotion to God and all facilities. But to die in the same way, without any progress, it is very bad. So, temples, churches, mosques, paGodas, etc., are all the kindergarten classes. Just like using the alphabet in the beginning. These are necessary things. But, if you stay at the same stage, learning the alphabet only, without making any progress, it is very bad. Then life has no meaning. So, one has to make progress. You have to rise up.

The church never speaks about meditation at all. And they don't know anything about it. Forty years ago, a Buddhist monk came to me to learn yoga. He had about forty monasteries under his control. He used to go to the universities to lecture on Buddhism. But the funniest thing was, he didn't know how to meditate.

Then again, one of the big organizations had a magazine and in that they were giving pranayama lessons to the public. And one of the brahmacharies, in 1950, wanted to learn pranayama from me. He was one of those giving lessons in pranayama and he wanted to learn pranayama! I got annoyed. I took him to task like anything. For one hour I gave him scoldings like, "Wretched people, what are you doing? You are teaching pranayama and you don't even know it yourselves. You have been teaching pranayama to the public. What a horrible thing!" Then I said, "I will not teach you anything today. Come tomorrow or the day after then I will see." Then he became afraid and he never returned at all. But they are all big "Gurus" giving pranayama lessons. That is the story going everywhere. There are so many Gurus, big Gurus. The paper propaganda makes them very big. Even the universe cannot hold them! It is horrible Gurus. This is a funny thing going on. It is a misfortune, rather. How many go mad? That is a thing to be seen. When they go further, they will understand.

There are so many others who are proud of their egos. They don't want to become disciples. They want to find new light in yoga. One young man was with me. He was proud. I asked him, "Why have you come?"

He had so many doubts. He had made a long list of all the questions. But he was proud. He didn't want to take a Guru or any guidance. Then what is the aim of coming to another? I answered one or two questions, and then I said, "You get out! I don't want to answer more. If you don't want a Guru, go and find out yourself. If you want to make a yoga school of your own, all right. Go on. Make a search." They don't understand anything.

Take another example. In physics, they started with the gross matter and they came to the Atom Theory. They came to the conclusion: there is the atom. And there are negative and positive currents which they called electrons and protons. That was the last point up to 1962. Then they split the atom. They know there is no matter. There is only energy. To come to this understanding has taken several centuries of experiments. There were thousands of men, not only one, who contributed little by little. If a man were to start from the Newton Theory, where would he end if he wants to found a new school, to do new research? What a stupid creature. He would not come to any conclusion. Within twenty or thirty years, he would die and that would be the end of his research. How could he come to this last point? How many of you have seen that particle or the negative or positive currents? Nobody. We have heard about it only. Like that, the child says, "I will make new research in yoga." They will read some books, that means, steal some ideas, and they will write something and people will think they are "big yogis". Their spiritual progress will stop. Many go mad and some more go to the madhouse, if there is any vacancy now. The Danish jails are full of hash people. They let many people out because there is no place in the jails and much less in the madhouse. That is the fun going on.

Reading: *Taking for granted that you have selected your Ishta-Devata and Ishta-Mantra and want to practise meditation, proceed as follows: Sit erect and worship your Guru and Ishta-Devata in the heart center and fill your mind with this idea: "Brahman the Supreme Reality is Formless but, at the same time, It can take numerous Forms also. Brahman is bigger than the biggest object and smaller than the smallest. Brahman is everywhere and in everything. It is Sat-Chit-Ananda (Existence, Knowledge and Bliss Absolute). The same Infinite* *and Eternal Brahman is in the form of my Ishta-Devata and my Ishta-Devata is my Atman (Self) in the heart center." Imagine and perceive that your Ishta-Devata is actually in the heart center seated on a full-blown lotus of eight petals, with a radiant body, smiling face and shining with silvery Divine Light. Now, select some of the good qualities that you want to develop in you to root out the evil ones. Let these be, truthfulness, brahmacharya (celibacy), pure love, charity, unselfishness, strength, good health, character, purity, contentment, etc. Meditate on them with all your heart and all your spirit.*

Swamiji: The easiest method will be in the time of meditation just to go on with your mantra. And then, in your spare time, when you are doing your work, some of these ideas must go on as a routine. It is more profitable to use them at such times. It is easy also. When you are sitting for meditation and doing mantra-jap, then go on and dive deep in the mantra itself. It will serve all the purposes. But besides this, if you want to develop some of these qualities, then go on repeating this process in your spare time when you are walking or doing some work in the garden or doing some other work, physical work especially. Some of the divine qualities which you want to develop, go on with them! Take one quality, brahmacharya, for example. You go on uttering the mantra four or five times and at the same time, think of perfect brahmacharya. Say, "I must gain it." Put some ideas in that way. Or take truthfulness or other divine qualities, whichever one you want to develop.

Disciple: Please give another example.

Swamiji: Suppose you are working as a nurse in the hospital. When you are doing that work, go on repeating the mantra mentally. If you want to be strong, say, "I have no more disease. I am strong. I am healthy." Give that suggestion. "I am not weak. I am strong, strong, strong." Give impressions in that way. By constantly thinking you are strong, you become strong. You have to negate all wrong ideas and create good impressions.

Disciple: What if the person at the same time is dying?

Swamiji: Death must come. At the same time, you say, "I am not dying. Death is only to the body." Put that idea. Why should you weep for the body? Why should you worry?

Disciple: It's just that you say, "I am perfect" and at the same time ...

Swamiji: Yes, say, "I am not dying. There is no death for me. Only the body is dying. Let it go." Put it off. It is just like an old worn-out coat. Throw it out! Why should you worry about it? You get a new coat. Death is like throwing the old coat away and putting on a new one. Who will weep for getting a new coat? Nobody will weep. One must be strong in that way. By habit, everything is possible. It is not mere exaggeration. By mere cultivation, by practice, if you go on doing this process, you will actually come to the high pitch. The mind gets established in that perfect Truth and nothing can drag you down. All these things will have no meaning.

Disciple: But if a person sits in an office where there is much talking?

Swamiji: What of that thing? Why should you talk? Let them speak but you go on internally with mantra-jap. Sit as if you were in the office but let the mind vibrate with the mantra. Then, why should you worry? If you are busy with your mantra, you will forget the talk. You will not hear the talk. That is the secret. Busy the mind! Engage the mind in thinking of the mantra again and again. Then you forget other things. We generally do this when people come and talk nonsense, they think we are hearing them but we don't hear. They think that, "He is hearing everything. He is very sympathetic, very kind, gentle and noble. He heard me, everything." We don't hear anything. That is the way and what about other work such as office work? Let there be talking there. Or say, you are going to a social gathering, all right. You are also there. Let them eat and drink. You sit there as if you are one with them. But you are in quite a different world. Act in that way. Then what more examples do you want?

Disciple: These were good examples.

Swamiji: A girl was telling, "I am working in a bank office. There are so many dirty things. I have a lot of extra time." I said, "Go on writing your mantra. They will think you are doing the office work." She took it up. It was all right.

In this way, you have to change it. Where there is a will, there is a way. If you actually want to make progress, you will find some time. And if you don't want to work, then you have so many lame excuses. Then you will say, "I have no time."

When I was a young student, nobody taught me meditation. I had no Guru or guidance. But I had a tendency to meditate even as a young boy. I was meditating morning and evening. We had to live in the hostels. There were some mischievous boys. Of course, these children of disciples here are fortunate. They have got good society, good encouragement for a spiritual life. But in India, it was terrible. We had to live in big dormitories. And all the mischievous boys would cut jokes and make a hell of the thing if you sat for meditation. So, I used to sit and meditate on my own bed in the evening, after they had gone to sleep, and in the morning before they rose. When the time came for getting up, I was pretending to sleep and pretending that I was getting up with them. So, nobody knew about my meditation.

It is always possible to cultivate meditation if you want. In this way, you can cultivate meditation wherever you go. But you must have the desire: "I must finish all those things. I must meditate. I must do mantra-jap." Even when you are travelling on a train with other people, you may do your sadhana also. It is possible. They may not know. Turn your face to the window and sit quietly as if you are seeing the outer things. But go on with your mantra. You can meditate also. In one corner, sit and meditate. That can be done, if you want to do it. If you have no mind to do it, then you have so many lame excuses. Any other points? Is it clear? Or any doubt?

Disciple: No, it is only to do it.

Swamiji: You have to do it. Every one has to do it. That is why it is said: first you have to hear and then to think over the matter. And then lastly, you have to act. Without action, nothing can be gained. That is a secret. Every one of you must first hear, then think over the matter and have a strong impression of what you have to do. Then meditate. Then you have to attain the Highest. That is a secret.

All right. Sit for meditation.

July 31, 1973

Disciple: Does the science of astrology come from the old Babylonia or from the Transcendental Plane?

Swamiji: It was an old science in India. Different people made different research on a variety of subjects. Especially the Brahmins after reading the Vedas, they used to devote their full time in meditation on a particular subject such as palmistry, astronomy and astrology. It is all made by the old Rishis. Rishi means seer. They might have concentrated on a particular thing and then gone to that region and found out the things. Or, it may be by samyama. It is another process. That is pratyahara, dharana, dhyana and Samadhi. You take a particular subject and then think over the matter and go into a sort of trance. When you come down, you have the knowledge of the subject. Many people have made use of that during the last war even in detecting Hitler's U-boats. That was all detected by the English people by this process. They got it from India and they were developing it secretly. They take a pendulum and concentrate on that idea and mentally they see the thing, the photo of that object and they can tell exactly which way it is going, how far away it is.

Disciple: Swamiji, will you tell us how to handle a person who is in Samadhi?

Swamiji: Keep him at least three days if a person is in Samadhi. Then try to bring him down.

Disciple: How?

Swamiji: You can utter "OM" into the ear slowly. That will have an effect, nothing else, only OM. Go on uttering, "OM". Slowly and steadily, that will bring him down.

Disciple: I think if it were me, I would rather stay there.

Swamiji: Yes, if you are disgusted with the world, you may think like that. There may be some others who want it. There may be different varieties of Samadhi. Nirvikalpa is quite different. Still, you can try there. But don't try for three days. After three days, if it is really Samadhi, the body will not get that bad smell after death. It will remain as fresh as anything. That is the state of Samadhi. Keep him for three days then he becomes perfect in that Samadhi state. After three days, you can bring him back by uttering OM. That is the only process.

Disciple: What is the meaning of the word atheist?

Swamiji: Those who do not believe in the existence of God, they are called atheists. But actually, there are no atheists in the world. It is all mere words. It is impossible. So long as you have the idea of disease and death, there can never be atheists. You may say there is no God but with all that, you know there is some power behind. The same man, who says there is no God, says there is nature or a supreme force. All different names but the thing is the same. From the heart of hearts, every man knows there is some power behind which controls him. So, how can you be an atheist in that way?

Disciple: If the mantra has been predominating during a lifetime, will the mantra automatically be there in the moment of death?

Swamiji: I am telling, if you get it you are fortunate but in order to get it, you have to practise it constantly. If you are lazy now, you can't remember it. Laziness will come while dying also. So, preparation must be there. Make it strong then. That will help you. That is why they often give God's name to children in India.

There is a story. There was a young boy, he was a Brahmin boy and he went to fetch some flowers in the forest. There he saw a man with a prostitute. They were having sex. He was hiding and seeing them and afterwards, he fell in love with that prostitute and left the Guru. They married and had a lot of children. Anyway, he gave the name Narayan to one of his sons. The father was going to die and he began to call his son Narayan. Then, the death God came there. He wanted to take him but when he heard the name Narayan, he got frightened and couldn't take him. He was saved by that word. Instead of going to hell, he went to heaven. That is a story just to explain the efficacy of that name. That is all. He could remember the name of Narayan at the last point and that saved him. It indicates how powerful God's name is. Generally, they give children one of God's names, that is the custom in India.

August 1, 1973

Disciple: In your book, you describe ten sorts of Gurus. What kind of Guru do you belong to?

Swamiji: I know only to chitchat and laugh. I know only that much with you people. So, I have not called myself a Guru. Who told you that I am one of the ten? Have I told it to anyone?

Disciple: No.

Swamiji: Then, I tell you, I don't belong to any of them. What kind of Guru do you want? I have not called myself a Guru. I am just a playfellow with you. Come here, then go back and sleep. That is all my work. If someone comes, I give one or two scoldings, then go, and I have finished the work in that way. So, there ends the question.

Disciple: I understand in that way that it will depend on the disciple how the Guru is.

Swamiji: You may understand it in that way. In whatever way you understand it, it will suit you. That is all.

Disciple: Swamiji, some time ago you told us that it was impossible to make any progress without a Guru and that we couldn't practise without a Guru? Now, you tell us that you do not look upon yourself as a Guru.

Swamiji: I have been saying there are different kinds of people. There are some people who have worked very hard and have come to a high pitch of evolution. Before attaining Samadhi, they have their death. Such people, when they come to the next birth, they easily find their way and attain the highest within no time. There are very few of that kind.

Then there are others who are born perfect, who have advanced more. Then comes death. Even after dying, they work in the subtle sphere. They continue their sadhana and lastly, they take birth as Jivan-Muktas, by birth itself. From the very mother's womb, they are Jnanis. That is another kind.

For ordinary people, there is a third grade. There are some people who worked also and they require guidance, you understand? It is the third grade. They require a Guru.

And then there is the fourth grade. They require hundreds of Gurus. So, there are four groups. The last two groups, they require a Guru. Without a Guru, they cannot make progress. Even with a Guru, they make so many blunders, so many mistakes, so many faults. The fourth grade, so horrible it is. There must be always a Guru behind them with a big stick to beat them. But the first, they are not in need of a Guru. That is what is meant. Is it clear to you?

Disciple: Yes.

Disciple: Will one become more clever at work and in life when meditating?

Swamiji: That is a fact. One will become more clever and more concentrated. You can do better work when you meditate. You have peace of mind and the mind is also well concentrated.

August 2, 1973
Reading: *If you want speedy results, you must sit down for meditation four-times a day: morning, midday, evening and midnight.*
Swamiji: But when you have heavy work, don't go for that process at all. It will be very dangerous. There will be terrible work. Many of you have to work the whole day and it will be very difficult. What will happen? You will have to sleep and sleep then sitting and dozing. It is given in that way. It is all right. Those who have got enough time, they must do it. When you have retired, say you have got all comforts, food and other things, then you have no other work. Such people must devote at last twelve hours. Then only your life will be fruitful there.

And those who have got heavy work, use your common sense. For example, when I was young, twelve hours was a minimum and sixteen hours a maximum. So, thereby, I don't ask every one to take it up in that way. It is not easy. You must be able to engage the mind. You must use your common sense at every step you take. When you have got very heavy physical work, two or three times, that is all right. In daytime, when you are doing all kinds of physical work, remember the mantra. That is the easiest. Thereby you don't strain yourself. That becomes an easy process. You follow it or not, every one of you? Those who have heavy work, don't go for four times. It will be a burden. Many people cannot handle it. Then it becomes rather disgusting – a monotony. Then every one wants to run away. No one wants to work. Even meditation also becomes boring, a sort of terrible devil. Instead of enjoying it, it becomes a sort of punishment. You say, "Oh, it is hellfire." Don't make it in that way.

At every step, you must be able to enjoy it. After meditation, every one of you must feel strength. Then you have progressed in meditation. That you can say. On the other hand, if you feel discomfort, weakness and drowsiness even after meditation that means you have not done anything. So, you have to use your common sense, every one of you. Thereby, never give up and say, "Swamiji told us to do it only twice a day." That should not be. Effort must be there. See your capacity first, how much you can do. Don't be easy-going. Another difficulty comes there. Many people will go in a wrong direction by saying Swamiji told us to sit only twice a day. They have an easy-going life. For everything, there is Swamiji. For all things, they will put Swamiji there. That is an end of everything. Laziness is from your side and you will put Swamiji there, like a target for shooting. That is wrong.

Reading: *And apart from these sitting hours, your mind must be kept fully and constantly engaged in thinking of your Ishta-Devata and the Ishta-Mantra.*
Swamiji: There is no lame excuse for it. Take the second point. Now make it strong, every one of you. Don't be easy-going. Even if you are doing work, concentrate the mind mentally. Don't gossip. Repeat the mantra constantly. That every one can do. There is no excuse for it if you fail. You have to engage the mind. Of course, those who are teachers, teaching and speaking, it cannot be done. But still, there is time. Start the work with mantra. Dedicate it to God. Offer everything unto God, think that it is His work. The earning and the pay are for God. In that way give it. If you adopt this method, then every work becomes a sort of worship. That is also a sort of progress. It will help your progress without any doubt. This, everyone can do. There is no lame excuse for these things. If you can't do it, it is only your laziness. That is all right.

Reading: *To begin with, the mind will wander restlessly. It would jump from place to place and from object to object.*
Swamiji: Every one has to face these things. In the beginning, every one will have this tendency. The mind will wander and many people get dejected. "Oh, my mind wanders here and there. I cannot meditate. I cannot concentrate." That is the complaint. So, it will wander, not only one, every one will experience it in the beginning. But if you have patience and work it out daily and regularly and systematically,

everything will come under control. If you are very sincere and work hard, even in fifteen days, there will be a lot of change. It will come to a standstill but there must be a hard struggle. Those who have work, it will take a little time. Even then, don't get dejected. Go on, have patience and perseverance, it should come.

Reading: *Innumerable desires and thoughts would rise up one after another like waves in an ocean.*
Swamiji: And then again, sometimes it is so terrible. You may get so many desires and thoughts you have never thought of. They may be evil or good ones also. That is due to your past samskaras, that means impressions in the chitta. Suppose, you take a pot of dirty water and keep it in one corner of the room at night. In the morning when you go and see the surface, it seems to be very clear but when you take a stick and stir it, the sediment, which is at the bottom, comes up.

Similarly, when you are not meditating, you are seeing the water from the surface. There are no more desires in the mind. It seems to be calm and quiet but when you meditate or after every deep thinking, you are stirring the chitta and things from the past life come up sometimes. Some thoughts may be very terrible which you have thought in the past life and that is why such thoughts come even when you have not thought anything like this in this life. Thereby, don't get frightened by these things. Only go on with your mantra. It will change you and it cannot disturb you. You must have patience and perseverance. So, every one will get it. In the beginning, there will be distractions. There will be innumerable thoughts coming up. But the only medicine is to purify the mind and the purification is mantra-jap. Go on with it. That is the easiest process. These are vital things which are absolutely necessary for every one to keep in mind.

Never forget all these things. Especially in the time of reaction terrible thoughts from past lives have a very bad effect on a person. But, if you keep this in mind, you understand this is reaction. Every one gets it; so, you must face it. Not by running away from the place. You have to work it out. You have done the mischief and who else will face it now, nobody. By running away, you will not do any good. On the other hand, you are injuring yourself more and more. Keeping that idea in the mind, face it. Whatever danger or difficulty comes, face it boldly and, after some time, your karma is gone. You have worked it out. You have paid the debt. Now, be simple and sincere. Work it out. Go ahead. Take the right and noble path. That is the only way to success.

Reading: *Many Sadhakas get afraid. They are full of fears for themselves. And in utter desperation they leave off work and give up all effort.*
Swamiji: That is still worse. A terrible hell it is to leave off work and go away, to stop meditation. It is very terrible. Then you have to pay double. For one hour's work, you have to work for three hours later on. Never do that. That is a very great mistake to do it in that way. Whatever may be going on, carry on the work. Success will come.

Reading: *Many even put the questions: "Why does the mind wander like this? Why do evil, wicked and vulgar thoughts arise during meditation?"*
Swamiji: Many people say, "I have committed a sin because such thoughts come." What a horrible state it is. Automatic thought currents are coming. You have no control over them. Then, it is also not a sin there. It comes. It goes. Kick it out. Have courage to do it. Never repent over it. Repenting means you are giving importance to such vulgar things. It will become stronger and stronger. Do kick it out. It comes and goes. It has come. Let it go. You are not responsible for it now. In that way be bold and work hard and walk ahead. That is the only way to get success.
Disciple: Swamiji, will the mantra destroy all the past impressions in the chitta?
Swamiji: It will purify. Even if the same thought may come, a bad thought, it has no power. It comes and goes. It has no meaning. It is just like a passing cloud.

August 3, 1973
Reading: *It is by constant and systematic meditation, therefore, that one can purify the mind and chitta.*
Swamiji: So, there must be steady work. Doing the work in a haphazard way will take a longer time. Someone was telling this morning, "I have been doing mantra-jap in a haphazard way for two years and I have not gained anything." Then I asked how many hours he had devoted. It may not be even one month combined. In one month, you want to attain without doing any kind of work. You only count the years, not the hours of work. That is dangerous. Be practical there. If you work hard and systematically, everything will come. I give a guarantee there. Those who are hardworking and don't get anything can come and ask such questions. But, without working and wasting your time here and there, if you want to progress, it is not possible. So, be practical, work hard and you will get the thing. If any of you have worked hard and did not get any result, come forward. You have worked hard?
Disciple: Sometimes.
Swamiji: Sometimes, not always?
Disciple: I do it now.
Swamiji: So, it is all gone. You have no right to ask it. You have to wait. If any of you have worked very hard, without any result, come forward.
Disciple: It is very difficult to know what hard work is.
Swamiji: Hard work is at least systematic work.
Disciple: For how long?
Swamiji: Since you took mantra. When you work, really work, you have satisfaction from inside and your inner voice itself, your conscience itself will tell you, "Yes, I have done my work." And if you don't really work, you have no satisfaction. You, yourself, say, "I have not worked very hard." Have you noticed all these things? When you actually work hard, on that day you have satisfaction. If you don't work hard, you have no satisfaction. You feel impatience and you, yourself, will say, "I have not worked very hard." Regulate your life. That is also necessary. When you go on working regularly and systematically, you get results. There is no one to withhold it.

Reading: *Thus, it is not easy to meditate in the beginning. The mind oscillates, one feels tired and meditation become insipid.*

Swamiji: It is a momentary stage. Then, there are other difficulties. When you really observe celibacy, the first thing is you get constipation and, with many people, the mind also works very dully. That is the first stage, as I told you the other day. While churning the ocean to get nectar, the first thing you got was the poison. In the beginning, some people get some sort of stomach disorder. All these things you get in the initial stages. One must be careful there. The remedy we have already given. If you have patience and perseverance, you can control it easily. That is the secret. Regulate your life. Take precaution about your diet during that state and everything will be okay. Never fall down. It is just like people smoking hash, they want to stop it. Then comes a dull state, a great temptation, the mind does not work. Then again, they go back. Let me have one pipe more, the last pipe, and that last pipe will never come to an end. They will go on and on, he is fooled. Never yield to temptation there in that way. Withstand it and it will run away.

Reading: *Some can easily meditate on the heart center, while others find it very difficult to do so. They should, therefore, learn to fix the mind on the crown of the head, i.e., the brain center, or in between the eyebrows.*

Swamiji: There is the danger. That is why I tell you the heart center is the best thing. If you want to know the secrets of the mind and it's working, you must concentrate in the heart center. It is the best. And then again, many people, when they don't get concentration, they strain the brain and that brings headache. So, avoid it. Don't force it in that way. The easiest method is to go on with the mantra, slowly and steadily. Then love and devotion increases. The concentration must be with love and devotion. Then it is fruitful and then you don't feel any kind of pain or strain. When the devotion becomes greater and greater, your concentration also deepens and you have more and more joy. And that is how some people have been telling, "If one gets a desire for doing more and more mantra-jap or meditation, during that time, allow it." There will be a sort of partial rising. The shakti must rise up there, when you come to that pitch and that makes you work hard without any strain. You feel pleasure. You feel happiness. And you may say you don't notice the time also. How many hours have passed in that happiness? When you come to that pitch, allow the mind. Not during the working hours, when you want to go to school and you get concentration, but other times. Those who stay at home, when they get it, all right allow the mind to stay in that pitch. It is helpful in that way.

Reading: *When once a particular part of the body has been chosen as the center of meditation and when a certain path as been chalked out for work, no change whatsoever should be made in them.*

Swamiji: But there, don't make a confusion. Sometimes, when you start in the heart, when the mind concentrates, it must go the third eye (ajna). If it goes automatically, without any strain, you can hold it there. Then forget the body. There, keep the point in the mind always. If the vision is there clearly, you can concentrate there. Don't drag it to the heart. Then there will be distraction in concentration. There you have to keep this understanding. Don't make mistakes. During meditation, the mantra may also stop sometimes but the image is still there in front. Don't drag the mind to the mantra again. Go on with the image, if the meaning is there. After coming to that point, again the mind may wander here and there. Then, take the mantra. If not, continue the concentration and that will deepen. There you will have to be careful. Don't make any mistakes.

Disciple: Where is the heart center situated?

Swamiji: There are four centers. There, many make a confusion. One is here in the center of the chest meant for meditation. The other is the spiritual heart center in the right side of the chest two inches above the heart-pit and a little below the right nipple. And the physical heart is in the left side. And the fourth is at the sushumna nadi. It is anahata chakra. There are four centers there in this region.

Reading: *The same is true of sadhana, if one goes on changing Guru, Mantra, Ishta-Devata and the mode of work. The fickle mind plays tricks and deceives.*

Swamiji: So, this applies to changing the mantra, changing the Guru and so many other things. Some will go from one Guru to another. Such people will come to no conclusion at all. That is a mere waste of time.

Stick to one principle. Work hard. It will come. Focus on your center. Go on. After some days, it will be easy also. Even if you find it difficult to start with, it will become easy. No center is easy in that way. When the mind becomes pure, subtle and one-pointed, you will succeed in all these things. Then you can concentrate on any center. But to start with, until you gain that perfection to a great extent, it is better to follow one method always and never change the mantra. It is very dangerous.

From the very outset, one must very careful. When there is any sort of propaganda, suspect the person completely. Where there is a display of all these things, the worldly things, think that there is something wrong. As a young boy, Benjamin Franklin was going to school. One day he was passing by the blacksmith's. He was mending the sickles, blowing the bellows. The fire was coming. The boy got interested. He began to look at it. The blacksmith was an intelligent man. He knew the boy was interested, so he thought, "I must have some work from him." So, he began to praise the boy, "You are a very excellent boy. You are a very good boy." The boy got puffed up a little. Now, he said, "Can you do this in this way?" "Yes, I can." "You don't know how to do it." "I know it," he said. "Let me see you try?" He began exactly like the blacksmith. "Oh, you know it." And he began mending the sickles. The boy got tired. He wanted to go to school but it was too late; so, he did not leave until he finished all the sickles. Afterwards, he said, "Now you can go", when all the work was over. He went to school but it was too late. The teacher gave him a nice beating. Since that day, he took it as a lesson for the whole life. Whenever people began praising him, he thought, he has some sickles to mend. When they praise you, think in this way. So, wherever there is propaganda, don't go to that region at all. That is very dangerous.

Disciple: But Swamiji, Guru Kripa is also necessary.

Swamiji: I tell you, without work, if you sit quiet, you will not get the Guru Kripa. You have to work. When you work automatically, without asking for it, it will come. Suppose there are two boats. One man has tied the sail. He has kept it well tied and left it as it is. And the other man has kept it ready and has opened the sails. The breeze is coming and it comes you both but the man who has worked, he goes to the other side. The man who has not worked, he does not get to go there. So, there is no difference between the so-called God's Grace and Guru's Grace. It is not a special thing for any man. The man who works for it, gets it.

August 4, 1973

Reading: *It is a time fraught with serious consequences. Many give up work (sadhana) altogether or take up some new path and new practices.*

Swamiji: Here one should be very careful, that is a common thing. Every one feels it. You have no interest. Then you may think, "What is the use of uttering this word? What meaning has it? It is better to give it up and take another." Stick to it. Stick to the mantra at any cost. Don't change the mantra. Stick to one principle, one ideal, and one method. Then you make progress. If you are careless there, you have to pay for it very heavily with compound interest. You understand, double interest? Interest for interest again. So, you should be very careful.

Reading: *Spiritual growth remains stranded, as it were, with these people and they generally degenerate. For, during the time of action, the mind works well, physical health remains normal, environments are favourable and everything looks very pleasing and congenial.*

Swamiji: Everything is all right, you say. "I am making progress." Some people will say, "I will reach Nirvikalpa tonight itself or in the next hour." They think like that. Suddenly, you will see you are down somewhere. You have lost all hope and it looks as a faroff thing. Then you will think, whether you will reach it in this birth or in ten births or in thousands of births. "Will I reach it at all?" Doubt comes. The mind plays mischief with you. In reaction time, every one feels like that but one must be strong, give up all weakness and stick to the ideals. Then you will overcome the difficulty.

Reading: *Weak and wicked propensities of the mind then remain suppressed and a man feels that he is progressing fast and that the attainment of Samadhi is only a matter of days.*

Swamiji: All weakness and other evil qualities which are in the mind, they remain suppressed, not controlled. They are waiting for a chance and when you give room there, in reaction time they come. They come up to kick you down; so, you must be very careful.

Reading: But then sets in reaction during which the physical health becomes subnormal.

Swamiji: Subnormal means below normal. You feel your health is not okay. You say it is not up to the mark. You feel disgusted. Everything becomes so horrible. You can't eat. Food is also disgusting to you. You have no attraction for anything. Your friends, their company, look so horrible also. For some, the reaction comes occasionally and becomes very strong for days together. Some have even months and years together. That is a terrible state, an unknown sorrow. That is really hell. For such people, it is very difficult to withstand. Mohammed, that Muslim prophet, he had it for three years. He never went out. His wife used to cover him with a blanket. For three years, she was covering him. If not for his wife, he would have gone to pieces.

Reading: It is the time for extreme carefulness and watchfulness.

Swamiji: Many people make a mistake there. They think, "It is my past karma that has brought all these things." It is not that exactly. How do you say it is past karma? To keep it or to dispose of it, you can do it. Why do you cling to past karma? It has no meaning. So, life is a mixture of these two, past plus present. At present you can do with it and without it. You can dispose of it or you can keep it. Both are with you. It is not owing to past karma. That would be wrong to say past karma about everything. Then there is no escape from karma. And whatever comes, you have to take it. But it can be avoided also. That means fresh karma is there with you.

August 5, 1973
Reading: The best way to tide over this period is to live in the company of one's Guru or, if that be not possible, one should move in

the company of holy and pious people, and observe light fasts with prayer.

Swamiji: Yes, reaction times, there are so many ways. Fasting will help you people very much. Absolute fast is unnecessary. You can take fruit, milk and live on a light diet. Keep the stomach empty. That will help you. Keep up your daily routine. Then you can overcome any kind of reaction. If you are strong in your mantra-jap and meditation, it will help you immensely. When the thing comes, you know it has come and you can easily overcome it. Don't get confused. If the thing comes, it will stay for some time and then it must change. Never give up hope there and continue your sadhana. It will be all right. Many people get worried for nothing in the time of reaction. It may stay for a day or two or even longer. Never lose hope. It must change. It will not continue forever in that way. This thing may come, the past karma. If there has been something very bad then it comes very strongly. That you have to face now. That every one must keep in mind. That will help you immensely.

Disciple: To have reaction, is that a kind of paying for earlier sins?

Swamiji: Yes, what else? How do you account for it then? Is it for merits? How do you account for it?

Disciple: In that way.

Swamiji: That is the easiest way to understand. Something has been done wrong in the past life. That is prarabdha and that you have to pay for. Face it now. Work it out. It will pass away. That is a good understanding to have in that way. You are safe.

Disciple: So, reaction is a kind of progress?

Swamiji: Yes, if you face it boldly, then you have worked out your karma. With many people, it becomes so severe they commit suicide. That is cowardice, a great sin. After committing suicide, you go back to hell. In the first state, you have to remain as a devil. What a horrible thing it is. Then you have to live that life — after that, death. Again, you take birth but you may not gain human birth. You may go to some lower life. So, you have lost the chance. That is very bad.

Reading: *During sadhana, if you succeed in fixing the mind at will to anyone place and are able to hold it at that particular place at least for a few seconds, you have certainly made good progress.*

Swamiji: You understand what is meant by pratyahara, all of you? Now you have been going on with the mantra, holding the mind, trying to fix it on the Ishta-Devata, whatever it may be, to a particular place. If you succeed in it, then you have really made great progress in your meditation. A man who has already attained to a great extent has a great will power also. Now, from pratyahara, you have to proceed further. From a place, you must go to a point and remain in that state for at least twelve seconds. That becomes dharana. And if you can keep it in that point for two and a half minutes, it becomes Dhyana and for at least half an hour, that is Samadhi. But, it is not easy. It takes a lot of time but it does not matter. Even then, proceed with it with courage. Progress will be there. Success must come. It will come.

Reading: *Your lips would be repeating the mantra but a major portion of your mind would be living in some external fascinating object.*
Swamiji: These things you have to keep in mind, every one of you. Now we are dealing with practical things. Don't lose the opportunity. That would be a great mistake for a sadhaka. For the last three or four days, we have been on a practical line. If every one will face the difficulty, you have the ready-made answers here.

Reading: *Go on with your mantra-jap and meditation. Let the desires come and go unceremoniously. Do not heed them. Do not pay any attention to them. Remain indifferent to them. But every now and then do drag the mind and put it at the feet of your Ishta-Devata.*
Swamiji: Watch the mind. Allow it. Let it see. If you allow it, the mind is so stupid. It does not want to go on with the mantra. It thinks it is to be caught; so, it will not work it out. Even if a bad thought comes, go and see that thing. What you want, allow it. What more do you want? See, you want filth, you want dust, you want dirt. Whatever you want to eat, come and see, allow it. Go further. Allow it in that way. Kick it, then it will get afraid. It does not want to run in that way there. So, it is afraid. It will come back. Allow it, whatever thought it may be. That is another focus.

Reading: *Use discrimination. When a thought comes, try to analyze it and see its ins and outs. Do not show any soft corner to it. Be merciless to it. Judge what is Real and what is unreal. Stick to the Real and discard the unreal.*

Swamiji: But this method is better to avoid during the time of meditation. Many so-called philosophers are using it constantly. Why, when, where, how that goes, avoid these things. It can be used in daytime when you are working. That is safe.

Disciple: Is it good to use the mantra the whole day?

Swamiji: Use it all the twenty-four hours, even in sleep. The more you use it, the better will be the result. The mind and chitta get purified and that is the easiest method.

Disciple: When you can keep the mind on one point for a few seconds, is that a steady thing?

Swamiji: Then you have to go further. When you come to concentration on one place, then you must take it to one point. Automatically it will go. You have to proceed with the point. You go further. Don't leave the point. Then there will be other experiences. Lastly, you get to Nirakara, formless aspect. That is the real state of God. To begin with, you have to take forms. Begin with form. You can't go to the formless aspect in the beginning. It is difficult. You will miss the point completely. Take the gross object and go to the subtle and then to the subtlest. Then there is no more form and no mind also. Everything merges. There will be only Consciousness by Itself. That is the last point.

Disciple: If while working you are too tired to keep the mind on the mantra, is it all right to talk about God with someone else?

Swamiji: You can do it. You don't get tired then?

Disciple: No.

Swamiji: Why?

Disciple: I don't know.

Swamiji: Why should you get too tired while repeating the mantra? When you are tired in that way, you must be tired in talking also. More tired?

Disciple: No.

Swamiji: You get refreshed?

Disciple: Yes.

Swamiji: All right. Have a chitchat.
Disciple: Thank you.

August 7, 1973
Reading: *Meditation on Om or the Formless Aspect of Brahman. First put to yourself the questions, who am I?*
Utter the mantra in full faith, and with deep and firm conviction. Feel whole-heartedly that you are not the filthy body and the senses but the Eternal, Infinite Spirit."
Swamiji: You have to feel it. The more you feel it, it becomes stronger and stronger. Then the time will come when you say, "All these things are false actually," and you will not care for anything. Your whole system will be vibrating with that great power. The body may not be strong, too big or fat. You may be lean and thin, full of power, and actually you feel it. This is not mere exaggeration. When you work hard, when you constantly live in that idea, your whole system changes. Then you can kick off the whole world single-handedly. When the mind goes to higher pitches, you actually see it is just like a dust particle, the whole world compared to Infinity. When the whole world itself becomes like dust, then who is rich, who is poor, who is king, who is the leader? You will kick it off like everything, like a football. That is the end of all these things – no fear, no attachment, nothing whatsoever. Actually, that power is there behind. Every one can feel it.

Reading: *The purpose is to hold the mind in Spirit or Brahman at all times and to impress it strongly with the futility of the evanescent sense-pleasures and their objects.*
Swamiji: Infinity cannot be described, where to begin, where to end, how vast it is. So, even by imagination, you think, millions and billions of worlds like this are nothing. It is only a speck when compared with Infinity, like dust particles, such is the vastness of Brahman. The man who takes up jnana-yoga says, "I am Brahman. I am Brahman. That is everywhere." In that way, you have to enlarge the mind's range of

vision. Then you become fearless with no attachment. Nothing can drag you down. One has to live constantly in that idea. That is sadhana. All these things come to naught when you go to Nirvikalpa Samadhi. There, there is no more thinking of anything or widening the range of mind or vision, nothing whatsoever. There is only One Thing. There is no more room for a second thing. The subject is too stiff. Any questions?

Disciple: I can't understand how you can kill the ego? I understand you can stop identifying yourself with the ego but how can you kill it?

Swamiji: What do you mean by kill? Take the spirit. You can't cut it with a knife or sword.

Disciple: That is what I mean. How can it be killed? That is impossible.

Swamiji: Killing does not mean in that way. If you can catch it, then also you can kill it. It is not a thing to be caught, in that way. One of the functions of the mind is ego. When the mind constantly identifies with the body, senses and other things, you call it ego. That is all. Now killing this, don't get attached to the body. Suppose you are doing a good work or you are doing sadhana itself. Somebody will say, "He is working very hard and he is really a great Saint." There, you only have to hear the word "Saint." "Yes, I have become a great Saint." That ego grows there. When people say like that, kill it in this way, "I am just a fool. And people, by ignorance, say you are a Saint." So, don't be proud of it. That is how you have to kill it.

If a man is rich, he thinks he is rich and the ego grows there. Suppose an ordinary man or woman purchases a new suit. When they put it on, they think, "This suit is so fine." They walk in such a way, that every one will catch a glimpse of it. If one has a beautiful watch, you go on looking at it, that it might be noticed. Though there is no need for looking, still you want to see it again and again. In so many ways the ego comes but don't allow it to play in that way. Some people will have a pipe and drive with one hand. Some will have a long cigar. Some people will be smoking a cigar. Sometimes when I go out, I rarely have the chance, but when I do go out, I sit quietly and see the fun, so terrible it is. Kill that ego. Then you are wise. Know that it is all false. You only sympathize with ignorant people how poor they are, how stupid and poor both. You sympathize with them rather.

Disciple: What can one do when one gets sleepy during darshan?

Swamiji: When all are laughing, you feel sleepy?
Disciple: She has worked so much in her house. She has just moved.
Swamiji: Oh, that is the cause. Does she want medicine for it? Have a thermos secretly. That is why you have been given the last place in the corner. Nobody sees you. When you feel sleepy, have a sip. Or, you have a chaddar, cover with it. Nobody will see you.

August 8, 1973
Disciple: Swamiji, what is Divine Will?
Swamiji: Is it only for ordinary people, it is said.
Disciple: Is it something to surrender to?
Swamiji: In order to control the mind, you have to use so many methods. The mind deceives you in so many ways. A devotee will say: "Divine Will, God's grace. It is His will. That is because he feels he is not strong enough to withstand everything as a Jnani does. A Jnani will never say Divine Will". An ordinary man feels weak and for all this weakness, he keeps God in front and he offers everything unto God. Such a man or devotee only says Divine Will, Divine Grace in the way. But with all that, there must be effort. Without right effort, nothing can be attained. But it is only in bhakti-yoga that they say all these things.

Suppose you tie a cow to a pole and there is a long rope in that area around which the cow can graze. The cow goes on eating and eating whatever grass is available on the ground. Beyond that circle, there is much grass also but whenever the cow tries the rope, it gives a pull. The cow tries this side and that side. All round the cow goes and tries. It is in vain. Lastly the cow understands that where the rope lets him wander, he can graze. Beyond that, he has no power. So, then he keeps quiet.

Disciple: Is that what they call fatalism?
Swamiji: No, not fatalism. It is not in that way. Fatalism is nothing but fate, prarabdha coming into action. That is called fate. But Divine Grace is just like the cow that is now waiting. It surrenders completely to the will of the owner. Until the owner comes and takes it to another place,

it keeps quiet. That is Divine Grace. It will wait for the grace to descend or come or enter, whatever they may call it. It is only a devotee who takes it in that way but a Jnani will not wait for such things. He will not say, "Wait for Divine Grace or Divine Will." He will say,"I will be doing. I want to do it. I will work it out."

Disciple: And he has no rope. Is he not tied with a rope?

Swamiji: He is not tied. Why should he tie himself? He is courageous. He is set free. He is beyond that master also. He does not want it. He is just like a jungle deer. It can go anywhere, wherever it likes. But, at the same time, there is a man waiting for something to shoot. He must be careful. So, he depends entirely on his fate. Whatever good or bad, whatever decisions he takes, he does not worry about God or dispensation, whatever you may call it. He does not depend on it. Come what may, if good comes, all right. If something bad comes, he will say, "I am responsible." He will not blame anyone else.

But normally, it is not like that. They will weep for God, "Oh God, save me, help me." Ordinary people feel weak every step they take. Such people, they take dwaita. Here, you have to come to adwaita, to Jnana Marga. There you must be strong.

As I told you yesterday, the man who has advanced highly can take up Jnana Marga. But for ordinary people it is safest just to have God in front and pray to Him. In the lower stages of life, they go to the temple, offer something to God, pray, weep, do all sorts of things. "God save me, help me, let me have your grace." It has meaning also. In the beginning, it is very difficult for a baby to stand on his own feet. There are so many pitfalls and dangers. They do not feel safe so they have all these things. When they go on slowly and steadily and come to higher pitches. Then one is free. The grace and all these things will have no meaning.

Fatalism is quite different. What you call fate, that is another word for prarabdha. Your past actions giving fruit now. Fate is your past effort giving fruit now, in this life. So, fate and effort go side by side. It is a mixture. Life is a mixture of these two things. These two are fighting just like two bulls: one, the bull of fate, the other, the bull of effort. That which is stronger will defeat the other. If your effort is strong and you have taken the proper path, you have success and you can defeat fate also. On the other hand, if fate is too strong and your effort is weak, it will defeat you and every time you do, it is a failure. Such people become fatalists. "Oh, my fate is such, I am doomed," in that way. This is a one-sided view. Many people give prominence to effort. That is a one-sided view. Both are necessary. Both are working in the life of a person. Fate and effort, both are there.

Disciple: So, a person who surrenders to God, is he not depending wholly on his prarabdha?

Swamiji: How can he? Even if he depends wholly and solely, it is not easy. Effort must be there. Even to depend completely for everything, it is also an effort in a deeper sense. You cannot entirely depend in that way. It is not easy. Always you have to check the mind, check the desires and check your movements. That is also an effort. It is just like somebody was telling, "Watch the mind. Never control it. Only become the witness of the mind." That is a very great effort there. It is much harder than your meditation and concentration. Constantly you have to live in that one idea. It is only a thoughtless word actually. If you think deeply, it has no meaning.

Disciple: Does it go only for the Jnani that God is in everything so there is nothing to avoid? There are certainly many things that ordinary people should avoid.

Swamiji: Even in bad things is there also God?

Disciple: Yes.

Swamiji: Then? If one will come with a sword to cut you, you will appreciate it then?

Disciple: We should rather avoid bad things.

Swamiji: We have been telling you from the very beginning to avoid bad things at any cost.

Disciple: But does it go for the Jnani?

Swamiji: Even a Jnani will also avoid bad things in the beginning. After having attained the highest, then good and bad has no meaning. That is another thing. Though God is everywhere, in a tiger as well as in a cobra, you have to avoid both the cobra and the tiger.

The Guru said to a disciple in a class, "Everything is Brahman. God is everywhere." And he took it by the word and forgot the meaning, that disciple. Next day he was walking on the street. On the way, a mad elephant was coming and the mahout was sitting on the top, he said, "Run away, run away. It is a mad elephant. Don't come near." The disciple said, "Yesterday, Guruji told me everything is God, everything is Brahman. Then why should I run away? I am also Brahman." He forgot everything. He stood there and then the mad elephant caught him and twisted him and threw him like anything so that he was unconscious for hours together. The news went to Guruji. They took the disciple to the hospital where he was nursed for three days. He regained Consciousness. He did not die, poor man.

Afterwards, the Guru asked the disciple, "What happened to you?" "Guruji, you told me 'Everything is Brahman,' and I stood there and the mad elephant Brahman caught me." The Guruji said, "All right, the elephant is also Brahman, you are also Brahman, the man who was on top of the elephant, he is also Brahman and that Brahman told you, 'Get away, get away.' Why did you not hear that?" Then the disciple understood. "Oh, that was the right thing." He forgot that Brahman. So, if he had obeyed that Brahman, he would not have been injured and he would have been a wiser man.

So, in the beginning, you have to discriminate between good and bad, right and wrong. If you mix all the things from the very start, you will get confused. You will go to pieces. You cannot make any progress. But, when you come to the last point, there is neither good nor bad. There is only One Thing. That is Brahman and Brahman alone. Then again it comes. All these things are the mind's creation. When you go to higher pitches, there is nothing good, nothing bad. All the pairs of opposites, they create all these delusions and the mind is the cause. There you end everything. There is only One Thing. That is a bit difficult to understand also.

August 9, 1973

Reading: *These are some of the methods for meditation on Nirguna Aspect (Formless Aspect of God or Brahman) of Brahman. But only very few are fit to take these up with success. In this process of meditation, the first and foremost thing needed is a very sharp intellect to gain which one must observe strict brahmacharya (celibacy) in thought, word and deed.*

Swamiji: If at all you want to make any progress spiritually, celibacy is absolutely necessary. The more you get established, the better will be the result and three-fourths of your sadhana is over. For such people, only one fourth remains. They can attain Samadhi easily. That is the secret. I have again and again been telling you that there is a close connection between brahmacharya and the kundalini shakti. The shakti cannot rise up to the head center without perfect brahmacharya. And without the shakti coming to the last point, there is no Brahma-Jnana or the highest kind of wisdom. Control of sex energy and mind-control go side by side. Here, on this point, modern education has neglected it completely. Don't make any compromise. Work hard and it will come.

Reading: *To be a real Brahmachari one must live a simple, pure life, follow the moral or ethical code of conduct in its entirety and exercise control over all the five senses.*

Swamiji: All are connected with one another. There is not only brahmacharya. If you want to follow only the word brahmacharya, it has no meaning. All the other things — how to live, how to eat, how to drink — also come. Suppose a man is earning in a very bad way, in a nefarious way. Then the food which you eat will make the mind impure. That is the secret. You will have a fall. So, one must work hard, live the life and it will come. It is only a question of time. It depends on you people to prolong the time or curtail the time. Suppose you want to go to Copenhagen. First, you can go by airplane. It may take half an hour, I think, or you can go by train which may take some hours or lastly by foot. It may take some days. If your effort is strong, you can cut short the time. If it is middle, it may take some time. If it is mild, it may take much longer. So, it depends upon you and what kind of speed you want to use.

Without a moral code, you cannot have peace. Without peace, you cannot meditate. By doing injustice to others or by living a wrong life, you can never have peace. There will be so many things to attack you. It is all joined together. So, one has to live a pure life, holy life, simple life. In this way, you have to build up.

Reading: *In fact, the very foundation of religion or spirituality rests entirely upon the bed-rock of morality and brahmacharya.*

Swamiji: Yes, that is the main thing. If that is gone, there is no religion, there is no philosophy and it has no backbone. It is just like making a big palace-like building on sand, without a foundation. One heavy breeze from this side and it will be in the sea. It is just like that. All religions say be good, be kind, be gentle, be chaste. Every one says but nobody follows it. That is the defect.

August 10, 1973

Reading: *Concentration. Cognition, emotion and volition must be unified in order to bring out all the latent possibilities of mind that lie dormant in an individual. Practice of concentration is therefore, the very kernel of religious evolution.*

Swamiji: Whatever path you take, it may be karma-yoga, bhakti-yoga, raja-yoga or jnana-yoga, the first and foremost thing to start with for all the yogas is to live a pure life. The rules of yama and niyama are common to each and every yoga. Suppose a man has been living a pure, holy and simple life and doing sadhana. The aim of sadhana is to make the mind, body and nadis pure. When you have gained purification to a great extent, the kundalini shakti also tries to rise upwards slowly and steadily. When it rises above the heart center, you will have deep concentration and there are no more impure thoughts. Then only can you have perfect brahmacharya. Without brahmacharya, there is no concentration of mind and the kundalini shakti can never rise up. Pay particular attention to this one thing, then all other things will come automatically.

Reading: *Real happiness results from right concentration.*
Swamiji: So, there is no comparison between the momentary sense-pleasures and when you really enjoy deep concentration. The peace and happiness there, you cannot describe it. There is no comparison. The ordinary man doesn't understand that side. They are merged in the world. They think everything is all right here in the world but it is an illusion.

Reading: *The man who has learned mind-control can, however, suppress emotions of all kinds at all stages to keep his mind in perfect equilibrium. This is the greatest boon a man can ever have.*

Swamiji: The word suppression is not properly put. It should be control. It is the proper word. Whatever kind of emotions may come, he can control it. That is the difference. An ordinary man cannot do it. People who practise mind-control, they have control over thoughts and can control any stage of an emotion.

August 11, 1973

Reading: *Mind-control at will is not developed and, therefore, not possible in lower forms of life. It is possible only in human beings.*

Swamiji: Now, after living a hard life, observing all the rules of yama and niyama and also observing perfect celibacy, a person goes on doing his sadhana. The body, nadis and mind, all these three things get purified. Then the kundalini shakti also tries to rise upwards, little by little. This partial rising is not as dangerous as it is by taking hash, LSD or alcohol. There, the up-going current is very strong, so you cannot control it. Until and unless the shakti rises upward, there is no concentration. That is why you sometimes have good concentration and sometimes not. There will be ups and downs. If you have good concentration in the morning, you may not get the same concentration in the evening. But still, the progress is there. Don't be sorry about it, but go on regularly. Secondly, occasionally you have very deep concentration when you are coming to a high pitch of that state. Then, for days together, you don't get such concentration, even if you work hard. Thereby, you are not losing anything. You are gaining ground. You are establishing your sadhana on a sound basis.

In that state, be firm, continue your sadhana, never give it up. And when you go on practising, the state of Samadhi may come at any time. There is no limit for it now. In deep concentration, many forget the world and the body idea slowly and then the breathing also comes to a stop. Then, the devil "fear of death" comes there and many people lose their concentration. That is the greatest misfortune a sadhaka can have. That is equal to suicide. Such a stupid man, he has to wait and wait for years together until he gets that state again. He has to pay for it very heavily. So, give up the idea of death. Even if you die, it does not matter. Have that firm faith in God and work it out and you go to the highest pitch.

While coming to that point, you have two stages again. On one side, you feel the body is going to melt, becoming smaller and smaller and you almost go to nothingness and you become one with Infinity. On the other side, sometimes you get the experience that the body begins to grow bigger and bigger and is becoming one with the vast Infinity. In the first state, the breathing becomes very slow and steady and when you continue further, it completely stops. There is a scientific reason for it. When the kundalini shakti is in the lowest center, muladhara, it supplies currents to all the different nadis. The nadis are going to the lungs that make you breathe. When the kundalini shakti rises up fully through the sushumna nadi to sahasrara, it is just like a wireless operation. All the nadis are cut off. They stop working. It is called kevala kumbhaka. That means without any effort there will be kumbhaka. Now you are landed. That is the last point.

Disciple: How to control sudden anger?
Swamiji: How can it rise suddenly, just like thunder? Why should you get it? Analyze it. When you watch the mind, there is no anger. Without cause, how can you get angry? There must be some cause?
Disciple: It grows quickly.
Swamiji: Quickly means it may come up suddenly. Whenever you have a desire and that desire is checked, you get angry. That is the secret. You like the work to be done in this way and the other man says in that way; so, your desire is checked and immediately you get annoyed. You have to watch it. There is nothing called sudden anger. You understand?
Disciple: Yes.

Disciple: In what state can you control the thought currents in dream?
Swamiji: If you can control your thought currents in dream, then you can control dream also. Then there is no dream.

Disciple: Yes, for instance, if you want to observe strict celibacy, you have to observe it in dream too.

Swamiji: When the mind is purified, you can't have bad dreams. Even if you have a dream, it will be a pleasant dream. You may see your Ishta-Devata or angels if you believe in that. As long as there is impurity in the mind, you have all those things. But mantra-jap will help you. Then all these defects will go away. Even before that, when you have some bad thing, you wake up suddenly. You will not allow it. You check it. Those who give a strong impression every day before going to sleep say, "I must have perfect brahmacharya." That firm determination wakes you up. In that way, give a strong impression to the mind. Whatever you want to win, constantly live in that idea, "I should be strong. I should be great. I should attain the highest." That will have much value. When failure comes, such things will help you very much.

Disciple: How to overcome this fear of death which arises sometimes?

Swamiji: Why should you allow it? Give firm conviction, "If I die, I will go to heaven." Put it in that way. Even if death comes, well and good. Come what may. That must be the attitude. "Even if the body dies, I am not going to die." Put that idea again. "I am the Self. The mantra is there to protect me. It will save me. What is death? Death to whom?" Put that question. Don't think of anything when you sit for meditation. Don't keep any small desires. That is the cause of your fear. You must be prepared for everything.

Disciple: Is it possible to reach Samadhi during meditation or by praying, letting the mind flow all the time by praying to God, talking to God? Instead of quieting the mind down, can you let it go by praying and talking?

Swamiji: Whatever may be, there may be better ways. If you follow any way, you must come to concentration. The prayer must stop somewhere and you have to go further. The prayer and all those things come with the idea of two things. There is only One Thing. With prayer you come to a certain pitch and you stop there. You may have some visions or other experiences. That is all tidbits. But, if you want to go completely to higher pitches, all those prayers stop halfway.

To quiet the mind, that is another process. If you can make the mind free, blank at will, that is not easy. But it is as good as other sadhana.

There are different methods. Mantra-Jap will be more efficacious than prayer. It may take you further, to higher pitches. When the mind goes deeper and deeper, you can't pray. The mantra will also stop there. Then comes the difficulty of how to proceed further. For that you have to train your mind. The idea of Samadhi and Nirvikalpa is unknown. They stop only in heaven by going to heaven. Even to come to that pitch is not easy. It takes a lot of time.

Disciple: So, you mean Samadhi is a higher state?

Swamiji: The last point.

Disciple: Is the mind always against you? When one meditates, the mind doesn't want to. And when you don't want to meditate, the mind wants to.

Swamiji: Your mind is playing tricks in the beginning but when you take some interest in the other side. Then you can't keep quiet. Then your progress will be steady. In the beginning, when you want to work, you will find some lame excuses. When you have no time, it wants to sit just to deceive you. So, regulate it. Don't be a dupe to it. And when you regularly do it, everything will be okay. Then you come to that point. Suppose you are regularly meditating and the time comes to sit. You may be doing any kind of work but all at once the thought comes there and you know the exact time is there. Then it forms a habit and it wants to work. Is it clear or no?

Disciple: It is clear.

August 12, 1973

Swamiji: We have been talking about the highest, or almost the highest, not the highest, but even to come to that pitch is not easy. The vast majority of people, they stay there and even many founders of religion, they are content with that. Coming to this point, many people have a vision of their Ishta-Devata or they may see some beautiful landscape they may call heaven, some sort of seven heavens. That is a dangerous state. That is one of the main causes of the so-called bloodshed and wars in the name of God and religion in the world. Many people say there is only dwaita. They never come to adwaita. They only have to love God. They must always be at the mercy of God. The so-called prayers come there.

Then again, there is another thing. Every writer says, "He is the only man. He is the last prophet. He is the last Messiah." It is nothing but a sort of propaganda. In India, every man has his own God and each God is quite different. They live eternally and He is Infinite and all-powerful. It is smashing away what you call philosophy. It is putting a big zero to it and saying it is all fanciful things. Many people are coming. They don't want to hear or argue because they say our books say that our Guru says only this much. They don't want to go beyond. They stay in that area. They don't want to cross it. Some others, they search for supernatural powers. That is the end of your further progress and you fall down. Some want to see where the kundalini shakti is working and so it is also gone.

These are some of the pitfalls and dangers. So, you must be firm. Don't stop there and don't hanker after anything if you want to make progress and go to the last point. Many of the so-called Gods and Goddesses are your enemies. They don't want you to go to the highest. They have not attained so they will play mischief with you people. They will try to pull you down. That danger is there. You must be careful. Don't be attached or dragged down by all these temptations. Make your mind free. Get rid of all your desires and don't be afraid of anything. These are the important things which every one of you has to keep in mind

Reading: *Concentration should continue to be carried on even after this state (concentration) till the light vanishes altogether and the mind merges in the void, a state in which there is neither light nor lightlessness.*

Swamiji: There you need not make any effort. Automatically, it will vanish when you continue your concentration. The light, the form of your Ishta-Devata and other things will all merge and come to a focus. It is just like you are switching on a flash light and focusing it on a point. It goes and goes just like a long path, as it were. You go to the point. You forget the body and your mind. Chitta, ego, everything will merge in that point. Then only, Nirvikalpa Samadhi can take place. The idea of subject, object and knowledge, they all blend into one and what remains is the Ocean of Consciousness by Itself. You know you are back to your Source. That is the last point. The breathing also stops automatically, without any effort on your side.

Disciple: When one reaches that state and doesn't breathe any longer, then one doesn't live any longer on this earth?

Swamiji: It is not necessary. One can come down also. That is another thing. Ordinarily, you are content. Where to come back to? Why should you come back? But, there is a "but" also.

Disciple: But in that state, there is no will.

Swamiji: Whose will?

Disciple: Then it must be God's will.

Swamiji: Whatever it may be, that is all right. You may have to say God's will. How to explain that state? That is nothing, only One Thing. There is only one thing, God and God alone.

Disciple: A "but" can only be in duality.

Swamiji: We are in duality now. All these explanations are in duality. When you are in Samadhi state, there is no explanation. There are no words to speak, with whom to speak? That is why we have been telling about the purified ego and the ordinary ego. You can make a simile with a rope. The ordinary ego is a rope, as it were, and the purified ego, is like a burneded rope. It cannot be used for binding.

Disciple: Do you have memory of any kind when you reach Samadhi?

Swamiji: Suppose you are going to deep-sleep-state. When you sleep, do you have any memory there?

Disciple: No, not in deep-sleep.

Swamiji: When you sleep, you don't say you are sleeping. When you get up, you make a bridge between the waking-state, before going to sleep, and when you wake up. In that way you say, "I had a very good sleep."

Disciple: Yes.

Swamiji: Similarly, when you go to Samadhi state, everything is merged there. There is nothing whatsoever. But, when a man comes down from that state, then he makes an idea.

Disciple: How can one avoid the mistake of thinking one has been in Samadhi, when one has not?

Swamiji: The inner voice will tell you that you have not reached the highest. There is something left behind. But, when you go to Samadhi, you have perfect peace. There is no more want, no more requirements, no deficiency. You have perfect contentment there.

Disciple: I don't know. Isn't it so that one could think just before reaching the highest that you have the choice, the chance to help suffering people?

Swamiji: If you have that idea of helping suffering people, you fall down. You can't go to the highest. It is not in your hands to help or to do. You must entirely give up all these things. Then only you can climb up. It is just like if you want to put a thread into the small needle hole. If there are some fibres, they may be very fine, if they are projecting here and there, it will not enter.

Disciple: Swamiji, you write that Freedom is our birth-right.

Swamiji: Yes.

Disciple: How to accept that in its full meaning? It is not possible as long as life is attached to the body. We can only accept that when we get Samadhi and we will only get that in the end.

Swamiji: You have to take gradual steps, slowly. You have to retain the body also. Before going to Samadhi, there are so many stages. In this stage, we do not disagree with the temples, churches, mosques or paGodas that are also necessary for ordinary people. But, don't stand there alone. It is the starting point. You have to rise up to higher pitches by mantra-jap, meditation and mind-control. That is what is meant. We are not against any religion. Different religions, all right, let them come. But never stay at the same point. Likewise, the universe can have only One God. There are countless radii coming to this point that you can attribute to different religions or paths. Many stop at the starting point only, at the circle itself. Some make a little progress and some reach the point. We say this is the best one and another man that his is the best one. It is a quarrel for nothing. If we have tolerance and patience, there is no more quarrel. Lack of common sense and understanding is the cause of so much bloodshed and quarrel in the name of God and religion in this world.

Disciple: Swamiji, who are these Gods and Goddesses who will not let one go into Samadhi?

Swamiji: It is just like human beings. They don't like that some of you rise higher up than them. So they will disturb you.

Disciple: Are there real living creatures in another vibration?

Swamiji: In this very atmosphere, there may be so many creatures. They walk on you and you walk on them. They are in different vibrations of prana.

Disciple: But if they can interfere with such subtle matters are they developed themselves?

Swamiji: They have done tapasya and they have come to a certain evolution but not the highest. Some are good. Some may help you also. Some others may disturb you and appear in the form of some terrible ghosts. Many people claim that when they meditate, they see terrible creatures coming and disturbing and some people even go mad.

Disciple: Can the same God appear to someone else or can they only appear to you?

Swamiji: It is possible to appear to someone else also. They can appear and disappear. It is just like human beings, maybe a bit better. Still, they are departed souls. They had a birth and then they must die also, all these Gods.

Disciple: Is there a connection between the place you get rebirth and the place where you were staying in your past incarnation. I mean geographically?

Swamiji: Your karma decides it.

Disciple: Only the karma?

Swamiji: Karma. If you have done good karma, according to that, you may choose the place which is similar to that particular karma and you may have a good birth in a very good family. That means everything is convenient for your progress and such people make speedy progress. If you have done something wrong, you may go down even to a lower life. It is left to you whether to improve it or destroy it. When you do yoga practice, mind-control, even if you don't reach the highest. Still, after death, you continue the practice, even in death. In the next birth, you will have very speedy results. So, nothing is wasted. Even if you don't attain the highest in this life, your work done is already in your bank balance. There is nothing lost; so, don't be afraid. The future is entirely in your hands. Now decide what you want. If you want progress, live the life. You must make a hard struggle. Then you have a chance. You must keep the idea, "I must reach it in this very life."

Disciple: Is it possible to be reborn as an animal?

Swamiji: Why not? Animal can become man and man can become animal. Both are possible.

Disciple: How can it be that one cannot remember anything from the past incarnation?

Swamiji: Why do you go to incarnation? Do you remember all that you have done from morning up to now?

Disciple: No.

Swamiji: Why? It is a wonderful thing. You cannot remember from morning up to now and you want to remember the past incarnation?

Disciple: I just ask why.

Swamiji: When did you get up? Is it so difficult? If you want to learn it, it also can be done. For that thing, mind-control is a necessity. By controlling the chitta, you can recall it. But it is a mere waste of time, mere curiosity.

Disciple: When the Ishta-Devata appears to you in a dream, is it dream or is it reality?

Swamiji: It is a good dream. That is all. During meditation time, you may have a flash. That is called a vision. Then again, in vision there are two ways. Sometimes, you may see it outside, really as you see other people. That is called objective vision and the dream vision is called subjective vision.

Disciple: Swamiji, why do these people in the madhouse call it hallucination?

Swamiji: That is another department. They are in quite a different world. Doctors can tell you better.

August 13, 1973

Reading: *How to concentrate on gross objects: Those who have chosen their Ishta-Devata for meditation, can make use of a picture of the same for the purpose of concentration. Have a beautiful picture of your Ishta-Devata. When you practise sadhana (spiritual practice) keep this picture in front of you and try to fix your gaze on any part of it.*

Swamiji: This process is known as tratak. Don't take it up all of a sudden. With five or ten minutes, one must be careful there. Start with one or two minutes and slowly increase it. There is another process. At night, you can keep a candle lit in one corner of the room and you can practise concentration on this also for a few minutes and then close the eyes. When you close the eyes, you can actually see the light inside also. It will help your concentration. When the mind is too fickle, when it wanders too often here and there, it will be very helpful. Or, at night, if you sit outside, you can use the moon or a bright star for concentration or you can take the distant light of a lamppost. These are some of the methods to make the mind steady. But don't be hasty. Don't take up the practice all of a sudden and strain the mind.

Disciple: Then to fix the mind, is that to think about it all the time or to stop thinking and just look?

Swamiji: When you are concentrated you can't think, only take the point. Practise first, see the difficulty and then come. Don't make guesswork now.

Disciple: Should this process be before or after pranayama?

Swamiji: You can do both. After meditation, you can also do it. Afterwards you can sit quietly. Don't get up suddenly and do any kind of work. That is very dangerous. The thing is that when you are meditating, automatically, there will be kundalini currents going up. When you have deep concentration, the shakti has been working well. That is the secret. If you get up suddenly, it will have a very bad reaction. The first and foremost thing one feels is abnormal sexual craving. That has a very bad reaction. There will be wet dreams. You are sure to get it. If you go to sleep just after meditation, you are sure to get wet dreams also. So, you must be careful. A little carelessness means gone. The whole life's work goes to pieces within a second. There is no one to give you any holiday. You must always be alert.

Disciple: Does it not bring disturbance when you have to meditate on that point and afterwards also the Ishta-Devata?

Swamiji: Oh, what a horrible thing. We are talking of the point and then coming to the Ishta-Devata. It will make the Ishta-Devata sit quiet without shaking. If your mind is steady, your Ishta-Devata will also be steady. If your mind is walking, that will also fly, poor creature. The Ishta-Devata will also run here and there along with the thoughts.

Reading: *Concentration on light at night is very profitable, for the eyes easily get fixed on light and the mind also easily gets concentrated because there are no other objects to drag the eyesight and the mind in darkness.*

Swamiji: In the waking-state, the mind drags the eyes out to so many different objects. That is why blind people have better concentration. Their mind is very sharp and when once they hear a thing, they don't forget it for years together. They can develop concentration very highly, those who come to this line and they have also speedy success.

Disciple: Swamiji, when one is working and one feels very fickle-minded, is it then good to sit down and look at a point?

Swamiji: Go on with the mantra. That is the easiest method. You don't have to concentrate there (at work).

Disciple: Before you also said it was good against fickle-mindedness.

Swamiji: While working, how can you do that thing? Suppose you are working in a factory and go on concentrating there, they will fire you. There, the easiest method is to take the mantra while you are working.

Reading: *In an advanced state of meditation and with the rising of Kundalini Shakti to the Anahata Chakra, you can clearly perceive (mental perception) an all-pervading steady silvery light all through your meditation. When you come to this state, catch hold of that light and try to fix your mind on it.*

Swamiji: How to catch hold of it? Sometimes one can see a spark coming out just like lightning or sometimes like a ball of fire or the moon. There are a variety of ways. When the Shakti rises above the heart center, you can see an all-pervading light everywhere. It is a silvery light. Focus the mind on one point. The light will also disappear and then you go and enter into the formless aspect that is neither light nor darkness. Hold it there and you have solved the problem. That is Nirvikalpa Samadhi.

August 14, 1973

Reading: *The breathing and the heart beats would automatically stop completely, and the mind would merge in Infinity, i.e., a void, which is neither light nor darkness.*

Swamiji: So, here you have to come. When you go on with the concentration, deeper and deeper, the kundalini shakti comes to the last point and shiva and shakti become One. You can't describe that state. There is no more mind. The mind completely merges together with the ego, chitta and intellect. To know a thing, there must be three things: the subject you, as the knower and the object, the thing which is to be known. These three things are necessary to get knowledge. Up to now, you have a small pot, a separate thing. It consists of mind, ego, intellect and chitta. The akasa is inside and outside the pot also. Going back to Nirvikalpa Samadhi means the pot is destroyed and the akasa inside the pot becomes one with the all-pervading akasa. You go back to your Source and become One with Infinity. Apart from that state, all other experiences have no value. It is mere ignorance to talk of so many things, a big dream. There ends the matter.

When you go to the last point, everything is eaten up completely. You have no fear. There is not a separate thing apart from it. That is your True Nature. The whole philosophy comes to a dead stop. It has no meaning to discuss. Discussion with whom? Every one of you has to go to that point. It may be today or tomorrow. It may be millions of births also.

Disciple: Swamiji, is it bad to want Savikalpa instead of Nirvikalpa?

Swamiji: Who told you that is bad? If you can't get Nirvikalpa, it is better to have Savikalpa. If you can't get a square meal, it is better to eat something, at least one or two apples. Who says it is bad? You are starving. Somebody gives you one or two apples. All right, take it.

Disciple: Swamiji, what is meant by Turiya State?

Swamiji: That is another name for Nirvikalpa. You know the thing. That is called Yuriya. Jivan-Muktas live in Turiya State. That is the experience.

Disciple: What can keep you from eating a good dish again if it was so good?

Swamiji: In spite of your dinner, somebody forces you. Rather, somebody pushes you. It is not your will.

Disciple: I also wonder what makes one go away from the very beginning?
Swamiji: How you have come down here?
Disciple: Yes, how?
Swamiji: That is the thing, the problem. That is a difficult question, you cannot answer. When you go there, there is no more. When you are here, there are so many things. That is the dilemma. So, when you go to that point, you can't say it is Moksha, Freedom. It has no meaning. So, as it is, you find you are bound, so many limitations you have, so many wants, so many requirements. But, when you go there, there is nothing. When you go to that point, there is only One actually. How that thing has become many has no meaning there. No question arises there. So, that will remain as a dilemma. When you go to that point, there is no bondage, no knowledge, nothing whatsoever. You are by yourself. It is better not to tackle that question. Now, try to get that point. Then you will see, all these things have no meaning. If you tell ordinary people that the world is unreal, they will say you are mad. They will laugh at you. So, avoid discussion for nothing. It is a mere waste of time. Work it out. When you go deeper and deeper, you will come to that high pitch.

Reading: *How to concentrate on Sound: If you are living near the seashore, or a water-fall or a roaring mountain stream, take the aid of the continuous noise it makes.*
Swamiji: Many people hear some sort of noise. The doctors take it to be a disease. When you hear some sort of sound, a ringing sound, it should be heard from the right side, not through the left. There is a nadi in the left side where the thoughts are going and that easily gets disturbed. When you hear it, concentrate on the sound. You can mix your mantra also with it. That sound can be taken to any part of the body. It may be head or heart. Bring it if you want.

Reading: *If you have a clock in your meditation room, catch hold of the tick-tick sound of the clock.*
Swamiji: It is all different methods. Don't try them all. Stick to one method. Don't go on changing. Stick to one principle, one idea. It is helpful, for example, that tratak can be done.

Reading: *How to concentrate on void: Sit erect in your favorite asana (seat). Thus seated, try not to think of anything. Make the mind void: free it from desires and thoughts of all kinds. Forget the body. Let the mind, will, ego, intellect, chitta and the senses remain in their respective places. Do no make use of them. Practise this for as long as possible.*

Swamiji: This practice can be kept by every one of you. As soon as you get up from sleep, it can be done. Then the mind is fresh. It has got strength. Make the mind blank. Do not even think of the mantra. Don't think of anything. That is a good habit, if you make it. You will have an idea if you succeed in making the mind blank at will that it is a great attainment. If you can succeed even for a few seconds, you have so much peace for the whole day. You understand what is meant by real peace.

August 15, 1973

Disciple: Swamiji, if we don't learn about reincarnation in Denmark, there will be so many difficulties and it will take thousands of years before we come to that.

Swamiji: Yes, you are not to wait. Automatically, it is all changing. The younger generation, they believe. Even if you go deeply into Christianity, Reincarnation Theory is there. In many places you will get it. All the things were changed and the Bible was re-written by Theodora in the year 535 AD. She was the courtesan of King Justinian and afterwards she became the queen. And, in order to hide her sins, she brought this theory. One or two popes stood against it and they had to give their lives for that reason.

Many of your western people admit, I think, Darwin's Theory of lower life coming to higher life. Then, what is the theory? Do you admit to the same thing completely? Many people agree with him in the Western World but stupidly they agree for nothing. It has no meaning. That also proves he is for reincarnation. There will be life. Then again, philosophically, logically, if you want to admit that something can never come out of nothing, it is impossible. Again, you say, they come for the first time and then, again, they will live forever. It is impossible. A thing which has a beginning must end somewhere. Also, the idea of heaven has no meaning there. Going to heaven and living eternally, it has no meaning at all. All these conclusions come to all conflicts.

Then again, the Dwaita Theory that God created the universe has no meaning there. When you say God is all-pervading, eternal and infinite, there can be only One. So, there is no room for a thing called dead matter or blind force. The all-pervasiveness of God is gone if you admit a separate thing is existing apart from God. Then your theory of this all-pervading — is gone. In every respect, all round, he will be caught.

So, that is why we say, at the last point, there is only One and I have concluded, "Without Consciousness, there is no force and that the Ocean of Consciousness by Itself is called God." Even the scientists have almost come to that but they are still some points away. If at all they can come, it is impossible to come to that point by study. It will never come under study. And if it comes under study, it is not God. It is not Infinity. So, it is impossible there.

There can be only One Thing and the last point is called God. Taking that point of view, then the word creation has no meaning. It is impossible to create, from where and how? So, when He is all-pervading, then how to create? All of you, do you catch the point or not? It is a subtle point. When you say it is all-pervading, there is not a single thing without it. It is full. It is Infinite. There can only be One such thing. Then, where to create? How to create? It has no meaning there. That is the last conclusion. Whatever science does, they must come to this point. Helplessly they have to admit there is only One Thing. It is a subtle point. So, that is the end of everything. The word creation or creator has no meaning. Coming to this point, that is Nirvikalpa Samadhi. Is it clear or any doubts?

Disciple: It is very clear. I have to begin to tell it to my own people.

Swamiji: Of course, it is the last point. It is very difficult to understand. Many people will not think of it. They think they will go mad even to think of it. People are merged in the sense-pleasures — eating and drinking. If you tell this highest thing, they say, "Oh, he is mad." They will make you mad. That is all. There, you can challenge even science. Come forward. It will take thousands of years. I have given this new thing to these people. All right now, work it out.

So, all these things I never expected. I never thought of coming. I never dreamt or thought or planned. Planning is a different thing. When I started my life, I had no idea about anything, about all these things, neither of books. I never thought I would become an author, oh horrible, to make an ashram in a foreign country and other things. I had not a single coin with me. So, that has come, people have come, everything has come. Work is going on without planning, without any desire on my part. Twenty years ago, they wanted me in America. They were prepared to pay all my expenses. I refused totally. I only laughed at it. "Ridiculous, horrible," I said. But anyway, here in Denmark, it has taken root somehow or other and caught me and that was only in a funny way. I never wanted to come. Somehow, by chance, they were talking of coming and going and other things. In a way they told me, "Yes," I said, "It is only fun." And that fun came into action now. That is the story. So, it will come. It must come. Truth cannot be hidden. It is only a question of time. It must come. If it desires, it will come. If it does not desire, who will worry about it.

I have given enough. Even in psychology, I have given original things. I never read any books. I never cared for all these things, going to great scholars to learn, book learning. I had nothing to do with it. When I wrote the books, I had no books also. Writers generally keep a big library for reference here and there. I had nothing. So, every bit of the work I was doing myself. Even now, also I do it. Without having a secretary for my writing or other things. I don't engage anyone. So, I am a secretary for myself. Everything I do.

The year before last when I came here, a typewriter was purchased. I did not know how to use it. I began typing then. So, in three or four days I picked it up though I use only one hand, not two hands. With that, I finish my letters. That is all right. I can manage with it. So, the other thing is, I don't write long letters. You see it is not possible. What you people write in three pages, I finish the whole thing in two lines. It has its purpose. In two lines what you want, you get it. All right, you are content. You will be happy. I don't repeat the words. It is not possible to write to each two, three, or four pages. There is hardly any time for me.

Disciple: How many disciples do you have?
Swamiji: I don't know. There must be some secretary to count it.
Disciple: Is it not a question of quantity but quality?
Swamiji: That is the quality, all youngsters. Every one coming and seeing you will be encouraged to see you with shining faces, working hard. All appreciate you people. That, itself, is a good symptom. Both boys and girls, young and old, they are all very pleased to see you people. They don't take you as beggars. This is almost a new thing I have started. I have given a new kind of sannyas. We are not depending on anyone. We are not beggars. We are not begging for anything. Every one of you is depending fully upon your own work and, at the same time, living the highest kind of pure life. It is really heaven if you can carry it out. I am not boasting. I am telling, it is really a great life for you people. And in a country like Denmark, to think about celibacy, it is terrible. In the middle of Denmark, we have this place. That is a great success itself.

In that way, come forward every one of you. Live the life. Rise up. Shake off your sleep. Come forward like heroes and heroines. A little hard work is necessary. The thing will come. We have got hundreds of real sannyasins, monks. They have renounced everything. Now they have come to this point. The first year that we came, we had more than a hundred who took sannyas. Last year, we had more than sixty. This year, there will be about fifty or sixty, something like that. That, itself, is a great miracle. Nobody initiated a hundred disciples as monks at one time. Nobody has done that. Every one of you must live to the point. That is what is wanted. We are not boasting in any way. That is not a boast. It is a real fact I am telling in this way. Now, come forward every one of you. There are only fifteen days. On the 31st, we will give sannyas. Then we will stop. The camp will end, you see.
Disciple: What will happen then?
Swamiji: All will go back to their respective homes and work hard, work it out.
Disciple: Another thing you say is, "Use your common sense."
Swamiji: I don't ask any to believe blindly. "Be rational," I tell them. In the book, "The Primal Poweer in Man or the Kundalini Shakti", I have written, "Don't believe me blindly." No author is in that way. Work it out and you will see the result and then only you believe it. It will

bring you results. That is all. So, again and again, I tell you people, "Use your common sense." When you work it out, you will understand, everything clears up.

I think it is time now. Sit for meditation.

August 16, 1973
Reading: *Pranayama is one of the yogic methods of controlling the mind and the attainment of Samadhi.*
Swamiji: By pranayama also you can raise up the kundalini shakti but it is not so easy. You have to control the prana. You have to take up the higher pranayamas. That requires that everything is well regulated there. Pranayama must also be taken up slowly and steadily and there must be a perfect teacher to guide you or else it is dangerous. Many people, by intensifying pranayamas, get a variety of diseases like piles or heart trouble. Your doctors cannot help them. They cannot find out the reason for it. You have to cure it by yoga alone. There are some pranayamas, number 1, 2, and 3 that are good for the health. Those, every one can do without any danger and it will help you people from pitfalls and dangers. Especially pranayama number 3, it is very beneficial for all sorts of people.

Reading: *Control of mind, control of prana, control of sex-energy and attainment of Samadhi always go together or hand in hand. One leads to the other almost simultaneously.*
Swamiji: So, those who actually claim some sort of attainment, there must be celibacy. Without celibacy, there is no success in any sphere of life. Even a man who makes a lot of money, self-made people, they have much less sex also. A scientist, when he is absorbed in his work, his mind cannot go for that thing. In any kind of sport like boxing, wrestling or athletics, go and study their lives. They have much less sex. The same thing with the great soldiers also. When you look at their lives, when they come to sex, their heroism goes to pieces. That is the most important thing. That is the strongest argument for you people.

Wherever there is brahmacharya, there is attainment. And to attain the highest, there must be perfect brahmacharya.
Disciple: But if these great heroes kill other people, how can they be called celibates?
Swamiji: It is their dharma to kill.
Disciple: What has killing to do with dharma?
Swamiji: Dharma is duty. As a soldier, he has to fight and kill. The more he kills, the better he will be. Fight and kill in a righteous war. What is the harm?

Reading: *Prana is the cause of sex-energy and of breath.*
Swamiji: So, when the shakti is in the lowest center, it is the sex-energy that goes out in the form of orgasm. It may be man or it may be woman. That is the greatest loss in the mental development. There is a thing called leakage from the dynamo. That means the body cannot get proper energy for circulation of the nerve energy. From the very start, it goes away. Such a man or woman suffers and is good for nothing. So, the whole world is merged in these three things. First, they want food, then they want sleep and then the third thing is sex. For an ordinary man, the aim of life is these three: food, sleep and sex. So, if you want to become human beings, you have to get the fourth one, mind-control. Come up now. In this way, rise up.

Reading: *So long as the kundalini shakti remains in the lowest center (Muladhara Chakra), tamo-guna predominates in an individual.*
Swamiji: In such people, tamo guna predominates. There can never be rajo guna even. In such cases, the kundalini shakti always takes the downward course easily. Such people are good for nothing. They are worse than animals also. Many of the animals are far better than these so-called human beings in that respect. Animals have sound health. Here, there is no health also. One cannot enjoy good health. They are always suffering. It is a horrible state.

Even the medical science knows if there is something wrong with the nerves, they cannot mend it. There is no medicine for it so far. Every orgasm means the body is squeezed out of energy. It starts from the brain center. The whole energy goes away. That is an irreparable loss. So, sex energy must be preserved and controlled at any cost. At least to call yourself a human being or to enjoy a good life with normal health, celibacy is necessary.

Reading: *Pranayama aims at regular and systematic breathing. It makes the practitioner healthy and enables the nerve-currents to function in a normal way.*
Swamiji: Whatever path you take, the essential thing is yama and niyama. Also, when you go on with pranayama, you will find out that you have to control food. If you eat too much, you can't do pranayama. You have to live a pure life. The sex energy must be controlled. One is connected with the other. Hash and LSD may bring a sudden push to the shakti and the after-effect is terrible. It attacks the kundalini shakti. There will be abnormal heat and you will have certain experiences but when it comes down, you cannot control it. The effect is mental derangement. That is the secret. In drinking, the same thing happens. The up-going currents will be too strong and they overpower the brain and the discriminative power cannot work.

Reading: *When It enters the Sushumna-Nadi, in Its upward course, the dynamo stops working.*
Swamiji: Thereby, never take up all of a sudden the higher pranayamas. That will be very dangerous. Don't go mad. Some years ago, a boy in Copenhagen took his own way of practising higher kinds of pranayama. He thought he would attain Samadhi. He thought, there was no need for a Guru and went on with full speed. And after some days, he went mad. He couldn't control it. He was living on the third floor and was going to jump but the owner was just passing and caught him. Then, there was a big hubbub. The police had to go with guns and they took him to the madhouse. What can the doctors do? They couldn't control him. Lastly his mother wrote me a letter about this and that thing. He was in a miserable state. Then we described for him how to control it. The only way was is to live on a milk diet and take some cold water hip baths. Afterwards, he got cured.

So, take precautions there. Go slowly. The easiest method is, without any danger, you can do mantra-jap and meditation. Even with little slips this side or that side, even in eating or drinking, just to have fun. Then, when you feel stomach pain, automatically you will say, "I will not eat more." So, never take up higher kinds of pranayama without proper guidance. The lower ones we prescribe for every one, even for curing disease. They are not dangerous.

Disciple: The body can also start shaking during meditation.

Swamiji: Sometimes when the Shakti rises up, it shakes the whole body. Some people have it.

Disciple: What to do then?

Swamiji: That is nothing. That will go away. Have patience. Try to sit straight. Some people jump. Some people fall. There are different things. It is all weakness of the body and nadis. Some people bend and bend out of emotion. Then they fall down slowly. That is why the seat should not be so high for ordinary people. It should be low, only this much; so, if you fall down there is not much injury.

Disciple: When you have pratyahara, does the kundalini shakti rise to the heart center?

Swamiji: That is not necessary, in that way. Even by coming to the second or third center, you may have some kind of experience. By practise, you go to a certain stage and later on, when the body is purified, it may go. It will first be travelling between the fourth and the last center. There will be movement up and down. Here it lives for some time. Then you have good ideas and the world also changes to a great extent. Then, if there is some mischief done by you, it falls down immediately. For such people, coming up and going down, it becomes easy. Whenever there is some emotional stir, it may come up to the heart center and then it falls down again.

Disciple: The hard struggle is to come to the fifth center.

Swamiji: Yes, that is a struggle. Actually, you gain. There is no fall then. When it goes to the fifth center only sattva guna works there.

Disciple: Is that the process of dharana?

Swamiji: Don't worry about dharana. Go on with your mantra-jap and all blessed things will come. When you go on with your daily mantra-jap and meditation, automatically all these things develop. The shakti will work by itself, don't drag it, don't guide it, don't meddle with it. That is dangerous. By going to watch it, you lose your concentration. That is a curiosity. If you lose it, you don't get anything. The best thing is to neglect it. Leave it aside. Let it do its own function. It will do it and you do your work. That is necessary. Is it clear or any doubt?

Disciple: Then it is not at all necessary to think of all those chakras?

Swamiji: Don't. It is not necessary, a mere waste of time. It is all momentary things. You see some illusion and your mind goes out. Instead of gaining higher concentration, you waste your time with all these things. Many people see some sort of visions of Gods. That is a natural thing. Some people see a variety of lights and some may hear sounds. Many people make a big hubbub over it and say they have seen God and they want to become Gurus then. That is an easy way. Other people, who have not seen, think that he is a man of attainment. He is an advanced man. That is how all this trouble comes. Falls come and you can't make any progress. At every step, you have to control it. All these silly things have no meaning. Some coming to higher pitches will have the tendency for poetry. You have got a beautiful imagination and you want to become a poet. That is also dangerous. You want to write this and that. A big circle is there. You are only wandering around the circle.

Then there is another thing called ecstasy, a sort of trance. By that you have got a better experience. You enter into the circle but you have not come to the center. Only Samadhi will take you to the center of the circle. There, you realize your True Nature. That is what is wanted. In all other things, you miss it but you can understand it. It is there still. All these things, you have to give up.

Disciple: Can these things not become help in your sadhana, for example, if poetry is directed towards the goal?

Swamiji: How can you direct it? You go on writing poems and poems. Where will you go? Your mind is engaged in this only.

Disciple: You can go to a certain point then you see it cannot take you further and then you leave it.

Swamiji: But how long will you waste time in that way?

Disciple: As long as it gives you good concentration.

Swamiji: There is no concentration. It is all imagination. You have to live in imagination, some flowery words. What is a novel? It is imagination. Just like poetry. It may be a good thing. It may be bad. Even the songs you make may be love songs or they may be devotional songs. That is all imagination. You may get some money, that is all right, but not the Truth. If you are satisfied with that thing, all right. That is also good.

Disciple: What about karma-yoga?

Swamiji: That is all right. If you take it in the right spirit, it is all right. When you go to higher kinds of concentration, then all these things will diminish. You will have to go further. You want to engage your mind completely in concentration. Generally, you feel it when you feel more pleasure in it. The other thing is a burden. Automatically you don't like it. Your selection will be for the higher things where you get more pleasure.

Disciple: How can it be that the intellect does not grow so sharp at the same time that one discriminates?

Swamiji: The intellect is sharp all right but you don't want it. In this way, all sorts of mischief you do. You are trained in that way. But when you are living a pure life, when you are training for higher things, then it will work in that way. There, it will not deceive you. That is what you call the "inner voice", the prick of conscience.

Disciple: Still, it is difficult to control, to take the right direction.

Swamiji: It also goes side by side. You have to control it. First you have been hearing it then you are practising it. It takes time. There will be ups and downs. Struggle is there. When you constantly discriminate between right and wrong, good and bad, pain and pleasure, all those things, and stick to the right one, automatically it will work in the right direction. The training is also there. That is what is meant by sadhana.

August 23, 1973

Disciple: Is it better to have a fixed time for meditation?

Swamiji: If possible do it. If it is not possible adjust the time. That is all right. Some people are very strict. They sit to the time. Whatever it may be, when the time comes, they will go for meditation.

Disciple: It is very nice.

Swamiji: A person who is indifferent, he cannot do that thing. He who has a strong will power will do it. When I was a young boy, then I would do anything and everything at a fixed time. Everything was fixed. I even had a time for winding my watch. In the morning at six, I wound it. And even if I was somewhere in meditation, after some time the watch came there. At exactly six I would see the watch amd wind it. By systematic work, the benefit is there. Even if you forget the fixed hour for meditation, at that particular time, you think of God. You may be busy somewhere, you may be travelling by train or airplane, wherever it may be. When the fixed time comes, you are aware of it. When you have heavy work in the office, it will be difficult sometimes. So, a little adjustment is necessary.

Disciple: May I ask something more? You talked some days ago about why we have forgotten our birth-right.
Swamiji: Then?
Disciple: Yes, why? Is it due to wrong training?
Swamiji: Mainly the mind, the habit of the mind. I have given the reply for it there, in the same chapter. I have given the illustration of the bee or butterfly. There is no why. The door is wide open. Nobody invites the butterfly. It enters the glasshouse, it sees the flowers and, being enchanted by the flowers, it enters through the door. The door is still open and coming in, it goes on seeing the beautiful flowers and it sucks the honey and other things. When the stomach is full, it wants to go out but it forgets the door. The door is still open but seeing light coming from this side and that side, it goes and strikes its head and it gets stunned and more confused. Now, instead of going to the door, it goes here and there. Many die in the room itself. Some may find the path also. For some others, the good gardener may catch them and throw them out. Anyway, the question comes, why it gets confused? Nobody has made it confused. So, the mind is the cause of all these things.
Disciple: Then it must be awfully stupid.
Swamiji: Yes, that is what I am telling. We are he most stupid and irrational sort of thing. That is why I say, "Oh miserable wretch." I call the man a "miserable fool." I tell him, "You have forgotten your True Nature. You are now working inside, going to that window, this door and up and down and here and there, so hopeless." Ordinary people think that by sense enjoyments they will be happy. They run away. That

is how the world is going on — mad after worldly things. The more they enjoy, the more kicks they get. Still, they don't want to turn back. They are busy with it. Money is only the means for these enjoyments and then comes the desire for name and fame. The whole world is nothing but a projection of your own mind. An impure mind is the cause of your bondage and misery and a pure mind leads you to Freedom and bliss, happiness - everlasting happiness. So, sadhana means to control this devil mind. Instead of allowing it to go out, now you are taking it inside. Go back to your Source and you will find your lost kingdom.

Disciple: Swamiji, you say that Freedom is also in the mind?

Swamiji: All understanding is in the mind. The idea of bondage and Freedom are also in the mind. When you go to the mindless region, there is not a thing called Freedom or bondage. Your Self is ever free but you have forgotten it because you are a slave to your mind and senses. That is the cause of your bondage. I told you long ago, it is not that you are not free or you are going to become free. It is not that you are not God or that you are becoming God. You are already That. Now find it out. The whole mischief is in the mind. So, control the mind and you will control everything.

Disciple: We should not have listened to that Reincarnation Theory; then, we would have finished sooner.

Swamiji: Even if you don't want it, it is there and it will be working. It will not leave you so easily. It is not an excuse. If you don't know it, ignorance is not an excuse there. Then, how do you account for all the misery from the very birth? One child is born so intelligent. Some are so idiotic. Some are born blind and/or deaf. How do you account for all that? You will have to make God responsible for it. It is only one birth theory. But the fact is not so. You are responsible for everything. What you have sown in the past in the form of desires, thoughts and acts, that you reap in this birth. That is past karma. If your present is owing to your past, your future is entirely in your own hands. So, we are not deceiving anyone. We say, "Work hard, be noble, be kind, live a pure, simple and holy life." We are not hiding facts. Now be prepared.

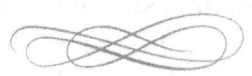

August 24, 1973
Reading: *Let us now see how one can control the mind and attain Emancipation through work. Work cannot be avoided by any living being. So long as one lives in this world one has to work even for the sake of bare maintenance.*
Swamiji: Don't make a confusion there and don't give up your work. If you are working in a factory, don't give up money and come back and then say, "Swamiji has said not to do it." Don't make a blunder. You will have to take money. "Don't expect anything," means a reward.
Disciple: How should the Ishta-Devata be thought of?
Swamiji: What do you mean by it? Take every work and think you are doing the work for God. Think the body and everything else, mind, senses, everything, belongs to God. When you do work in that way, then you have got love for the work and you do not neglect anything. When you go to the office, think that the earning is meant for God. Suppose you are a married man, say "I am serving Him through wife and children." If you go to the field, when you are working there, it is all meant for God, "It is all His work I am doing." It is the easiest way to kill the ego.

Reading: *One must work whole-heartedly with one's whole mind, will and heart but one must not hanker after or expect anything in return. One must work like a master – work for work's sake, without expecting anything in return as its fruit.*
Swamiji: And there must be a hard struggle too. It is not so easy. The devotee puts God in front. For everything, he says, "Oh God, I am only the servant. You are the Master." That is thou and thine. Constantly he puts that idea. A karma yogi will not worry about the fruits of the action done. In this way, the mind gets purified and the shakti rises upward. It is all the different paths of purification only. That is sadhana. The aim is to purify the mind. That is the main thing.
Disciple: Swamiji, to offer your work to God and not to expect anything as a result, is that not a kind of abstract thinking? Isn't it very difficult to convince yourself to do that?
Swamiji: In the beginning, you may find it difficult. Difficulty is there. But when you go on with this slowly and steadily, it becomes a habit.

Then you don't care for it and at the same time you don't neglect the work also. That is what I mean.
Disciple: Yes.
Swamiji: Many people may think that without interest or without desire, how can you work? It is impossible. Suppose you are going to school. You are teaching the children. There you handle it properly. Work it out and do your best and, at the same time, leave it as it is. Don't expect that you should get a promotion or something else, for example, some sort of praise or other things. If somebody does not praise you or if you do not get the expected raise, then you are sorry. That is not karma-yoga. But, if you work without interest, you have done your duty. That is all right. You have peace of mind. That is the secret. If somebody gives you praise, it does not matter. You are not worried about it. If somebody criticizes you, then also, you will not be worried. Take both equally. Think it is God's will. That means ups and downs, in all pain and pleasure, in all the pairs of opposites. You will have equipoise. The mind remains in balance.
Disciple: Yes, but before you can do karma-yoga, you have to have a certain perfection in work. You must really know how to handle it.
Swamiji: Whatever work you take, not only karma-yoga, every work can be made a sort of karma-yoga. Suppose you want to sweep this room, you understand?
Disciple: Yes.
Swamiji: So, you have been given this work. Say, I ask you from tomorrow to take care of the room, to keep it neat and clean. All right, you have taken the work. Do it carefully and nicely to your utmost satisfaction, not in a hasty way. If you have to finish the work in a hurry, you run out this side, that side and you have some new desires. Do not do it in that way. Then you have no satisfaction. On the other hand, someone has been given the work of the toilet and that may be a bit dirty work. Still, he does it with full love, so carefully and nicely, putting his whole energy and concentration there. He keeps everything neat. And here, you have not done it carefully. You have done here and there without much shraddha, just to finish it. But he has done the work with full love. So, his work is far better than this work then. That is karma-yoga. At the same time, don't expect that someone must praise you or lift you up. Don't expect anything.

Disciple: If you stand in a factory on the production line and it goes very fast, there it is nearly impossible to make karma-yoga. You cannot get in touch with it and you have to be very busy.

Swamiji: When you begin the work, take God's name and begin and then merge yourself in the work. At intervals, if you have time, remember your mantra. When you finish, offer everything. Be busy, forget everything, it is all right. You can do it. When you finish every work, offer it, the whole work and its fruits. In this way, you have to proceed.

Disciple: I mean that not all kinds of work are so simple.

Swamiji: It is not a question of simple. Whatever comes unasked for, do it. If you desire the work and you do not get it, that is very terrible. And if you select the work then also the mind deceives in so many ways. There is a thing called monotony. If you sometimes do the same work, after some days, you will feel disgusted. You want a change. That means from one work to another. You go on changing and it is difficult to adjust. The mind deceives you. You have no satisfaction. It is also dangerous there. Stick to the work, whatever has come. You have selected some job. That is all right. Go on with it.

Disciple: But Swamiji, you can have a kind of work, where you have no idea how the work should be done but you are bound to work together with another.

Swamiji: Suppose together, that is all right. You have the control. Carry out the work. And, if someone else is controlling you, yield to it. That is all right. You have no responsibility there. When there are equal partners, there is little difficulty.

Disciple: Not a little difficulty, a big difficulty.

Swamiji: There is difficulty but if you know how to adjust, see which is right, which is wrong. If you are wrong in some way, all right, let him have the idea.

Disciple: If two people have a job for a big thing and one says, "If we do so, we will jump over." And the other says, "No, we will do so," and then they both fall down.

Swamiji: For that thing, give a little sacrifice. Let him have a choice first. Let him jump first. If he knows how to jump, all right. He is the leader there. If he fails, then you have the right to check him. Next time you have the choice.

Swamiji: Who of you is the composer?
Disciple: He is not here yet.
Swamiji: You must read it also. You people must sing it. I don't know how to sing.
Disciple: But Swamiji has composed the words.
Swamiji: It is all right but the meter must be there. I don't know your meter. There are different meters. It must be done tomorrow.
Disciple: Should it be read?
Swamiji: Read it. Just let them have an idea.

Regaining of Your Lost Empire:
written by Swami Narayanananda

Wake up My darlings, wake up
Wake up from the long-lasting slumber
I have brought you the grandest news
The news of the lost Empire – God or the Ultimate Truth
Your innermost being itself is God
But by thinking of your sins and sinful acts
  you have become sinful
By thinking of your weaknesses and drawbacks
  you have become weak and stupid
For, as you think that you become
And what you sow that you reap
You have come from God, in God you live
And in the end, you go back to God
Your Self is ever pure and free
It remains in the body as a witness only
And the universe is only a projection of your mind
Desires are the causes of your bondage and misery
And the ego is the cause of the desires
The mind becomes weak and impure
  by evanescent sense-pleasures
An impure mind is the cause of your bondage and misery
And a pure one leads you to liberation
To regain your lost Empire
A pure mind elevates you

and an impure mind drags you down to bondage
Now, live a pure, simple and holy life
Keep up sadhana and control your mind
And regain your lost Empire
Wake up My darlings, wake up.
Wake up from the long-lasting slumber.

Swamiji: The lost Empire, what is that news? It means you've lost your Empire and now I am bringing the news of that Empire. That is the Eternal Truth. You have forgotten the thing so you have been suffering. Now, wake up from sleep. So, God or the Eternal, that is your innermost being. Your innermost being, itself is God. That you have forgotten. It is just like a lion.

A pregnant lion goes to hunt a sheep. She jumps and gives birth to a baby and the mother dies. And that helpless baby lion, "pup" you call it, was brought up by the shepherd. They used to give it milk and grass only. And it began to drink milk and eat grass instead of meat. So, it was bleating like the sheep and goats, just like their young ones. So, it entirely forgot it was a lion. One day, even when it became a very big, it used to run when there was a little noise like the sheep and other goats used to run. It also used to run and it became a coward. It forgot its true nature.

One day another lion went there. It was hiding from a distance just to catch some of the sheep and goats. But it found this terrible fellow much bigger than him but he was acting just like the goats and sheep. Whenever they began running, it also ran and it was eating grass. Poor creature, the lion took pity on it. It was just watching. Some way or other, when the grass-eating lion was coming, it jumped and caught it. The grass-eating lion began to tremble with fear. "Please leave me alone," it was crying with fear. The lion said, "No. You are not a sheep, you are not a goat, you are a lion, king of the forest, come forward." The grass-eating lion could not believe it. It said, "No, no, please let me go." It was shivering with fear, "Let me go." So, then the lion took the grass-eating lion by force and went to a place where there was a water tank. Then he said, "You see, you and I, we are equal." Again, it forced it. And lastly, the grass-eating lion understood it was not a sheep but a lion.

Likewise, you people have forgotten your True Nature. You have been sleeping. Now wake up from sleep.

August 25, 1973

Reading: *A person in whom the feeling faculty predominates takes to bhakti-yoga for sadhana (spiritual practice). Bhakti means love and Yoga means union. So, bhakti-yoga is the union of the individual Self with the Supreme Self through love.*

Swamiji: Like pouring honey, you have seen pure honey or castor oil, for example, if you pour it from one bottle to another, there will not be any break in the continuity. That is called bhakti, when your love is constantly flowing. If there is a little break or you forget to think of God, even for a second, it is as if you have forgotten Him for some years together — such a big gap, painful thing. That is called real love. The further it goes, you hear the name of God, you get goose bumps out of emotion. And the further it developes, one really forgets the body idea completely when hearing the name of God. These are different developments. The symptoms of pure love are: it knows no hatred, it knows no bargaining and it has no fear. It is free from all these three things.

Is it clear? Any kind of yoga means that dirty ego, small ego, must die. These are different methods to kill the ego only.

August 26, 1973

Reading: *But, when once a real Guru has been accepted the disciple must have infinite and implicit faith in him and in his power and wisdom and carry out his instructions to the letter.*

Swamiji: Then only His instructions will bear fruit. If doubt comes again and again, then you are nowhere. You cannot work and you will lose your path. That is the secret. When once you accept him, follow him, whatever it may be. If he asks you to jump from a housetop and give your life, be prepared. Don't ask why. It is His responsibility. The man who gives the command to jump from the rooftop must be able to save you also. So, obey Him. If there is something wrong, if you die, then it is left to Him. Let Him take the blame. That is faith. If that faith is there, the success is speedy.

Disciple: But to do everything exactly, it is very difficult.

Swamiji: Then your ego is deceiving you. That "I am," that "I" is hiding and externally you must make a show of it. "Oh, I believe my Guru in every respect. I am prepared to give my life, everything," you will say. But when the time comes, nobody wants it. The ego is deceiving you. That plays mischief. That is the test.

Sikh Guru Gobind was the last Guru there. He had a big congregation and then he secretly hid four goats, big goats with beards. In the public lecture, he said, "I want at least four people who are very, very faithful, who are prepared to give their lives. I want to sacrifice them here today." Then he showed a big sword also. "How many are prepared?" There was much difficulty then one stood up. "Yes, I am prepared to give my life." "All right," he said. "Take him inside and cut him." They went inside and cut a goat and he showed the sword with blood and also the beard he showed. "Here, one man has died," he said. "I want three more who will give their life." Four people came forward in that way. They were selected as his first-class bodyguards afterwards. Later on he said, "It was only a test." So, other people now understood their lives were preserved and those people were selected as his foremost disciples. And they had much work to do also. So, every one will say, "I can do it." But when the time comes, very few want to do it. So, there you fail. You must be strong.

Reading: *Stick to one Guru, one Guru-Mantra and one Ishta-Devata. Otherwise, you are sure to miss the goal.*

Swamiji: These are all practical things every one of you must keep in mind though we have to hurry up in dealing with the subject. You will not get this chance or this teaching always. It is not possible. Many of you have been very fortunate. I should not praise myself. It will be stupidity to say such words but I have to speak also. It is not easy, even if you spend thousands of kroners. If you go to India, you go here, there.

All right, you will see some and come back and have heard some cock-and-bull stories. Perhaps, you don't find much value but that you will understand later on. All right.
Disciple: Also, now!
Swamiji: If you cannot take up the proper line, proper work, everything will go to pieces. One boy came this morning, he was practising pranayama himself, also number four. It is forbidden. He was so haggard looking. Then he was asking, "What about Mahapralaya?" Mahapralaya means the whole universe coming to naught, complete destruction of the universe. It is impossible. If that is possible, then you can know God and when He started His game. Then He must have a beginning and an end also. So, everything is illogical. Everything will go to pieces. Pralaya is there. At every moment, it is going on as you see it in the universe or in the world itself. So many creatures are taking birth. So many are growing and so many are dying. This triple function is constantly going on. But, if the whole universe were to come to naught, it is impossible.

Reading: *A Sadhaka must observe very strictly the code of moral conduct. He must be always truthful, kind, gentle, unselfish and charitable.*
Swamiji: Yesterday there was a charge against you people that you are not hospitable and not charitable enough. But the other side has completely misunderstood. You people have been working very hard. You have been struggling to get concentration of mind. For three months, you have been working. It is natural, when you are deeply interested in any kind of work, not only here. Suppose as a teacher you are busy making preparations for your study for a class. It may be your closest friend who comes to you. Even to attend to the person, you can't speak to him. You have to hurry up with the work.

Similarly, a man is busy in his field and a stranger comes and asks him, "What do you grow? What is the season? How to preserve it?" It is not possible for him to answer so he will say, "Please go away." "Here is the manager, the camp chief, go and ask him," he will tell you. So, he will say, "Oh, the people are so inhospitable. They are not at all kind. They cannot explain even this much." They do not understand the difficulty. So, when one is absorbed, it is natural. You cannot expect that thing. As I told him yesterday, "Tivoli is not here. It is not the purpose here. Every one of you will be busy. They have hardly any time."

I have realized myself that when I was a young boy, I had no time even to speak with other people. I would ask them from a long distance, "Have you got any work or have you come only for gossip? If it is for gossip, then don't come here. I have no time. If you have got any work then come to the point." When you are making progress spiritually, even to speak, it becomes so painful to you. If you were to give a hundred thousand kroner for one minute even, you would pay that and use that minute for God-Realization. It is so fascinating. It is so charming and so powerful also — the bliss of concentration. I remember that period, so I can understand the difficulties of other people. And it was an injustice in a way to accuse them in that way without knowing the other side. You have got the discipline also in the camp, not to speak loudly, not to disturb other meditating people. They have saved money for the last year to make use of these three months in the camp for meditation. So, it should be understood in that way also.

Reading: *To attain the Highest: Brahmacharya is the very first thing to look to; while loss of brahmacharya is surely the greatest fall in spirituality.*
Swamiji: That is the first and foremost fall for a sadhaka. If perfect brahmacharya is established either by man or woman, then three-fourths of the sadhana is over. For such a man, only one fourth remains. They can attain Samadhi easily. That is the secret. That is a herculean task in the beginning but when you go on with your mantra-jap and meditation, it will come up. You will go on gaining ground, gaining strength. You can tell lies, thousands of lies and still you are not caught. You can try to escape it but there is no escape. Immediately you have a fall. You cannot hide it.

Reading: *Hard physical and mental labor militates against meditation and mind-control.*
Swamiji: But we cannot avoid it. Thereby, don't make a hubbub over it. You have to adjust. You have to work. You have to keep both the things or we can't eat. That we have to see now but the fact is there. Those who work very hard, they feel tired and when you meditate too

much, you cannot work also. The thing is there but you have to make a compromise between these two things. Those who have got enough money, who can devote much time, that is another thing. For such people, it is there. They can make use of it. But here, in the country, it is not in that way. It is very difficult. So, until we get opportunities, we have to make adjustments between both. Work and meditation must go side by side.

Disciple: Swamiji, does that mean those who have money and really use it the right way, they could sit meditating very much and will reach it much quicker than all of us who have to do a lot of work?

Swamiji: Yes, that is a fact.

Disciple: Isn't it a bit unjust?

Swamiji: It is not unjust. Because they have worked hard in the past life, they have got it now. This life they got a chance. If that money is misused, they go down again. They become pigs in the next life. When it is misused and they lead an animal life, gone. So, it is misused there.

Disciple: I think it is very interesting and very complicated.

Swamiji: Because people do not believe in reincarnation, they think only of one birth theory. It will make it complicated. Then you must think God is responsible for everything because he has created one birth, such a horrible God. It is of no use worshipping such a God. So, people get annoyed with him now. They think there is no need for such a God. That is why they revolt, the younger generation. A God who has made someone rich, someone else a king, some others starving and others hash smokers. What a horrible God it is. We are not in need of such a God. You are responsible for you own good and bad, progress and degeneration. Both are within you. Here, you can explain it in a proper way. Better than the so-called one birth theory.

Disciple: Swamiji, what about mercy?

Swamiji: Even to have mercy, that is all your own doing. Everything comes from within. When you pray to God, "Oh Lord, have mercy," you will try to mend your life also. If you are sincere in your prayers, you must work hard also for that for which you pray. So, you will get mercy.

Disciple: So, in a way, is it the impure mind?

Swamiji: It is all the tricks of the mind. When the mind is purified, it becomes stronger and stronger. Mind has infinite powers and whatever you will, it will come. It is there. It must come.

Reading: *Free mixing with all sorts of people is very injurious; for, during the sadhana period when the mind is in the act of gaining purity, it is like a well washed white piece of cloth which takes any colour almost immediately.*

Swamiji: So, here the danger is this. Suppose you are mixing with a variety of people for talking. Some have the habit. Then even a small mistake may look like a big thing. It is natural then. So, you must be very careful. When the mind revolves on that, "Why has this thing happened, why has he done that thing?" It is offensive. You get annoyed. So, a lot of time is being wasted there. So, take precautions in all these things. That is why free mixing and free talking is forbidden. It has a very bad effect. When the mind is purified, you have a meaning for every sort of thing. So, you must be very careful there.

Reading: *A doubting mind can never reach the goal. It is better to have a bullet through the heart than to allow a doubt to arise in the mind.*

Swamiji: Don't take any bullet. Catch the spirit, not the bullet. That means it is very bad to have doubt. Whenever it comes, kick it out. That is what is meant.

August 27, 1973

Reading: *After a little hard practice and with a little steady progress, there comes the unconscious desire to preach dharma (what one has known) to others. This is a very dangerous game and should be avoided.*

Swamiji: It is, "I have gained something; so I must give something to the world," that comes. Many people are weak. They have not got a clear understanding. That is also one of the attractions. You want to become popular. There are some fools and you will try to be a wise man. You will talk so many things. You want to convince them. You will say, "Ah, miserable fool, they are so worldly-minded. They don't want to come to God." So many things you will say. The whole force goes away in talking. It is all mere attractions. It is better to avoid such things in the beginning or else you will be stranded. Many people want to pose as Gurus themselves.

Reading: *One can do real and valuable service to the world by leading a pure, holy and ideal life. Example is always better than precept and an ounce of practice is worth tons of theory.*
Swamiji: Here you have to understand this point every one of you. Don't go to preach in the beginning. That will have a worse effect.

Reading: *To extol one's spiritual attainments and to narrate them to one's friends is a very bad habit.*
Swamiji: There is no common mind, common understanding, common companion. All these things have no meaning there or you will be stranded. The easiest method there will be to have a common understanding, common background, common mind, hash and a chillum. That will make the common understanding there. Have one big chillum and hundreds of people have one puff. That will be the common mind. All have the common experience then. That will be the best thing. But here, if you want progress, it must be secret. It will be necessary here or else the friends, themselves, will become enemies.

Suppose you have some progress and the other man, he might have started the game long ago, many years before you, he says, "Oh this fellow, he has got so much experience. I have not gained anything." Another man will say, "Oh, I have worked ten years and I have not gained anything and he has got it. He began yesterday and he has got it. He is a fool." So, all will have is a tug of war there. So, it is better to keep quiet. Such things will not help anyone.

Reading: *Otherwise, one loses what one has already gained and must struggle hard over again for it. This is no understatement. It is a warning which the author would like to sound as a result of actual tests with many sadhakas.*

Swamiji: When you go on telling your experience, then you have a great fall. If you want to come to that point again, it will take several years. You have to weep and weep. There are so many cases of that kind. So, you must be careful there.

Reading: *Another alluring practice which proves a stumbling block in the way of spiritual progress is the use of supernatural powers.*
Swamiji: Curing of diseases comes under this category. When you make use of it, it will disappear. It can't stand long. Then you have to pretend. Many people keep up prayers. It is very dangerous. They have to give their life for it. Every one has got that power. It is only a question of time. With the full rising of the shakti, these siddhis manifest but it should be kicked out. Don't use it. You know it. It is there, but control it. If you are weak, you will go to pieces, never to rise up in this life again.

Last year I was in Rungsted. One man said he had certain siddhis. One of his friends was suffering from heart disease. He knew he had that power, so he passed his hand over his chest. He got it cured and he got the disease himself. He was telling even after so many years that he is suffering from the same disease. He had to pay for it. Likewise, there are so many minor siddhis. There are so many major siddhis also.
Disciple: What is the difference between minor siddhis and major siddhis?
Swamiji: There are major siddhis. They can disappear at will from the body. They can become lighter than air or heavier than the earth and they can walk on water. There are some austere siddhis like that. The minor siddhi is you can see things from a very long distance or you have the power of oratory or you can speak so wonderfully. One man could move a piano. These are all small ones you may have even from the very birth. Never go for all those things. Be normal.
Reading: *Very often sadhakas make the mistake of living in secluded places for a long time in the initial stages of their sadhana.*
Swamiji: So, one can go occasionally, once in a while. Sometimes for three or four days, even ten or fifteen, not more. Don't speak, observe mouna, eat little and meditate. It will help you people. But don't go for a month or two. It is very dangerous. Even amidst the people, you can develop yourself. Only you have to control your speech and your diet every day. That is the best thing.

Reading: *In conclusion, let it be said that a sadhaka must always be cheerful. He must have infinite patience, perseverance, courage and hope.*

Swamiji: It is necessary. Don't weep and don't laugh, also, too much. Be normal. You must be joyful also. Have contentment. That is what is meant. That is one of the rules of niyama - contentment. If some failures come, don't worry so much. Take precautions not to fall down again. So, resume the work. In that way, you have to proceed.

There were two sadhakas. One was doing so much tapasya, sitting under a tree always meditating. Then there was another man who had contentment. One day the Deva Rishi Narada was passing on his way to Vaikuntha, the abode of Narayan. The first man, he asked, "Please ask Narayan how long I have to wait to get God-Realization." "When I come back, I will see you," Narada replied. He proceeded further and met the man who had contentment and he also asked Narada, "If he could ask Lord Narayan how long he had to wait." After six months, Narada came back and he met the first man who was meditating. He asked, "What did the Lord say?" Narada said, "You have four births more. You have to meditate." He began weeping. "So much? Horrible, how long I have to wait." Then Narada proceeded to the other man. He came running and said, "What did the Lord say?" Narada said, "You see that very big tree with all the small leaves?" "Yes," he said, "I see it." "You see how many leaves it has? It may have millions. After millions of births, you will get it." Oh, he was so happy. "At least, at last, I will get it." He began dancing out of ecstasy. He was so happy. Then immediately, Lord Narayan had to come and take him to heaven. That is a story of contentment.

Work hard and leave the rest to God. Have contentment. Don't go to extremes. Always take the middle course. Many people make a mistake and kill the body. They don't want to kill the mind and senses and desires. They fight with the body for nothing. After all, the body is only a machine. It is just like a house for you for living. Keep it, but never get attached to it and, at the same time, go on. The desires have to be controlled and the mind is just an instrument like a watch. You have to keep the body neat. You have to give it food, rest and clothing, everything. Always take the middle course. That is the safest.

August 28, 1973

Reading: *But in spite of all his (Ramahrishna's) sincere prayers, he had no response and, at last, life becoming unbearable to him without a vision of the Mother - he resolved to put an end to his life.*

Swamiji: Don't do it in that way, any of you. One brahmachari in Rishikesh, he might have heard all these things. One day he went with a big axe to a small jungle. He prayed to God and put his leg saying, "If you don't come, I will cut off the leg." God did not come so he gave a severe blow so it broke. It was the end of his devotion. So, don't imitate in that way. It is not easy to have complete faith. When you come to the last point, that is another thing. So, just to pretend, "I am going to die", you are making a show there and that is very dangerous. So, don't imitate in that way.

Now every one must struggle. We have given the most beautiful expression and those things must be kept in mind always. Many people, when they come to a certain point, they make mistakes. I have been warning you again and again. Don't be stupid and weak. Every one of you must be strong there. There will be a lot of temptations also before coming to this point. That we have been discussing last week. Many people slip down. They go into a dream state. They will go to so many heavens. Such people get confused and their followers become bigots. They say,"Our founder says only in this way. Our books say in this way," nothing further. So, if you want to break down in the middle and enjoy, you will have a lot of fun. A lot of coming and doing and you will have an easy-going life in a way. So, now decide what you want at the start. Don't bend your knees half way. Don't stop there. Always think, I must have the last point, not all these intermediate states.

August 29, 1973

Reading: *After attaining this state of Samadhi once, there is nothing more to gain, nothing more to acquire on earth or in heaven. For such a man, there is no want, no longing and no deficiency of any kind. He enjoys complete satiety.*

Swamiji: So, there is the answer. You were asking one day, "How to know whether one has attained Samadhi or not?" After attaining Samadhi, you have perfect satisfaction all round, no want, no requirement, no desires, nothing whatsoever. You are complete or full by yourself. What more do you want? You want to die? There is no more death for you. Any doubts still?

Disciple: How often do you enter Nirvikalpa Samadhi?

Swamiji: How often? There is no limit for it.

Reading: *He gets absolved of all obligatory duties, goes beyond the idea of time, space and causation and beyond the three gunas (sattva, rajas, tamas). To gain this state of Samadhi, is the aim, the end, the goal and summum bonum of life.*

Swamiji: So, if anybody asks what is the aim of life, here is the aim. Every one is struggling to attain it. First ask whether you want it or do you want something else. If you want filth, all right, the world is full of that. Go on. Have as much filth as possible. If you don't want that, the path will be clear. Follow it. Nobody is compelling you. The choice is with you and nobody is misguiding you. Have a clear-cut idea and work it out. The path is open to all and the selection is with you individuals. There is no God to make you or misguide you. Your mind, itself, is the cause of everything.

Reading: *Therefore, we cannot consider a Jivan-Mukta to be under the influence of prarabdha karma; as he would, then, be doing both good and sinful acts which is absurd.*

Swamiji: Many people make a mistake. They read books and come to the conclusion that they have realized God. Then they make a hubbub and they make disciples and do all sorts of evil. They say, "Even by doing everything, the body is doing, I am not doing". Some will say, "This is prarabdha-karma. The karma is there. Let it go on. I am not worried in that way." That is all hypocrisy. It is a wrong way. That is why the chapter has been given.

Reading: *The vast majority of so-called Brahma-Jnanis have not attained Nirvikalpa Samadhi.*
Swamiji: You have to go on saying, "I am not this thing. I am Brahman." You go on and you become Brahman. They don't admit that Nirvikalpa Samadhi is a necessity to attain Brahma-Jnana. They go on reading books and they miss the point.

Reading: *Nirvikalpa Samadhi and real Brahma-Jnana always go together.*
Swamiji: There was a King. He invited all the Brahma-Jnanis of the land. There were some thousands. All were Brahma-Jnanis. He made all the arrangements for their food and living and they were all happy. The King went in the evening with his Prime Minister to have the darshan of all these Brahma-Jnanis. So, all were there. He went and prostrated and paid his respects. Afterwards, when he returned, he said, "I am so happy. So many Brahma-Jnanis are in the country. So many have come here. I am blessed." But, the Prime Minister was a wise man. He said, "Out of so many thousands, you see, I don't know whether there are one or two real Brahma-Jnanis." The King said, "How can you say that? They are all real men, so great." "Well, if you will permit me, I will test it within no time," he said. "Yes, let me see." "All right." He went and set fire to the camp. It was a big camp. One side he set fire with another man on the other side shouting, "There is fire, fire." All the Brahma-Jnanis began to run here and there. They wanted to save their lives. Only one or two were unmindful of the fire, "What can it do?" They were sitting quiet. All others ran away from the camp. Then he told the King, "Now you see how many Brahma-Jnanis you have, only one or two." Then the King understood.

There are many who pose like that. They speak of that but, actually, there are very few who go to the highest. They are satisfied with tidbits of success. They have no patience. They don't want to work and they have the desire for name and fame. They leave the work. They are satisfied if they get a little name and fame, some praise, some disciples. They are content with it. So, they will avoid all further troubles when there is some comfort. Let us see. This life passes on easily. Let us see next life.

You know your True Nature. That is only Jnana. Many people understand that a Jnani must write books and give lectures. There is nothing like that. Jnana means wisdom. That is just like striking a match and getting light. When you go to Samadhi, you have that wisdom. That is the secret. "I am Brahman." That is Jnana. To know your True Nature, that is wisdom, nothing else. When you come to this point, there is no room for your supernatural powers also. It is as filthy as anything. On whom are you going to use it when you see God or Brahman? You are going to help God? What a horrible thing. It is blasphemy. That means you are seeing something else. The real thing is forgotten. That you have to keep in mind, every one of you. Then the question of serving the world, helping the world, it has no meaning there. But still, the Jivan-Mukta's life goes on. It is very difficult to explain, how you can live at all. He is just playing a drama. That is all. Some people may speak so many things, but if you know the real facts, then you know the depth of the person. Immediately, you know he is a fraud. It is all real facts which you people must keep in mind. It will serve you in so many ways.

August 30, 1973
Reading: *He whose mind is not shaken by adversity, who does not hanker after happiness, who has become free from affection, fear and wrath, is indeed a Muni (man of meditation) of steady Wisdom. He, who is everywhere unattached, not pleased at receiving good, nor vexed at evil, his Wisdom is fixed (He does not praise or blame).*
Swamiji: Don't make a confusion there of praising and blaming. Sometimes you have to speak the Truth, then what happens?
Disciple: People will criticize.
Swamiji: How?
Disciple: For blaming.

Swamiji: You are stupid. When it is real fact, it is not criticism. That you must understand. Many people like that understanding. Suppose you speak a certain thing about a person, a place, whatever it may be. You speak the Truth and that Truth may look like criticism to other people. It is not criticism. That you have to understand. It is the fact about the thing. Criticism means you are unnecessarily scolding or doing something, even it may be good or bad, you neglect it. You have your own way of talking. That is criticism. But speaking the Truth is not criticism. Every one of you must understand it. Many people misunderstand that thing.

Reading: *In a Jivan-Mukta, the mind naturally lives in Turiya-State where one sees unity in diversity. In the purest and the highest kind of intuition there is no reasoning process at all. Intuition transcends reason but does not contradict it; on the other hand, it fulfils it (reason).*

Swamiji: So, that is all right, that state. But when you become a Guru and live with others, then it is not there. You have to scold, you have to beat, you have to do all such things. It is a horrible thing or else the disciples would go astray. So there, you have to pretend, you have to hiss. He has to take a stick also sometimes. To some, he has to slap, some he gives scoldings to also. All these things must come there. So, don't become a Guru. It is a horrible thing to become a Guru and take a big burden for nothing.

Reading: *The Gist: If we minutely study all the activities of the multifarious living beings of the universe, we find that they all tend towards one object, which we may call Freedom, Happiness, Peace or Bliss. In a deeper sense, all these different words mean one and the same thing.*

Swamiji: That is all right, that is the gist there. We have been talking about it long ago. Every one is struggling to get peace and happiness and how to get it. Many people think it lies in sense-pleasures but the more you enjoy sense-pleasures, the more you suffer. There is no peace. Even fabulous wealth will not make you happy. The hidden desire for name and fame will also not make a man happy. Then comes the question, "Where does that real happiness lie?" It lies in knowing your

True Nature. So, the attempt made to know your True Nature is known as religion or philosophy. In order to know your True Nature, you have to exercise control over all your five senses because the mind and senses are interlinked. Until and unless you control the senses, you cannot control the mind also. That means you have to live a pure life. Also, the rules of yama and niyama automatically come. Without that, you cannot make progress. You come to that conclusion.

So here, those who want to make progress, have to live the life. Don't succumb to temptations. Don't be a slave of your senses and mind. By living the life, you go step-by-step. That is, in a deeper sense, what is meant by sadhana. Everything ends here in Nirvikalpa Samadhi. In that state only, you know your True Nature. All illusion, all ignorance, everything is destroyed there.

So, all of you become heroes and heroines. Wake up! Don't stop half way. You have taken the right course. You have selected the path. Now work it out. Don't be afraid of anything. Success must come. It will come. But don't fall down. In winter many go to pieces. All evil comes in winter, not in summer. In summer, people wake up. In winter, they don't know what to do. In the long winter, the devils come. The idle brain is the devil's workshop, they say. Then also we told you, during that time at least, every one of you write the mantra to keep the mind engaged. Read some good books and take up meditation as much as possible. The climate is also good. It is cool so there is no danger of the head getting heated. You require some cold so there is not that danger. Utilize the time but never fall back to animal life.

That is the last conclusion. That is the gist.

Disciple: There are more than four billion people on earth. How many have attained Samadhi?

Swamiji: The modern education does not teach about Samadhi at all. They don't know what is meant by Samadhi. That is the difficulty. The world is so attractive for them so why should they go leaving all these pleasures to gain Samadhi. So very few know it. It is all kept secret. Really, if people try, they can get it. It is not a hard thing. If the children from childhood are taught properly, proper education given, then you can mend the nation. The whole world can be mended easily. When childhood is neglected and when they grow up and become young men and women, by that time everything is exhausted. Brahmacharya is wasted like anything. Such people find it very difficult because the vital force is gone. They have to work it out again. It is an uphill task. If they are taught from the beginning, there is much hope. You can improve nations. Many people can attain it. One man from Australia wrote to me once after reading my books, he was aged, "I have squandered everything. Now I got this book. If I had gotten it when I was young, I could have done miracles." So, many people understand it when they are very old.

Disciple: So, does that mean that the time has become ripe for many to go?

Swamiji: Let us see. Make use of it. It is for you people now. Come forward.

Disciple: What we are fighting for in this room must be very exclusive. I mean is there a future for the whole human race to learn about these things or will it always be for a few hundred?

Swamiji: That is all right. Even now, we are not disappointed. Even if one can come forward that is also good among so many. If one or two can come forward, they can also do much work.

Disciple: I mean, we must have some kind of obligation to spread the message to the world.

Swamiji: That will come if it wants. All obligations and other things, everything will come if it wants. If it does not want, we shall not worry.

Disciple: I think there are millions of people who want it. I am thinking that it is the start of a revolution.

Swamiji: If it comes, it is well and good. If it does not come, it is also good. So be content. There is no claim whatsoever. I have given the thing freely so I don't expect anything. Live the life, all of you. That will help.

Disciple: We are talking so much about astrology. Is it a fact or is it some nonsense?

Swamiji: You see, it is a fact as well as it is sometimes a bogus thing also. Because many of the alterations, they have not made. Some thousands of years ago when there were the same planet conditions, there were some alterations that they have not adjusted. An expert can adjust properly but it is a life long struggle to become an expert in any department. It is not at all easy and if it is corrected, it has its facts and figures. You have to study so much. The whole life is wasted. You have to utilize the thing.

Disciple: Swamiji, are the sun and stars conscious beings?

Swamiji: How will you say they are not? Life is everywhere. An ant may not understand an elephant. The ant will think, "What is this elephant? It is some huge stone or rock or hill." Likewise, they are all conscious beings. They may be breathing. Life is there. Everything is there. Even the sun or moon is too hot for our life to be living there. There may be some different kinds who are not burned. So, life is everywhere.

Disciple: How can you look into the future and change something by right effort?

Swamiji: Future changes also. If you have will power, you can change the future also. Mind has got all powers.

Disciple: Yes, but when can one change his destiny with his will power?

Swamiji: At will, such a man can change the future also. When the man has that will power to change his future destiny, destiny also changes there. What is the difficulty?

Disciple: But then you can't perceive the future now?

Swamiji: Yes, you must be able to see the future, that such and such things are going to happen. You use your will power and change it. That future has changed also. Now, when you see what is next, that future is no more destiny. You catch me or no?

Disciple: Yes.

Swamiji: Say, there is a ghost in the corner and you are firing from here with your will power and the ghost dies. Now, you are seeing the future. The ghost is no more. You have changed destiny. The ghost has died.

Disciple: Intense sadhana, isn't that the same as changing one's future?

Swamiji: Yes, that I have been telling you people. It is just like two bulls fighting one another. One is your prarabdha, past karma, and the other is fresh effort. Whichever is stronger will defeat the other. By intense sadhana, you can cut short all those things. All your dangers can also be controlled. It is possible.

Disciple: Then if each one of us really kept our sadhana and only had one thing in our mind, then we could change Denmark.
Swamiji: Yes, really. Not only Denmark, the whole world.
Disciple: Swamiji, that leads me to the question, many worldly-minded people often think that we are egoistic people.
Swamiji: If there had not been great people in the world, who were absolutely unselfish, the world would have gone to pieces. It is their will power. It is their good wishes that are sustaining the world. So, to live the life is not easy. They are doing the highest kind of good to the world. Only ignorant and stupid people can talk so much. Without knowing anything, they talk some nonsense. If all were to live the life, that is a mighty force. It can work miracles.

Disciple: Concerning the egoistic thing we talked about before, does that mean that if you have got Realization you automatically help thousands of people?
Swamiji: Yes. It is just like a beautiful rose you have in the garden. It helps by the very appearance and people who go there smell the fragrance. They are so happy. In this way, a man of God-Realization helps automatically.
Disciple: Also, if you cannot see him?
Swamiji: That does not matter. He may live inside a cave but still the thought vibration is there. The thought aura is there. They help the world, not only the world, the universe. In olden times, they had so much high regard for the saints in India. Now, they are forgotten. They have followed the western world so they are going to pieces. They think that what the sadhus are doing, they are mere drones. They call them drones and I call such people who say this stupid. I call them face-to-face idiotical sorts of people, muddy-headed brute-like people who have become leaders without knowing anything. They talk so much nonsense. I tell them the same thing without fear. They think it is all the so-called Ahimsa Theory and by the monks coming and preaching, they make the nation a slave. That is their stupid argument. Those people, they have come to the western side. They have studied in England and America. They are westernized. Such people are leaders there and they destroy the whole thing. They are getting kicks also. Such a man had to die when China attacked from the back. He got a stab. He

went mad almost. Though he was a powerful man, he went mad. So, there is no fun in all these things.

Disciple: There must be hope now. Many young people are not going wrong.

Swamiji: That is a very good hope. Just to see many young people, both boys and girls, coming forward. It is a good hope. I have not lost hope.

Disciple: Swamiji, there is one thing that is difficult for me to understand, that is that everything is a mixture of good and bad. Isn't it possible to do something which is absolutely 100% good?

Swamiji: If you have got anything that you can mention, we shall look at it. Let me see what is 100% good.

Disciple: I mean if a man is trying to kill an innocent woman and you come there and stop it, have you done something bad then?

Swamiji: You have stopped it. It may be good you have helped the woman but you have not helped the man. On one side, you are not good. The man is annoyed. So, you have done an injustice to the man. So, a bad thing is there. He is sorry.

Disciple: I think if I had a bomb now, naturally Swamiji was not here, but if I blow up the house?

Swamiji: Then?

Disciple: Then I think it would be a very bad thing I did.

Swamiji: All right then. It is a major portion bad and then there must be some portion good also. There may be some who want to die; so, you have helped such people. On one side, you have done a bad thing and on the other side, a good thing also for those people. So, both things are there, always mixed. A thing which brings more good and less bad is called a good act. And a thing which brings more bad and less good is called a bad act. Suppose many of the youngsters are coming in this line. That is a very good act. But there are so many parents who are very miserable. They are weeping for these youngsters. They are sorrowful. In this way, everything is a mixture.

Disciple: Is it only good when it leads to Self-Realization or is it good when it gives people food under certain circumstances?

Swamiji: What are you talking about? There is good and bad mixed, I am telling. There may be some who may be helped but others may be squeezed having to give food to them and there may be an injustice done to so many other people. In that way, you will feed the idiots and you will kill other good people and snatch away their money and give it to idiots and hash smokers. You will feed the drunkards and hash smokers. It is good to feed all, all right. Make them work also. Let there be no hash smokers. Let them not be idlers.

Disciple: Swamiji, in karma-yoga, you offer your work to God. Isn't it a kind of fraction because you are God yourself?

Swamiji: Offer the Self also to God. The body is meant for God-Realization. So, everything you do for that thing. Let it be a sort of worship. It is all just to tame the mind, all these varieties of methods used, that is all. When you go to higher pitches, automatically without any strain, without much difficulty it goes on. You don't get attached. For an ordinary man to get detached from all these things, there are various methods adopted. When you make progress, then you go deeper. Then, all these things have no meaning. Automatically, it goes.

Disciple: You have asked us to offer the meditation also. I don't understand it.

Swamiji: Even the meditation, even the fruits, everything, offer it to God and remain indifferent. You get peace of mind. If you have got that idea, "I must get prosperity, I must get concentration," this and that thing, that ego is there. Offer everything.

Disciple: I think you can say to yourself, "Now I am starting a kind of work and I offer this work to God." But how can you know that you are not fooling yourself?

Swamiji: You have to watch it. Mind will deceive you in the beginning. If somebody praises you, say, "Oh, yes, I have done the work." It comes there. Then check it. In this way, in the middle of the work also remember the mantra. Remember God again and again. Then, after some time, it cannot fool you. It becomes a habit and you don't get elevated by anything. If somebody praises you, say it is all stupid things. It has no meaning. In the beginning, there will be difficulty when all these problems arise. Be steady. Work it out. Then, everything becomes easy.

If name and fame comes that is all right. Don't get worried. That is God's. That also offer. Think that it is nothing. Don't take the responsibility there. Good and bad, success and failure, everything is all God's. That "I" is no more. If you want to take the credit, then you must face the failures also so don't take either. Give them unto God. "It is all right. I have done my work. If success has come, it is all right. It is His will." Struggle is necessary in the beginning.

Disciple: As a teacher, you are in a dilemma because you have to make these little children's egos strong if they shall survive in the world or they will be crushed by other children.

Swamiji: Not in that way. How do you make the ego strong?

Disciple: By self-confidence. We call it ego therapy.

Swamiji: That is a wrong idea. Tell the child, if you get one blow, give two. Tell it in that way to the children. If he gets one blow, he gives two blows. In that way, make him strong. You are not weak. It does not mean that you make the ego strong in that way. You must defend yourself. Don't injure others.

Disciple: What is strong then?

Swamiji: Your mind. Be strong there. Don't make them weak by telling them, "You are weak, you are so low," this and that. Not in that way. "You are strong, you are powerful," in that way make them strong.

Disciple: Is it possible to work scientifically and at the same time have a sadhana?

Swamiji: Yes, why not? They can easily get concentration. A scientificly minded man has been devoting so much energy in concentration on certain objects to find out some new things. The same energy can be converted here also. Both can go. They can get better success. So, concentration has gone in different directions. That can be done by practice. Bring it by will. They can easily succeed.

August 31, 1973 – Sannyas Day

Disciple: Will you speak a word or two to the new sannyasins?

Swamiji: That they have been hearing for the past three months. In the navel cord of the musk deer, there will be a small bag-like sack and it weighs about one hundred grams. Out of that, they make incense. It is very costly. That is a very strong fragrance and that deer smelled that musk but it did not know from where it was coming. It was so tempting. That smell was so wonderful. It went on smelling from tree to tree, jungle to jungle. It went all over, wherever it could go and lastly it found out the fragrance was from its own body.

So, where to find God now? It is within you. You have to search. All the while you have been searching here and there. You thought sense-pleasures would make you happy. It is not making you happy. You thought some other things were making you happy but they are also not making you happy. All these things are a mere waste of time. You have already wasted a lot of time. Now, as we have been telling all the while, you have to be strong. I have been telling again and again, strength is life and weakness is death and weakness is the most terrible sin in the world. Don't be weak. At the same time, don't be proud of your strength also. There must be humility. So, keeping up this thing, don't yield to temptations, be strong. Be strong in your meditation. Be strong in your daily routine work. And, at the same time, do not neglect your job also. Keep it up.

It is a new type of sannyas we have started. You have to stand upon your own feet and earn your livelihood. Do not be a burden to any man, either to the government or to any person. You are free. If you follow the simple life, you are really doing a marvellous thing. That is a new type of sannyas we have been creating. We have been working it out and it is successful work. Nobody can blame you. You are not to depend on anyone. Now, as the world situation is there, it has become too shaky.

The old type of sannyas was to renounce everything and go to the forest and live there. Nowadays, there is no forest also. To live, you have to earn. So, there you understand the spirit. Don't get attached to anything. Have the spirit of detachment always but, at the same time, never neglect your work also. In this way, by doing your sadhana, live a pure life controlling your mind and senses. Slowly and steadily, you go to the last point. So, as we have been telling, again and again, the aim of life is Freedom and that Freedom you have lost. How? By going after sense-pleasures, you have lost it completely. Now, you have to revive it, control it, and regain your Lost Empire. All of you have been living it. Never yield to temptation, to weaknesses and stupid things. Every one of you be heroes and heroines. The same thing we have been saying and saying all these three months.

Again, in conclusion, also I say, I have full hope for every one of you that you never disappoint me. You disappoint yourself that is all. So, never degrade yourself. Rise up now, every one of you. Make up your strong resolve. I have given you the daily dictum.

Remember the Following Dictum Every Day
1. There is only One God and That is The Ultimate Truth.
2. God, Guru and The Ultimate Truth are one and the same.
3. The aim of life is Freedom or, in other words, God-realization.
4. This Freedom can be got only through Nirvikalpa Samadhi.
5. To attain Nirvikalpa Samadhi, one has to live a pure, simple and holy life and live in life long celibacy.
6. I select this life by myself. No one has compelled me. So, I must live the life at any cost.

Written by Swami Narayanananda,
Coorg, South India, 3-16-1972

Every one of you, read it before going to sleep is what you have to do. This life you have selected. Nobody has compelled you. I have not asked anyone to take up sannyas. I have only given the Truth.

I have told you again and again that broadly speaking, we can grade humanity in three groups. One is the animal man, the second is the man and third is the superman. For the animal man, those who want to live, eat, drink, beget and do whatever you want, we have no argument with such people. I told you the second man, if you want to become a human being at least, then, you have to observe the moral code, rules of good conduct. Live a pure life, holy life and at least those married people who cannot control themselves, they have to regulate their sexual life also. That I have been telling again and again. And if you want to be a superman, sannyas means you want to. You are trying to become a superman. There, absolute brahmacharya is necessary. There is no compromise with it. Fall of brahmacharya means gone. Your whole life goes to pieces. Be careful in that way. Avoid temptations. Follow strictly the rules of brahmacharya and that will help you. The coming winter is the most dangerous period here. You must know how to adapt and engage your time. Don't waste your time unnecessarily. If you cannot meditate long, go on with mantra-jap. If you cannot do mantra-jap, write the mantra or read the mantra. In this way, engage the time and try to control yourself.

So, we will meet again. Next year also we will be coming and all of you must be prepared as well. Every one of you must be heroes and heroines. Have courage now. Have hope and courage both. We are leaving you in a better position now. So, now, every one of you, resolve to live a pure life. Help will come. Everything must come. There is nothing in the way. Don't get discouraged. Work hard now. Then what else to say?

All of you, Wake Up! That is a good thing. Rise up now from your long-lasting slumber. Wake up!

Om Shanti! Shanti! Shanti!

Glossary

Adwaita	Non-duality, One without a second.
Anahata	Heart chakra.
Ajna	Third eye chakra.
Apasiddhasapnasiddhas	Enlightenment in dream.
Arjuna	Warrior in Hindu mythology who struggled with his Dharma.
Arya Samaj	Indian Hindu reform movement.
Asana	Seat for meditation, a hatha yoga posture.
Ashrama	Monastery.
Atman	One's true Self.
Bhagavad Gita	Core text of Hinduism and Indian philosophy.
Bhakti	Yoga of devotion.
Brahmacharya	Completeness and purity in thought, word and deed; celibacy, austerity.

Brahman	The unchanging, infinite, immanent, and transcendent reality in Hinduism
Brahmin	Highest of the traditional castes of India, priests.
Brahma-Jnana	Knowledge of God or of the spiritual Self.
Bhiksha	Food obtained by asking for alms.
Camp	Spiritual Training Camp in Gylling, Denmark.
Chaddar	Meditation shawl.
Chakra	Subtle center in the body from where the life energy works the body, senses and mind.
Chitta	Mind-stuff or storage of memory.
Chitta Akasa	Mental Space
Coolie	Unskilled worker.
Darshan	Meeting with a holy man.
Dharana	Hold the mind on a point for at least 12 seconds.
Dharma	Duty, Righteousness, Way to Perfection.
Dhyana	Contemplation, Concentration for two and a half minutes.
Dictum	A short statement, especially one expressing advice or a general truth.
Durga	One of the ten names of the Divine Mother.

Dwaita	Duality
Gunas	Three kinds of attributes of all things and beings.
Guru	Spiritual guide.
Guru Kripa	Grace of the Guru.
Guru Mantra	Mantra a Guru gives to his disciple.
Gurudev	Divine Guru.
Guru Purnima	Indian festival dedicated to Indian teachers.
Gylling	Town in Denmark near Swamiji's main ashram.
Hatha Yoga	Yoga of physical exercises or postures called "asanas".
Initiation	Special instruction by a Guru. Diksha.
Ishta-Devata	Chosen deity or an aspirant's spiritual ideal.
Jiva	Living Being.
Jivan-Mukta	Living Liberated One.
Jivatman	Individual soul.
Jnana-Yoga	Yoga of discernment and knowledge.
Jnani	One who possesses Self-Knowledge or Knowledge of Liberation.

Kali	The female aspect of the Supreme Being or Shiva.
Karma	Action. Sometimes also: the results of past actions.
Karma Phala	The results of past actions.
Karma-Yoga	Path of selfless action.
Kroner	Danish currency.
Kevala Kumbhaka	Unprompted stop of breath that occurs within a samadhi state
Kshatriya	Second of the traditional castes of India, warriors.
Kula Davata	Household deity in Orthodox Hindu family.
Kumbhaka	Retention of the breath in pranayama.
Kundalini Shakti	The primal power in man.
Kutir	A small cottage.
Lakshmi	Hindu Goddess of wealth, fortune and prosperity.
Madcap	A person who acts like a maniac; a reckless, wildly impulsive person.
Mahapralaya	Complete destruction of the Universe.
Mala	108 beads + meru bead (guru bead) strung together and used for mantra repetition.

Manipura	Third chakra, area of the navel.
Mantra	Repetition of God's name corresponding to an aspirant's Chosen Deity.
Mantra-Devata	Particular universal force toward which a mantra is directed.
Mantra-jap	Focused and (usually silent) repetition of the mantra.
Markata Vairagya	Renunciation like a monkey.
Maya	Divine illusion hiding the Truth.
Moksha	Freedom from suffering, Self-Realization.
Muladhara	Root chakra.
Mouna	Non-speaking, silence.
Nadi	Nerve currents through which the energies of the body flow.
Narayanananda	Sannyas name of Swamiji.
Nirvikalpa samadhi	God Realization. Highest spiritual attainment.
Niyama	Habits and activities for right living.
Ocean of Consciousness	God or what is eternal, infinite, without beginning, middle or end.
Padmasana	Lotus pose. Cross-legged sitting pose.
Para	The immaterial, efficient, formal and final cause of all that exists.

Pashyanti	Ability to see deeply.
Prana	Sanskrit word for "life force".
Pranava	*Om* or the last of the spiritual sounds one hears.
Pranayama	Control of the breath to aid in mind-control.
Pranayama	**#1: To purify the nadis**: Close the right nostril firmly with the thumb of your right hand. Inhale as slowly as possible so no sound ix produced. Fill the lungs with as much air as you can. Now close the right nostril with the help of your ring and little finger and exhale very slowly and noiselessly through the right nostril. After exhaling through the right nostril, inhale slowly as before through the right nostril, then exhale slowly through the left nostril with the right closed. This will constitute one round. Do six rounds at one sitting.
Pranayama	**#2: To produce heat**: Close the mouth, inhale quickly through the nose and without holding the breath inside, exhale quickly. While inhaling and exhaling, let a hissing sound be produced and let the chest expand and contract like a bellows. Do this pranayama ten times (inhale and exhale ten times). Now begin to inhale and exhale very slowly two or three times. These two processes constitute one round. Do two such rounds to start then slowly increase to six rounds. **#3: To cure disease:** Inhale slowly through both nostrils to fill the lungs with air. Contract the throat by taking the chin back towards the neck. Then, force the air upwards by dragging the stomach and the lower abdomen backward

towards the spine and upwards and hold the breath between the heart and the throat as long as possible. Now close the left nostril with the ring and little fingers of your right hand and exhale slowly through the right nostril. Do this combined process five times. Then inhaling as before each time, breathe out through the left nostril five times, closing the right nostril with your thumb. Gradually, the number of this kind of breathing-out can be increased to ten times from each nostril.

Prarabdha karma	Results of actions performed in the past.
Prasad	Sacred food.
Pratyahara	Concentration of mind at will.
Prem	Pure love.
Puja	Worship, ritual.
Rajas	Quality that drives motion, energy and activity.
Raja-Yoga	Yoga of concentration and meditation.
Ramakrishna	Indian mystic and saint (1836-1886).
Rishi	Accomplished and enlightened person.
Rungsted	Suburb of Copenhagen where Swamiji stayed.
Sadhana	Spiritual practice, spiritual work.
Sahasrara	Static center. Chakra at crown of head.
Samadhi	Concentration for at least 30 minutes.

Samskaras	Tendencies inherited from one's past births.
Samyama	Attaining knowledge of a subject after trance.
Sandhya	Sending good thoughts and vibrations to departed people in India.
Sannyasa	Renunciation of one's attachments. Monk or nun.
Sannyasin	A person who renounces. A monk or nun.
Sat-Chit-Ananda	Existence, Knowledge and Bliss absolute.
Satsanga	Satsang is a sitting together with an enlightened person. Holy company.
Sattva	Quality of purity, light and harmony.
Savasana	Resting pose in hatha yoga.
Savikalpa Samadhi	Samadhi with support of an object or form.
Self	God or universal consciousness, according to Advaita Vedanta.
Shabda-Brahman	Transcendental sound.
Shakti	Power, energy.
Shanti	Peace.
Shiva	Hindu God of destruction.
Shraddha	Faith and belief in God.

Sickle	Sharp tool used for harvesting.
Siddhasana	Meditation seat.
Siddhis	Supernatural powers.
Static centre	Sahasrara Chakra.
Sudra	Lowest of the traditional castes in India, laborers.
Sukhasana	Easy pose.
Svastikasana	Sitting cross-legged.
Swami	Nun or monk.
Swamiji	Affectionate name for Swami Narayanananda.
Tamas	Quality denoting darkness and ignorance.
Tank	Pond.
Tantra	Range of ancient Indian religious traditions.
Tantrics	Practitioners of Tantra.
Tapasya	Self discipline to achieve Self-realization.
Tratak	Meditation method of staring at a point such as a candle.
Turiya state	Superconscious state, attained after Nirvikalpa Samadhi.
Upanishads	The philosophical and spiritual texts in the Vedas.

Vanaprastha	Retiring to the forest.
Vedanta	Hindu philosophy.
Vairagya	Dispassion, renunciation.
Vaishyas	Third of the traditional casts in India, traders.
Vedas	Ancient Hindu scriptures.
Vishista Adwaita	Non-dualism of the qualified whole.
Vishnu	Hindu God of preservation.
Viveka	Discrimination.
Yama	Ethical code of right living.
Yantra	Geometrical design.
Yoga	Union of the individual soul with the Universal Soul.
Yoga Paths	Karma Yoga: Path of selfless action. Raja Yoga: The path of concentration and meditation. Bhakti Yoga: The path of devotion. Jnana Yoga: Path of discrimination and knowledge. Hatha Yoga: physical exercises and postures called "asanas".
Yogi	Practitioner of yoga.

Brief biography of Swami Narayanananda

Swami Narayanananda was born on April 12, 1902 in the hill country of Coorg, South India. Despite his enjoyment of childhood activities, from a young age he regularly sat quietly for meditation for a half hour in the morning and in the evening. He developed this practice instinctively without any outside guidance. This early practice of regular meditation established Swamiji firmly in spiritual life.

After finishing his studies, he renounced the world and became a sannyasin (monk) because his mental state had completely changed after he experienced deep concentration of mind for over an hour. Soon after, he gave away all his possession and left home in 1929 in search of a Guru (spiritual teacher). After a long and exhausting journey, he arrived at the Ramakrishna Mission in Belur Math, Calcutta and met his Guru, Swami Shivananda, who was a direct disciple of Sri Ramakrishna. After a few years, his Guru sent him to the Himalayas for tapasya. He lived in a small hut in the jungle near Rishikesh, India and practiced meditation and mantra-jap for 12-16 hours a day. As a result of his sincere effort, Swami Narayanananda was rewarded with the attainment of Nirvikalpa Samadhi on Shivaratri, February 22, 1933, the night of Shiva worship all over India.

After this rare attainment, Swami Narayanananda lived a solitary life and started to write down observations from his own experience. It was not until the partition of India in 1947, with the bloodshed and horror, that he felt a need to help and began taking disciples. Among his first disciples were a family of four Pakistani orphans. They read his books and, even though there was no money, decided to publish them. This was a difficult time but Swami Narayanananda remained calm and unruffled.

Swami Narayanananda was reluctant at first to develop ashrams but understood, over time, their value to provide support for those on a committed spiritual path. Eventually, an ashram was started in Rishikesh, India then other ashrams soon followed. Many Danish disciples came to know of Swami Narayanananda though his books and began visiting him at his ashrams in India. In 1971, the Danish disciples convinced him to visit Gylling, Denmark to give a much-needed boost to sincere Truth-seekers. And so began his travels from India to his ashrams in the west located in Denmark, Germany, Sweden, Norway and America. This continued every summer for 17 years.

At The Free Spiritual Training Camp in Gylling, Denmark, all were welcome to join the daily program of four meditations, hatha yoga classes, study groups and daily private darshan where personal questions were discussed. The camp was a unique chance to live a simple life in tents, keep silence, do spiritual practice and absorb the all-pervading, peaceful energy that surrounded Swami Narayanananda.

In the early years, Swami Narayanananda gave public darshan every evening followed by meditation. Later, he joined for common darshan and satsang only on the weekends. These were hours filled with spiritual discussion, stories and lots of laugher. His goal was to teach Truth and to offer all possible assistance wherever and whenever possible to sincere Truth-Seekers.

Swami Narayanananda established "The Universal Religion" to teach Truth regardless of caste, creed, sex, nationality or race. He wrote a total of 36 books which focus on philosophy, psychology, religion, spirituality, meditation, yoga and the kundalini shakti. And he created a new kind of sannyas, order of monks and nuns more suited to western customs, who work and earn an income and are independent and self-sufficient. He gave Mantra-Diksha (mantra initiation) to thousands of disciples around the world and Sannyas-Diksha (initiation into sannyas) also to many. He encouraged everyone to thoughtfully consider the path he was offering, to not make a choice blindly but to fully understand and make a conscious decision. As is written in the text of this book, he said, "This is all your own choice. To come to this line nobody has compelled you."

Swami Narayanananda was a rare being. A Saint in our lifetime, who taught Truth as he knew it regardless of the consequences. If his goal had been to attract followers, he would not have taught about brahmacharya. He could have continued to live a secluded life in India but he came out of isolation to offer, from his own experience, a way to inner peace and the essential goal of life, Freedom or Nirvikalpa Samadhi. And now, with this book of darshans, there is the possibility to sit at his holy feet and absorb his words and his energy but, most of all, to dive into his resounding message about the possibility of total and complete Freedom that we all seek.

Swami Narayanananda died on February 26, 1988 at his ashram in Mysuru, India.

www.ingramcontent.com/pod-product-compliance
Lightning Source LLC
Chambersburg PA
CBHW070419010526
44118CB00014B/1824